WOMEN IN INDO-ANGLIAN FICTION

Women in Indo-Anglian Fiction

Tradition and Modernity

Edited by

NARESH K. JAIN

MANOHAR
2026

First published 1998
Reprinted 2025, 2026
First eBook edition 2025

ISBN 978-81-7304-217-1 (Hb)
ISBN 978-93-6080-953-9 (ebook)

Published by
Ajay Kumar Jain *for*
Manohar Publishers & Distributors
4753/23 Ansari Road, Daryaganj
New Delhi 110 002

Printed and bound in India

Contents

Acknowledgements

Grateful thanks are due to the following for according copyright permission to reprint the article noted against each.

The Sahitya Akademi, New Delhi and Shashi Deshpande for her article 'Of Concerns, Of Anxieties' published in *Indian Literature*, October-November 1996.

The Indian Institute of Advanced Study, Shimla, for Malashri Lal's article on '*Baumgartner's Bombay*: The Feminization of a Hero' from her book *The Law of the Threshold: Women Writers in Indian English* (Shimla: Indian Institute of Advanced Study, 1995).

Makarand Paranjpe for his articles 'The Crisis of Contemporary India in Nayantara Sahgal's Fiction' published in *World Literature Today* (Spring, 1994) and for the article 'Cultural and Political Allegory in Nayantara Sahgal's *Rich Like Us*' published in *Indian Writing Today* (New Delhi, 1996).

Sarla Palkar for her article 'The Politics of Gender in Raja Rao's The Serpent and the Rope' published in *The Indian Panorama* in its first issue.

I am also grateful to the Indian Institute of Advanced Study, Shimla for permitting me to visit the Institute as an Associate for two short spells in 1991 and 1994 to fill in the gaps in my reading and writing my contribution to this volume.

I must also thank my friends Professor T.N. Dhar, Dr. N.P. Singh and Dr. Kamal Bhasin, for help in preparing the volume for publication.

Ramesh has as usual been more than a publisher and I am particularly happy that he agreed to take up the publication of the anthology after the project had run into difficulties and delays for various reasons.

NARESH K. JAIN

Tradition, Modernity and Change

Naresh K. Jain

The value of a study of this kind lies in the recognition that in any society women are the chief preservers of tradition, and in a sense no change howsoever momentous becomes complete or real unless it involves them and carries them along. The sexual revolution in America in the twenties, for instance, chiefly liberated the male and it required another revolution in the sixties for the idea to gain ground that sexual desire in a woman was normal. So a study of women fictional characters' response to change in their lives and in the lives of those around them and their quest for selfhood could provide a valuable glimpse of India in transition. Also the study would throw into bold relief questions of woman's identity, self-fulfilment and sexuality.

While calling for papers for the anthology I had written to the contributors to examine how women characters in Indo-Anglian novels coped with change in their lives and with the rival pulls of tradition and modernity in their search for identity, independence, fulfilment and love whether within marriage or outside it.

I now realize that while I recognized the copresence of tradition and modernity I also suggested through the use of the word *rival* that tradition and modernity were antithetical and that if one wished to be modern one must discard all tradition. Alternatively, one must resist modernity and remain rooted in tradition. In this view tradition is equated with old outdated ideas and beliefs and customs and practices, and modernity with progress and new ideas. This Eurocentric view is, however, a colonial construct. It is being increasingly recognized that tradition and modernity need not be dichotomous. Pointing to the Western fallacy of seeing 'an all but unbridgeable chasm between tradition and modernity', Heesterman says: 'We are prone to overstress the stability of traditional societies and the upheaval caused by modernization. On the other hand we are apt to play down the capacity of tradition for initiating change and accommodation to modern circumstances.'[1] The *and* between the two key words therefore need not always mean *versus* but also *plus.* The initial impetus towards modernity in India came from the West but being modern is not the same thing as being Westernized. Indeed the modern West need not be the model of social change. We also need to distinguish between modernity and mere trendiness. The freedom of a woman to choose her own life partner or life goals is a modern value but smoking by women in the name of equality or sexes is being merely trendy.

Before we go further, it will be proper to talk about Indian tradition. Can we talk of an Indian tradition in the singular? In that case we must also recognize that besides the Hindu tradition which is its major constituent, there are several other traditions that have contributed to what it is today. Then, the Hindu tradition itself is not homogeneous. The Vedas, particularly the *Rigveda,* point to a society that was free of the inhibitions of later Hinduism. The Vedic *rishis* as well as the laymen relished beef and alcoholic drink. Nor is there in the *Rigveda* any mention of child marriage, ban on the remarriage of widows, the caste system, *karma,* rebirth or *avatar.* In considering the compatibility of the Hindu religious tradition with the spirit of modernity, therefore, one has to be clear as to which particular tradition one has in mind. The dominant Hindu tradition that I, and I suppose, the other contributors have had in mind is the one that has governed, and continues to govern the attitudes to women in India today, namely, the framework of ideas, attitudes, and institutions as codified by Manu.

Undeniably, there is much in this tradition that is fit to be consigned to the scrapheap but because of the presence of vital elements in it, it is capable of providing direction for the future. Bhikhu Parekh has provided a synoptic view of the critical resources of the Hindu religious tradition. Many of the nineteenth-century reformers, he points out, made use of these resources to successfully challenge unacceptable practices.[2] For instance, Raja Rammohun Roy appealed to the Upanishads to argue against *sati,* Ishwar Chandra Vidyasagar to the *Parasharsmriti* (in place of *Manusmriti*) to struggle against the ban on widow remarriage, and Swami Dayananda to the Vedas against image worship. Secondly, they invoked *Sadharana-dharma* which could broadly be called universal moral principle; they also appealed to the unique problems and needs of the prevailing *yuga* and insisted that *Yugadharma* (historical specific principles) was to be determined in the light of *Sadharanadharma* or *Manavadharma*. Finally, they invoked the concept of *Loksangraha* (preservation of society) and argued that these practices would weaken the Hindu social order.

In more recent times, Vivekananda used the distinction between *Sanatandharma* (eternal principles) and *Yugadharma* to attack several Hindu customs. Witness Gandhi too. He used the traditional symbols of Hinduism to mobilize the Indian masses and forged a mass movement for the freedom of the country.

It is clear therefore that confronted with the challenge of new situations, individuals and cultures go back to their past, sift the vital elements in them, modify them if necessary, and use them in order to prepare themselves for the future. The movement towards modernity is therefore not always linear. Then, modern developments often go to strengthen tradition. For example, the modern means of communication such as the TV made it possible for Indians to go back to their traditional roots in the form of mega serials like the *Ramayana* and *Mahabharata*. Aminocentosis is a modern scientific technique but its use to kill the female foetus is a return to primitive bestiality. Moreover, it is not always possible to separate the new from the old and decide their relative value. There is a yoga, for instance. Shall we call it traditional because it is rooted in India tradition? Or shall we call it modern because it has come to us with the sanction of the West? Or because it is extremely important in resolving some of the problems created by the modern industrial society? Similarly, the traditional Indian concern for environment is a modern concern. The dividing line between tradition and modernity is therefore often blurred. The attitudes that these terms signify may overlap and may often coexist in the same individual in a state of tension or otherwise. For instance, Bankim Chandra Chatterjee's *Samya*, a powerful attack on inequality published in 1864, did not include untouchability among the 'four great social evils' of our society.

The tradition-modernity question gets further complicated on account of the heterogeneity of our society and the asymmetrical growth and development among different regions and sections of it. What may be modern in a rural setting may be traditional in a city. The whole question is highly complex and can best be studied not in terms of tradition-modernity dichotomy but in terms of social and cultural change and interaction between the two.

II

We could, I suggest, discuss the different dimensions of the tradition-modernity issue with reference to the following nodal points:

1. Subordination—Autonomy,
2. *Dharma*—Personal goals,
3. Sexual purity—Sexual emancipation, and
4. Silence—Speech

The points on the left, namely, subordination or acceptance of male authority whether of father, husband or son, *dharma* or duty, sexual purity both premarital virginial and marital fidelity, and silence—are all cherished Indian values sanctified by tradition and particularly enjoined upon women. All the points on the right are the directions in which women could be seen moving under the impact of new ideas. Though for the sake of clarity, the points have been separated, they are interrelated and overlapping.

1. Subordination—Autonomy

In childhood a woman should be under her father's control, in youth under her husband's, and when her husband is dead, under her sons'. She should not have independence. *The Laws of Manu*,[3] 5.148

An Indian woman's self-perception as also the society's expectations from her have for long been largely determined by the complex of ideas and values and beliefs codified in the *Manusmriti*. In mythical terms the dominant feminine prototype still is the chaste, patient, self-denying, long suffering wife, Sita, admirably supported by other figures like Savitri and Draupadi.[4] (Another ideal wife recalled by Shashi Deshpande's Jaya in *That Long Silence* is Gandhari who covered her eyes to become blind like her husband, Dhritrashtra.) The values embodied in these ideal figures loom large in the consciousness of women even when they reject these role models. The injunctions relating to women in the *Manusmriti* and the Sita/Savitri prototype together provide a framework within which the response of women characters to male domination could profitably be studied.

There is a considerable variety in the women characters' attitudes reflected in the novels. These range from passive sufferers like Savitri in R.K. Narayan's *The Dark Room* (1938) to those like Daisy in his *Painter of Signs* (1976) who defying traditional wisdom about marriage and family intend to plough a lonely furrow. Between these two extremes lie a lot of attitudes combining acquiescence and protest in varying proportions.

Narayan's early novel *The Dark Room* is significant for two reasons: it brings out a woman's helplessness poignantly by showing Savitri returning home after a brief rebellion; more importantly, because it spells out the issue of a woman's dependence effectively. In a moment of illumination, Savitri says that women are willing victims, and proceeds to point to the economic basis of a woman's servitude: 'We are responsible for our position; we accept food, shelter, and comforts that you [the men] give, and are *what we are*'[5] (emphasis added). (Her protest against her husband's brazen philandering will be referred to in full later.) The dark room (reminiscent of the *kop bhavan* to which the queen Kekai had retired to register her protest against king Dashrath's decision to declare Ram as his heir) to which Savitri retires in order to protest against her husband becomes a symbol of a woman's fate from which escape is impossible except through her own volition and sometimes not even then. The image of a cramped enclosed space to indicate a woman's lot in the traditional Indian set-up from which the characters long to escape is widespread in the novels, e.g. as the Bow Bazar house in which Monisha finds herself trapped in Anita Desai's *Voices in the City* (1965), as the *haveli* in which Jaya finds herself trapped in *Inside the Haveli* by Rama Mehta and as the Big House in a Bengal village in *Music for Mohini* (1952) by Bhabani Bhattacharya and in many other novels. The image is widespread in the novels of Shashi Deshpande also. The *purdah* or the veil is only a concrete variation of this sheltered suffocating existence that women lead in Attia Hossain's *Sunlight on a Broken Column* (1961) and Gita Mehta's *Raj* (1989).

Escape through suicide which is also a protest of a kind is one of the several options available to women who feel oppressed at home. Monisha's suicide in *Voices in the City* is an example. A great many women characters, however, while questioning traditional values are in favour of adapting themselves to their situations *within* the framework of the family.

Two examples of women who are both educated and city-bred and who make a space for themselves within a traditional home—

after marriage are to be found in *Inside the Haveli* and *Music for Mohini.* The fact that two writers geographically located so far apart should deal with an identical theme shows that the dilemmas faced by these women are not theirs alone. These novels show how modern attitudes infiltrate and modify traditional values even as these values are questioned and severely criticized.

A more radical response to male oppression is the resort by women to divorce, a theme that three of Nayantara Sahgal's novels deal with. Divorce in these novels—*This Time of Morning* (1966), *Storm in Chandigarh* (1969) and *The Day in Shadow* (1971)—provides the writer with an occasion to castigate Hindu tradition where a woman's life is hemmed in by a web of duties to her husband, her *pati-parmeshvara* and where she is conjoined to stay faithful to him irrespective of his character or treatment of her. ('A virtuous wife should constantly serve her husband like a god, even if he behaves badly, freely indulges his lust, and is devoid of any good qualities'. *The Laws of Manu*, 5.154, p. 115). Divorce is also presented as an assertion by women of their need for personal freedom including sexual freedom.

One of these divorced women, Simrit, in *The Day in Shadow* is described by Nayantara Sahgal as 'a passive creature to whom things happen. Simrit is not an individual—she is culture, tradition, a patient enduring passivity'.

Sahgal's women are educated, middle class and therefore more self-aware and have greater inner resources to fight for their rights. They can be seen moving towards autonomy. But there is a sense in which women characters however independent need male support of survival. Witness Raj's help to Simrit in *The Day in Shadow.* Significantly Raj, a sympathetic character, is a Christian and brings Christian values to bear on his criticism of Hinduism. In the novel he offers a contrast to Simrit's husband Som and on the tradition-modernity issue he stands for modernity, which in the scheme of things means justice to the weak, and for full development of the individual, among other values. This apparently indicates Sahgal's own predilection for the Western Christian values. This, however, is not an isolated phenomenon because Kamala Markandaya also has an Englishman Dr. Kennington as the agent of change in the *Nectar in a Sieve* (1954).

Divorce is a potent weapon of revolt but it is not exercised by the women characters to any large degree. A large number of women don't give up, and fight for their rights as a wife and as a person *within* the framework of marriage and family. Shashi Deshpande's novels belong to this category. Her women protagonists are professional women—two are writers, one is a doctor. We need to take an illustrative example. *That Long Silence's* central character, Jaya, like Betty Friedan, calls into question the whole issue of a woman's domestic life and its failure to add up to a meaningful existence. When she introspects she finds that she had finally to blame herself for her own acquiescence more than anybody else: 'With whom shall I be angry? With myself, of course' (p. 192). In acknowledging this complicity in deciding a woman's fate, she recalls Savitri in *The Dark Room*. But Jaya will now speak up and erase 'that long silence' between herself and her husband. The earlier image in Jaya's consciousness of two oxen yoked together automatically stands rejected. So also are the mythical analogous of Sita, Savitri and Draupadi: 'I remember now that he [Mohan, her husband] had assumed I would accompany him, had taken for granted my acquiescence in his plans. So had I. Sita following her husband into exile, Savitri dogging Death to reclaim her husband, Draupadi stoically sharing her husband's travails . . .' (p. 11). Instead she prefers Maitrayee, sage Yajnavalkya's wife who rejected her husband's offer of half of his property and who asked him 'Will this property give me immortality?' (p. 25).[6] This is an example of a character seeking strength from a more vital part of our tradition in order to move towards greater autonomy and greater mutuality.

Shashi Deshpande doesn't like to be categorized as a woman writer and I think that if the term is used restrictively it does her less than justice but I hope she would permit us to say that as a writer she takes us inside the consciousness of women characters and deals with what she herself calls, 'The vulnerability of women. The power of women. The deviousness of women. The helplessness of women. The courage of women.'[7] We almost see women's minds in their undress. She is above all concerned with empowering women. If knowledge of the self is power, she arms her central character Jaya in *That Long Silence* with it. Towards the end of the novel she recalls Lord Krishna's words to Arjuna: 'I have given you knowledge. Now you make the choice. The choice is yours. Do as you desire' (p. 192). Implicit in this is the recognition that a woman's destiny is ultimately in her own hands.

At this stage the emergence of the 'new woman' typified by Daisy in *The Painter of Signs* needs to be noticed. But before we talk about her it would be helpful to mention a character in Anita Desai's *Clear Light of Day* (1980) who in her repudiation of marriage as a woman's ultimate destiny anticipates Daisy. The character is Bim, the older of the two sisters: 'I can think of hundreds of things to do instead [of marriage]. I won't marry,' she recalls telling her younger sister Tara when they were young. Later she says, 'I shall work—I shall *do* things, I shall earn my own living and look after Mira-*masi* and Baba and—be independent. There'll be so many things to do—when we are grown up'. . . .[8] She remains unmarried and as a college teacher she has been trying 'to teach them, *train* her students to be "different", from what we were at their age—to be a new kind of woman from you or me. . .' (emphasis added, p. 155). Daisy is autonomous because she is not only not dependent on male help but she abjures marriage, love, even sex in the single-minded pursuit of her self-imposed mission of spreading the family planning message. As Syd Harrex says, 'the novel raises important issues like sexual politics, romantic love, marriage, family planning and women's liberation and does so in relation to a conflict of values of traditional customs challenged by an activist sociology.'[9] Daisy doesn't think much of romantic love. She will not marry Raman in the traditional manner but only in the Gandharva[10] way, a kind of live-in-arrangement. She doesn't want any children either and her work would always come first. In all this she is challenging the old myths of marriage, wifehood and love symbolized by Sita. Daisy to be sure is a strong woman but she is seen entirely from the outside through the eyes of young Raman who is in love with her and is bewildered by the new phenomenon.

Throughout the novel Daisy is described in a variety of ways as a 'puzzle,' a 'she-devil', 'temptation', a 'female warrior' and a 'general'. To the love-sick Raman she is 'a furnace of conviction' and in his bafflement he tries to fit her into various images and stereotypes with which he is familiar—as a river, Mohini, a monomaniac, a Queen Victoria, Rani Lakshmi Bai, a general planning a campaign, a goddess and an automation.

The distance that R.K. Narayan keeps between himself and his creation enables him to look at the new woman ironically. One suspects, however, that Raman's bewilderment at her precipitate departure at the end of the novel with a cryptic 'marriage is not for me' reflects at least partly the writer's own bewilderment and in that sense is a prime example of male incomprehension of a woman who is a rebel.

On the other hand Nayantara Sahgal's new woman Sonali in *Rich Like Us* (1985) is presented sympathetically from the inside. Like Bim and Daisy, Sonali is a single woman trying to survive in a male-dominated society. In an assertion of her independence, she resigns from the IAS and is far from being the clinging ivy that we meet in the earlier fiction.

The important question of the relation between education and gender identity needs to be raised here. Formal education, a marker of modernity, is by itself perhaps hardly ever adequate in enabling one to view oneself or others in the right perspective. So much depends on socialization which is, as Karuna Chanana says, 'basically the process of construction of a woman's reality in the home'.[11] This process of value internalization begins at birth and moulds a person's self-perception' so the important questions to ask, according to her, are:

1. What is education expected to do *to* women and *for* women, subjectively, in terms of their self-perceptions, identity and role, and objectively, in terms of others' expectations from educated women and the perceptions about their identity and role?
2. *What* does education actually *do* for women and why? What does it *not* do and why?
3. How does socialization react to and interact with the process of education and how does it affect women?

Examples of the right kind of socialization may be seen in *Raj* and *Rich Like Us*. Both Jaya and Sonali, though grounded in traditional values, have been trained by their fathers to think aright and indepdendently. As a result Jaya goes through the ordeal of fire which is her marriage and comes out successful. At the end of the novel she is not afraid to be a loner in the male world of politics and greets the future with a triumphant laughter that resounds all over. Sonali after the defection of her college boy friend Ravi Kachru decides to stay unmarried. Both have definite goals before them. Staying within marriage or walking out of it or staying single does not by itself help us decide who is modern and who is not. What matters is what a woman makes of her life and how far she is able to go towards selfhood and decide things for herself. The arrival of a Jaya (in *Raj*), a Daisy, a Sonali doesn't however mean that dependence has given way to autonomy or that the movement has been linear. All that can be said is that a majority of characters are shown as struggling towards greater self-awareness of their situation as women and as persons. Women characters who are writers are a late arrival in the novels. But such representation does not necessarily mean liberation. Many of them are engaged in the quest for identity and also creating more space for themselves in terms of self-fulfilment and individual goals.

2. *Dharma*—Personal Goals

Integral to the larger question of subordination—autonomy is the urge towards living freely and this includes living so as to realize oneself and so as to be happy. The Indian woman's psyche, it needs hardly be said, has traditionally been determined by the need to do one's duty or act according to one's *Dharma*. A wife, according to Manu, must live for her husband and children. Verses 27 and 28 of Chapter 9 of *The Laws of Manu* are relevant here:

> 27. The wife is the visible form of what holds together the begetting of children, the caring for them when they are born, and the ordinary business of every day.
> 28. Children, the fulfilment of duties, obedience, and the ultimate sexual pleasure depend upon a wife, and so does heaven, for oneself and one's ancestors' (p. 200).

Clearly, Manu does not give a woman an existence apart from that of her husband or his family. In these novels questions of self-awareness do keep rising but it is only later that the issues of personal fulfilment and individual happiness come on the agenda of women characters. Raj in *The Day in Shadow* raises the question of personal goals and happiness when he asks the recently divorced Simrit: 'What do you want out of life, Simrit?' Simrit's answer—'Permanence'—does not satisfy him. In actual fact as he points out, she has had no time to find out what she really wanted. This is how the writer concludes Raj's meditation on the subject: 'Had she ever been avid, really avid about anything at all? She simply could not go through life like this, letting other people's ambitions and actions overwhelm her. First it had been her husband. Next it could be her children. *Woman for use had been the rule too long*' (emphasis added pp. 37-8). Vishal Dubey in *Storm in Chandigarh* voices the same concern calling women 'the subdued sex' 'for whom the adventure of self-expression had not even begun'.[12] But once personal goals enter into a woman's consciousness and become a reality, they can pose a challenge to male ego and be a potential cause of marital conflict as in Shashi Deshpande's *The Dark Holds No Terrors* (1980). In this first novel there is role reversal also because Saru the doctor wife earns not only the butter but most of the bread as well[13] and the husband tries to compensate for his failure by being a sadist in bed (p. 102). Jaya's serious writing in *That Long Silence* disturbs her husband Manohar, which induces her to take to writing a safe column entitled *Seeta*.

When does happiness enter the agenda of a woman? The goal of self-fulfilment includes happiness but perhaps the clearest example of happiness as an overriding goal is to be found in *Jasmine* (1990) by Bharati Mukherjee. We must remember two things here: first that Bharati Mukherjee avowedly an American writer has presented Jasmine as having internalized the American goal of happiness and, second, that Jasmine pursues this quest in America. In *Paro* by Namita Gokhale and the novels of Shobha De the quest for happiness appears disguised as a more or less frantic effort to make the best of the passing moment—the unabashed pursuit of sex. But these novels concern only a small fringe. Obviously a life of domesticity is no longer enough to absorb all of a woman's energies. While not quite a central concern, the question of happiness including sexual happiness is slowly edging its way past several other concerns into the frame.

3. Sexual Purity—Sexual Emancipation

Chastity has been a traditional means of patriarchal control of a woman's sexuality. Our mythical prototypes in this respects are Sita and Savitri—Sita who did not yield to the persuasions of the demon king Ravana to marry him and who later proved her wifely virtue by coming out unscathed from the ordeal of fire, and Savitri who because of the power of her chastity[14] could bring her husband back from the world of the dead. The ancient Indian ideal enshrined in *Manusmriti* has been an abiding influence on man-woman relationship ever since.

The question of a woman's sexuality is central to any

consideration of tradition and modernity. The idea of purity and chastity is still the norm and any deviation is generally deeply disturbing to the male psyche. Male promiscuity is however tolerated and dismissed as a sign of masculinity. But there are clear signs of change. This includes a growing awareness of a woman's sexual needs.

Narayan the traditionalist favours chastity among his sympathetic women. Even Mulk Raj Anand in spite of his iconoclasm keeps his Gauri chaste. There is some attempt at redefinition of a virtuous woman in Kamala Markandaya. In *Nectar in a Sieve* Ira feels no hesitation in selling her body if it can help her feed her sick brother. Her answer to her father's shocked discovery is ringing: '[She will go out] tonight and tomorrow and every night, so long as there is need'.[15] Nayantara Sahgal's central characters have no hangover of guilt when they have extramarital affairs. Gita Mehta's Jaya finds in sex with Arun Roy the sexual fulfilment that her husband had denied her in marriage. There are several other examples in Shashi Deshpande. Clearly extramarital sex has come to be looked at with greater understanding.

But Nayantara Sahgal goes a step further. She redefines a virtuous woman by deflecting attention from life-long fidelity to a husband to a more essential quality, essential to a woman's autonomy—courage. Her remarks made in 'Meet the Author' programme of the Sahitya Akademi deserve to be quoted in full:

> My on-going theme would probably be freedom. Then I have another which could be called 'the virtuous woman'—by which I mean that in every novel the heroine has moved one step further away from the stereotype of the virtuous woman into a new definition of virtue. In *This Time of Morning* Rashmi leaves her husband when her incompatible marriage becomes intolerable. In *Storm in Chandigarh* Saroj advances the cause of emancipation. Though she is pregnant with her third child, she leaves her insanely jealous, unreasonable and unfaithful husband, taking her two children with her. In *The Day in Shadow* Simrit who has a large unspecified number of children, walks out with all of them when she is divorced by her husband and hung with a crippling divorce settlement. Our children are among the chains that bind us to the status quo. They are used in blackmail against us. Saroj doesn't succumb. She leaves taking them along. What does these women walking out have to do with their virtue? The meaning of *sati* is a virtuous woman. And this is synonymous with self-immolation—a tradition arising out of the concept that woman is her husband's property and has no other life. Traditional virtue lies in staying put, suffering. The

new woman does the opposite. No more *sati,* she is determined to live, and to live in self-respect. Her virtue is courage, which is a willingness to risk the unknown and to face the consequences. ('Passion for India')[16]

Clearly, *sati* as a dread symbol of a woman's chastity stands rejected. Gita Mehta's Jaya in *Raj* goes further by reinterpreting the idea of *sati** in favour of life and service.

The new definition of a virtuous woman and the sympathetic portrayal of premarital and extramarital sex shows that women are becoming more conscious of their sexual needs and their fulfilment. The advance lies not only in the characters enjoying greater freedom but in fairly close depiction of sex in the novels. Even the usually sedate Narayan who holds that the sex act is a private act and that we should not be peeping into bedrooms goes to the extent of showing Raman fumbling with Daisy's clothes—without of course crossing the *lakshman rekha*—thus far and no further in *The Painter of Signs*.

Nayantara Sahgal and Shashi Deshpande take us inside the bedroom and also inside the consciousness of their characters giving us details that were taboo earlier. The characters are aware of their own sexuality and the effect it has on their relationship with men. Passion in a woman hasn't been accepted for long. When Jayant in *Roots and Shadows* makes this discovery about his wife Indu, he is resentful. Indu responds by pretending to be passive and unresponsive: 'I am still and dead.' She describes herself as an 'anachronism'. 'A woman who loves her husband too much. Too passionately. And is ashamed of it.'[17] She ultimately finds sexual release in the arms of Naren, her cousin, and a confidant,

I lay down impelled by his thrusting body feeling at first a passive languor. Oh, blessed, blessed hardness. An ecstasy filled my body and I could not be still any more. There was a joyous sense of release, of passion I could experience and show and participate in. I clung to him convulsively, marvelling that I did not have to hold myself back. (pp. 151-2)

This is a fair illustration of how descriptions of sex with varying

*Curiously the idea of *sati* finds a place in the consciousness of Mira Cheriyan, the Christian protagonist of the *Salt Doll* by Shourie Daniels. 'Despite my Nazarene background I myself dream of a time when flinging oneself on the funeral pyre of one's husband was a national idea. My self-image not less than his, would have required it. I don't know why, but deep inside I regret the loss of the *sati* ideal', New Delhi: Vikas, 1978, p. 115.

degrees of explicitness are integrated with the narratives in Sahgal and Deshpande. Shashi Deshpande's characters are more open, more frank with themselves and with others. This makes it possible for a daughter to confess her marital rape to her father in *The Dark Holds No Terrors*. Saru's confession is self-conscious:

> 'Does it shock you to hear such things? I know you're my father and I'm your daughter and there's nearly thirty years between us, but still. . . . You're a man and I'm a woman. Can we talk of such things?'
>
> 'Why not?' he said and his voice came out husky. . . . 'Do you know, Saru, I often feel sorry that we left so many things unsaid, your mother and I . . . . Now. . . . Go on, tell me. Tell me everything.'
>
> *'He's cruel to me . . . in bed'* (emphasis added).

The old barriers are breaking down.

When we move on to Namita Gokhale and Shobha De, we enter the world of the affluent and the aspiring middle classes with a new sexual morality and their uninhibited language. Products of consumer culture, the women who hold centre stage in the novels have an enormous appetite for life. Setting aside past inhibitions not always without guilt feelings, they insist on the right to have sexual life of their own both before and after marriage.

Namita Gokhale presents two new kinds of characters in her *Paro* (1984). First there is a bitch goddess heroine who is greedy for life and sex: 'Her need to live was so total, greedy and heedless that she would doubtless have exhausted anyone in the sexual fray'.[18] Priya the narrator, who belongs to the lower middle class, in describing Paro's life vocalizes her own secret longings and fantasies with disarming honesty. Here are two pieces from Paro and one from Priya. The difference between them is partly the difference in their social backgrounds:

> 'See what this prick [her young admirer Avinendra after a violent quarrel] has done to me!' she shrieked, throwing her breasts open to all to see and beating on them frenziedly. 'Do you want to see my cunt as well? He thinks I'm a whore—I'll show you what a whore's cunt looks like!' (p. 48)

> 'You sneak,' she [Paro at the discovery of Priya's diary] would hiss, 'you little spy, you bloody lesbo, you don't even have the guts to live your own bloody life, always creeping about me and Bubu . . . tell me, who turns you on more, me or your darling B.R. [Paro's former husband]? Hah, B.R. that miserable prick, hah!' (p. 101)

> 'I napped lightly for a while and then I began to masturbate. I did not

fantasize but sometimes I became Paro, and sometimes I was myself. Sometimes I was B.R. devouring Paro, and then B.R. tenderly loving Priya, and then I became Suresh who was ravishing Paro, and then Paro with Suresh in slavish possession, and intermittently, Suresh copulating with Priya who was actually Paro. I was all these people; fragments of their thoughts, feelings, terrors passed through my writhing body. . . .' (pp. 52-3)

Compared to Namita Gokhale, Shobha De is even more audacious and violent in her language with little reserve in her description of human anatomy.

This explicitness also includes mention of sexual feelings considered unmentionable in themselves earlier. Anita Desai describes Bim's incestuous feelings for her retarded brother Baba in *Clear Light of Day* which are perfectly consonant with her character and her situation and which have been brought in with great artistry:

She felt an immense, almost irresistible yearning to lie down beside him on the bed, stretched out limb to limb, silent and immobile together. She felt that they must be the same length, that his slightness would fit in beside her size, that his concavities would mould together with his convexities. Together they would form a whole that would be perfect and pure. She only needed to lie down and stretch out beside him to become whole and perfect.

Instead, she went out. (p. 166)

There is a novel of Shobha De's that I wish particularly to mention here, *Strange Obsession* (1992) that deals with the difficult subject of lesbianism. While the novelist shows a certain boldness in taking up this subject—there is perhaps no other novel in Indo-Anglian fiction that does this—the treatment is wholly traditional and the end is wholly melodramatic in the style of a Bombay film. Minx's (Meenakshi Iyenger's) passion for a Bombay model Amrita is presented as an abnormal, weird, unnatural passion of a pervert who has a pathological need for possession. Twice we are given a close-up of Minx's lesbian love-making with Amrita who feels 'trapped' and wants to be rescued. She is ultimately rescued and is married off in a traditional way to Rakesh but not before Minx has chased the new couple to the place of their honeymoon and has tried to burn their room down. There is no attempt on the part of any character either to explain this sexual phenomenon or present the other side. The two exceptions to this are feeble. When Amrita goes to seek help from a friend, Partha, he describes Minx's lesbianism as 'alternative sexuality': I won't call her a lesbo. The correct term these days for them is . . . people who practice *alternative sexuality*[19] (emphasis added), but this line is not pursued any further. The other is the brief explanation of Minx's strange obsession offered by her father towards the end. Was the writer too busy in titillating the reader to worry about doing justice to her creation, Minx? Or did she lack courage to take a sympathetic view?

4. Silence—Speech[20]

Silence—Speech dichotomy can be useful in locating women on the tradition-modernity axis. How do women characters respond to male hegemony? Is it silence or is it speech? Not to talk back is part of the culturally inherited value of modesty and is considered essentially feminine. In this sense silence is a symbol of oppression, a characteristic of the subaltern condition. On the contrary, speech signifies self-expression and liberation. This would depend on their self-perception and self-awareness. But silence and speech may not always be diametrically opposites. Silence which results from a freely chosen refusal to speak may signify displeasure, resistance or suppressed anger, and speech may mean collaboration with the oppressor. Moreover, an alternative to silence may be action, not speech which may be dismissed as mere words. The whole question of women and language is complex and deserves a fuller treatment than is possible in this introduction.

Here I wish to suggest that Indo-Anglian novels furnish examples of a whole range of attitudes from silence to speech and/or action and other variations. I have chosen four texts to indicate this range. An early example of female acquiescence is Rukmani in Kamala Markandaya's *Nectar in a Sieve* who accepts her husband's extra-marital affair tamely within the space of a few sentences: 'Disbelief first; disillusionment; anger, reproach, pain' (p. 120). And when she speaks she absolves her husband shifting the blame on the other woman: 'It is as you say a long time ago I said wearily. 'That she is evil and powerful I know myself. Let it rest' (p. 120). Significantly the character's silence is matched by the writer's silence on the subject. Savitri in *The Dark Room* is another patient sufferer but when provoked even she speaks up. In words that are reminiscent of Clarissa's passionate words to her seducer Lovelace ['the man who has been the villain to me that you have been shall never be my husband'], she tells her husband: 'You are not having me and her at the same time.' Her words before she leaves home are a revolt against man—be he a husband or a father. When her husband points to some ornaments saying that they were not given by him, she grandly says: 'Take them away. They are also a man's gift.' But her protest is unavailing because it is not backed by any effective action. Perhaps the text that best examplifies the silence-speech dichotomy is *That Long Silence*. Here the acquiescent Sita image and the image of two oxen yoked together are both rejected. Jaya's past has been one long story of acquiescence in her husband's will. Her husband objected to her writing and she stopped writing and instead took to writing 'middles' and then a safe column by 'Seeta'. But at the end she will break the silence of centuries and speak a different language: 'While studying Sanskrit drama I'd learnt with a sense of outrage that its rigid rules did not permit women character to speak Sanskrit. They had to use Prakrit—a language that had sounded to my ears like a baby's lisp. The anger I'd felt then comes back to me when I realize . . . that *I have been speaking Prakrit*' (emphasis added, pp. 192-3). Jaya's recognition that women are responsible for their own fate recalls Savitri's realization but Jaya looks forward to supportive action.

Here Bharati Mukherjee's *Wife* (1976) needs to be mentioned because it shows a woman moving from silence to action without recourse to speech. Dimple is trapped in a loveless marriage with Amit with whom 'she talked in silences'.[21] The only person she could talk to was Milt Glasser, her American friend, in whose arms she finds love in her New York apartment. Towards the end her frustrations at being imprisoned in the deadening routine of her bourgeois existence erupts into a chilling act of self-assertion—she knifes her husband. With Casca in *Julius Caesar* she could say: 'Speak hands for me.' Dimple is of course an extreme case but clearly women characters have started unlearning to not speak and asserting their individuality and even taking decisive action.

As for the anthology an attempt has been made to make it representative. While a large number of novels chosen focus on women in an urban setting, several of them deal with women in small towns or even villages. Two are partly located abroad. Again while most are concerned with different eras of British and post-colonial India, Gita Mehta's *Raj* takes us to the princely India. Muslim women are represented in Salman Rushdie's *Shame* and Shama Futehally's *Tara Lane*.

The anthology presents novels written by both men and women. Interestingly, but perhaps predictably, not many men have written about women in a central way. Mulk Raj Anand's *Gauri* and R.K. Narayan's *The Dark Room* and *The Painter of Sing* are the notable exceptions. It is only with the arrival of women writers like Kamala Markandaya, Anita Desai, Rama Mehta, Nayantara Sahgal, Shashi Deshpande and several others that women have moved centre stage. Some of these writers take us inside the consciousness of their women characters to present their plight, fears, dilemmas, contradictions and ambitions. Shashi Deshpande's article has been included because it puts some of the issues relating to writing on and by women and the grooming of a woman as a writer in a wider perspective. For reasons beyond our control the article on her novels was unfortunately withdrawn at the last moment.

The last two decades have seen the emergence of writers of controversial merit like Namita Gokhale and Shobha De who present their versions of the newly liberated woman and who demand attention. In one view these women writers have sensed the state of flux within the new bourgeois society they belong to. 'They write to describe the process that proclaims: "We are different, notice us. We have a secret life and longings we must speak about."' 'Their narratives, their characters and their language are part of a pattern that emerges whenever a social order changes, when suppressed voices find utterance and a new world opens.'[22] Clearly, the new urban female with her insistent sexuality is finding utterance, but the experiences of underprivileged women still remain largely blocked off from the Indian novel in English.

The fault, dear Brutus, lies not in our stars but in the situation of our writers in English. Analysing this situation, Meenakshi Mukherjee points out that historically English has been the language of privilege and has had an aura of exclusiveness and is not a value neutral medium of communication. The women writers in English still belong to the urban elite for 'proficiency in the language is determined by the cultural class and incidentally, the levels of economic affluence'.[23] She goes on to acknowledge that

> all the new and exciting writers that have enlivened the Indo-Anglian literary scene in the last couple of years. Amitav Ghosh, Upamanyu Chatterjee, Alan Sealy, Vikram Seth, and Shashi Tharoor—are almost all products of a single college in Delhi and possibly a couple of exclusive public schools. To state this is not to marginalize their works but to precisely locate them in the

cultural context of India. There are not many women among the remarkable crop of young writers, but when they fo emerge, . . . the same socio-economic deteriments will be operative in their work as well perhaps even more acutely.

This is not a very happy prognosis. We can only wait for the emergence of a woman writer who has a room of her own and adequate amount of money but who by an act of imagination can empathize with the lives of her less-privileged sisters and transmute their experiences into works of art.

NOTES

1. J.C. Heesterman, *The Inner Conflict of Tradition: Essays in Indian Ritual, Kingship, and Society* (Delhi: OUP, 1985), p. 15.
2. *Colonialism, Tradition and Reform: An Analysis of Gandhi's Political Discourse* (New Delhi: Sage, 1989), p. 17. See also on p. 16.
3. Tr. by Wendy Doniger with Brian K. Smith (New Delhi:1991, rpt. 1992), p. 115.
4. *That Long Silence* (New Delhi: Penguin, 1989), p. 11.
5. *The Dark Room* (New Delhi: Penguin, 1991, rpt. 1992).
6. The reference originally in to *Brihadaranyaka Upanishad* (IV. V. 4). Another example of a character going back to the past is Jayadeva in *Music for Mohini*, who sees some mystic resemblance 'between Maitrayee and Mohini' (p. 71). See also: 'If only she were his Maitrayee, his fellow traveller they would have worked together in complete harmony' (p. 124).
7. 'On the writing of a Novel', *Indian Women Novelists*, Vol. 5, ed. R.K. Dhawan (New Delhi: Prestige, 1991), p. 34.
8. (New Delhi: Allied, 1980), pp. 140-1.
9. 'India' in *The Commonwealth Novel Since 1960*, ed. Bruce King (London: Macmillan, 1991), p. 75.
10. 'It is to be recognized as a centaur [gandharva] marriage when the girl and her lover join with one another in sexual union because they want to, out of desire.' *The Laws of Manu*, 3.32, p. 46.
11. Introduction, *Socialization, Education and Women* (New Delhi: Orient Longman, 1988), p. 7.
12. (Delhi: Hind Pocket Books, n.d.), p. 189.
13. (New Delhi: Vikas, 1980), p. 182.
14. The legend of Kali is yet another example of the power which chastity confers on woman.
15. (New Delhi: Sagar Pubs., 1968), p. 137.
16. *Indian Literature*, Vol. XXXII, No. 129, Jan.-Feb. 1989, pp. 83-4.

17. 1983 (New Delhi: rpt. Disha Books, 1992), p. 83.
18. (London: Pavanne, 1985), p. 121.
19. (New Delhi: Penguin, 1992), p. 113.
20. For this section I am indebted in Rajeswari Sunder Rajan's discussion of this subject in her *Real and Imagined Women: Gender, Culture and Post-Colonialism* (London: Routledge, 1993), pp. 83-98.
21. (New Delhi: Sterling, 1976), p. 191.
22. Ira Pande, 'Literature of the baby-log', *Seminar* 384, Aug. 1991 (New Writing in English Issue), p. 38.
23. These remarks were a part of keynote address delivered by Prof. Meenakshi Mukherjee at a seminar on Women Creative Writers organised at Jodhpur in March 1990. See *Between Spaces of Silence: Women Creative Writers*, ed. Kamini Dinesh (New Delhi: Sterling, 1994), p. 18. See also Mulk Raj Anand, 'In Yama's Hell': Indian English Writing about Women, ibid., pp. 1-5.

Of Concerns, Of Anxieties

Shashi Deshpande

I once heard Salman Rushdie say in a TV interview, that it is the first fourteen years of one's life that are of enormous importance for a writer. Most writers will agree with this. It is what happens in these years that has the greatest influence on one, that in effect shapes one as a writer.

There are three things in my early life that have shaped me as a writer. These are:

That my father was a writer.
That I was educated exclusively in English.
And that I was born a female.

When I speak of my father's being a writer having influenced me, I do not speak of genetic factors. How big a role the genes play in this, how much it has helped to make me a writer, I do not know. Nor do I mean by this that I was consciously shaped by my father to become a writer—the way musicians or dancers are. The influence was far more subtle and indirect and I can see it only now, through the space of time that separates me from my childhood. The number and variety of books at home, for example, and their accessibility. To read soon became as necessary as to breathe or eat. Ever since I can remember I was an addict. And there was the atmosphere in our house, the company my father kept, the kind of friends he had, the conversation and discussion that went on over endless cups of tea, the play-reading and rehearsals that took place at home—all this created a world of words and ideas I was happily submerged in.

Equally important were my father's ideas and beliefs. He was born in a very orthodox family but had very early moved away from it. His hatred of blind faith in orthodox beliefs and superstition stayed with him till the end. A great advocate of rational logical thinking, a four-year stay abroad gave him a love of Western liberal ideas. And, on returning home in 1930, he fell in love with Gandhism. All these ideas, practised by him, not preached, formed part of my childhood.

However, the greatest gift he gave us, his children, was intellectual freedom. There was never any attempt to impose any ideas on us, no attempt at shaping our thinking, no hard and fast rules laid down for behaviour. There was this too: that my father being a writer made writing real to me. It was not just a profession, it was a way of living. For me too, ever since I began writing, writing was serious work, it was never 'just a hobby' which is what it is invariably regarded as. Specially when you are a woman and a house-bound woman at that, it becomes the equivalent of flower-arrangement, or embroidery or things like that. It was never that way for me.

Today, when English education is so widespread, it may seem odd to speak of my being educated in English having made a difference. But in those days most parents sent their children to the regional language schools; that was the norm. There had to be some reason for not doing it, for sending your children to an English school. That my father, who had such a great love of his own languages and literatures, did it seems a bit surprising. Perhaps it was because my mother and he had two different languages that he decided to opt for a third, a neutral one. Perhaps it was so that we would not have to be confined to Karnataka. However, I think that the truth is that his years abroad had given him an admiration for Western, specially, English ideas, language and literature. And so we went to a 'convent'. In those days one could get away without learning the regional language—incredible though it sounds now. There was a second language, which for me was Sanskrit. But I hated it—the hairsplitting grammar, the compound words, the endless sentences became the bane of my life. And so, by the time I was seven or eight, English became my language. I read enormously, from children's books to Jane Austen, the Brontes, Dickens, George Eliot, Hardy: before I was out of school I had gone through them all. Strangely, I came to the lightweight stuff later—I read romances and detective novels in my teens, Enid Blyton only with my children, and now I have moved on to Asterix, Tin Tin, Beetle Bailey, Hagar the Horrible and all those other characters who make the morning paper bearable.

But ours was by no means a Westernized household. Apart from the fact that we lived in a small town, in a middle class family, there was the fact that my father taught Sanskrit in college, he wrote in Kannada, read English and had married a Marathi wife. Home was a harmonious mixture of languages. Kalidasa and Bhavabhuti, Shivaram Karanth and Masti Venkatesh Iyengar were names as familiar as Ibsen and Shaw. And if in school we did Wordsworth and Tennyson, at home we had to learn the *Amarkosha* by heart. Nevertheless, all reading was in English.

Let me say it aloud: I have no regrets at all about having been exposed to English literature. What I do regret enormously, more and more now, is that I was cut off from my own languages and literature. In effect, it meant that I was cut off from a whole literary tradition, my own literary tradition, which is an enormous loss for a writer. There was a backdoor entry, of course, which I took: I read everything translated into English that I could get my hands on (and discovered that Sanskrit was more than just grammar. *Svapna-vasavadatta* gave me the same thrill Jane Eyre did.). But this was very limited—translations were very few then. I did learn on my own to read both the languages we spoke at home—Kannada and Marathi. But English was and remained the language of my thinking, it was the language in which I expressed myself. Therefore when I began to write I wrote in English. There was no question of choice. I am so very often asked this question: why do you write in English? I guess the question comes to me more often than it does to other writers in English, perhaps because my father is a known Kannada writer. I am always aware that it is a loaded question, that it carries political overtones. But the answer is a very simple one. I write in English because it is the only language I can express myself in.

I myself have never felt the need to defend the fact that I write in English. But I must admit that writing in English in this country, specially at the time I began writing, did confront me with certain problems. I am not speaking of the problems of writing about this cultural milieu in a foreign not alien—language, of writing in a language which most of your characters will not be speaking. These are problems one learns to cope with, there is a kind of challenge in facing them. And English is an amazingly flexible and versatile language. My problems were different. There was a sense of isolation. I was part of no writers' group, neither physically nor literally. The English writers of the day were not my role models, nor did I feel any kind of literary kinship with them. The only common factor was that we were Indians and that we wrote in English. And so in a sense I wrote in a vacuum.

This was true in another sense as well. I was nearly thirty when I began writing. I had written nothing until then, not a short story, not an article, not even a poem. I had never thought, imagined or dreamt of becoming a writer. I just began writing. I wrote three articles which were, amazingly, published. This was the beginning. I joined the Bharatiya Vidya Bhavan Journalism course after this and found out, suddenly, how much at home I felt in this occupation. It was as if something lying dormant in me through the years was suddenly wakened. I wrote a short story for a magazine I briefly worked with and then it was one short story after another. But all this writing was done in a total isolation. I had no one with whom I could speak of my writing, no companionship of like-minded people. There was no feedback to tell me whether what I wrote had any merit. Cloistered in a house with two young children, I had the additional disadvantages of low self-esteem and indifferent health. And most frustrating of all, time for writing was never available at a stretch. It came in little bits, in between chores, when the children were sleeping or at school. And even these tiny bits were subject to constant interruption. And, of course, there were always rejection slips.

But there was no time when I felt I could give up. And there were assets—I had a good Parker pen, a brother-in-law gave me an old writing table and I had the use of the typewriter in my husband's office after office hours. And I wanted to write and could write. Soon I found that the women's magazines of the time—*Femina* and *Eve's Weekly*, began to publish my stories. At first it felt good. I was writing and getting published. Later, however, I was not so happy; it seemed that writing for women's magazines deprived me of recognition as a serious writer. I became known as one 'who writes for *Femina, Eve's Weekly*'. It took me a long time to get away from that. Now I have turned round again. I know that the fact of publication helped me to grow as a writer. Just writing, without publishing, is like acting in your room before a mirror. It is never the real thing. Acting before an audience is the real thing. And I got a readership, the extent of which I have been slowly discovering over the years. So that when I began writing novels, I was not totally unknown.

It was a short story 'The Intrusion' that was the turning point of my writing career. V.S. Naipaul, in his 'Enigma of Arrival', mentioning a moment early in his writing career says, 'all at once material, tone of voice and writing skill had locked together and began to develop together'. This is exactly what happened to me with 'The Intrusion'. It was a story that almost wrote itself. For the first time I had a sense of power within, the knowledge, as Graham Greene puts it, of the unconscious collaborating with me. To have the unexpected happen in your writing, to find surprises waiting for you as you write is, as many writers have said, a heady experience. With this story I broke through another barrier—there were never any inhibitions, or consciousness of my writing being associated with me personally after that. It was years before I dared to call myself a writer, but the beginning of that knowledge was here.

This consciousness of one's own voice is a very important development for a writer; until then, most writers are groping, feeling their way, imitating other writers. I certainly was doing this. But after 'The Intrusion', it was my own voice that I began to speak in. The stories I wrote then, and the novels that followed, marked me out as a 'woman writer', as a woman who wrote about women.

I must admit I have very mixed feelings about these labels. Yes, I did and I do write about women. Most of my writing comes out of my own intense and long suppressed feelings about what it is to be a woman in our society, it comes out of the experience of the difficulty of playing the different roles enjoined on me by society, it comes out of the knowledge that I am something more and something different from the sum total of these roles. My writing comes out of my consciousness of the conflict between my idea of myself as a human being and the idea that society has of me as a woman. All this makes my writing very clearly women's writing.

Gender is, undoubtedly, one of the most important factors in our lives. The first question asked when a child is born is 'boy or girl'? Our lives are to a great extent shaped by our gender. So are our experiences related to it. But these gender-related experiences are a part of the human experience. And, as a writer, I deal with these experiences the same way any writer does with any experience. I expected such writings to be of interest to all human beings. However, I found out, very early in my writing career, that women's experiences are believed to be of interest only to women, that women's problems, ideas and lives are specifically and narrowly considered women's problems, not human ones. It is male problems, male ideas and male experiences which are human. I also realized that in a world dominated by male values, while the class and the class struggle are taken seriously, the gender struggle is not. In fact, the women's movement is the only one, I think, against which the weapon of ridicule has been consciously, consistently and fairly successfully employed. If it is not a joke, it is a boring kind of mass moaning, a mass scale nagging.

For quite a while, I believed—a belief that came from all around me—that men's lives are more important, more significant. And, therefore, that serious writing is done by men and is about men. That women's writing, like their lives, somehow lacks weight and substance. That there was something embarrassing about such writing and one had to feel apologetic about it. For long, I had to fight against the feeling that my writing is second class writing for the sole reason that it is about women. Yet when I wrote *The Dark Holds No Terrors* I never thought of it as a women's novel. It was difficult to write, it was different from the other novels I had read written by Indian writers, it was, I hoped, good, it satisfied me as much as one's writing can satisfy one. But all the reviews that came spoke of it as a novel about a woman, a middle class woman, a professional woman, etc. In effect, a novel about a woman. And then I wrote *That Long Silence.* A lifetime of introspection went into this novel, the most autobiographical of all my writing, not in the personal details but in the thinking and ideas.

With the writing of this novel I crossed another barrier. It was with this novel that I, as Naipaul says 'defined myself through my work'. It was with the articulation of all that had been in me through the years that I came to feminism, to a consciousness of myself as a feminist. I read a great deal after this—Simone de Beauvoir, Germaine Greer, Betty Friedan, Kate Millet, Virginia Woolf—whose *A Room of Ones Own*, along with Simone de Beauvoir's *The Second Sex* have been the greatest influence on me. But it was not these books that made me a feminist; they were only confirmatory. My idea of feminism came to me out of my own life, my own experiences and thinking. To come to an awareness of yourself through your own knowledge is a great feeling. It is like drinking Asterix's magic potion. You feel full of power. No more feeling that my gender made me or my work inferior.

And yet the problem of women's writing being marginal remains. For it still is, and continues to be, a man's world. And therefore a woman is seen as not-a-man, her mind is not-a-man's-mind, her writing is not-a-man's-writing. The very letter the Sahitya Akademi wrote to me about this meet wrote of the writer 'speaking about himself, his struggle, his achievements, his view of life as presented in his works'. It's no use saying that he includes she. That kind of usage is no longer possible. If man includes woman, why do we have two separate words? Why do we have the comprehensive word 'human'? The insensitivity of language towards women is but one telling aspect of the whole problem. The problem faces me all the time for I am constantly referred to as a 'woman writer'. Why is the word 'woman' necessary? Do I, as a writer, have to always carry my identity tag of 'woman' round my neck? Why is it relevant? Would the phrase 'male writer' have been used for a man?

The fact is that one is always put in the context not of writers but of women writers. This kind of ghettoization makes me angry. To categorize literature on the basis of gender is ridiculous. And if we have to separate writers on the basis of gender, we need to have two categories—men's writing and women's writing—not writing and women's writing. Things are changing a bit. Women's writing, if it is feminist writing, is to some extent being taken seriously. But at the same time, because it is feminist, it cannot belong to the mainstream. A Catch 22 situation, if ever there was one.

'To be a writer is not a state of competence or achievement or fame or content at which one arrived and where one stayed', Naipaul's words. It's true. One never arrives. Each novel, each short story is a new beginning, it is the first, it never gets easier. The thought that you have to begin, to do it all, out of what is in you, 'your own internal resources' as Naipaul calls it, is frightening.

But there's the other side of the coin. To start on any writing, a novel specially, is like embarking on an adventure. You don't know what lies ahead. There are surprises, you suddenly make discoveries. Whatever it is, it is certainly never dull or boring.

But there's also this, that you feel guilty as well. You are privileged. How many humans are able to do work they enjoy? Writing often seems like self-indulgence.

And again, there often is a sense of futility. What purpose does this writing serve, whom are you doing it for? If you never wrote a word, no one would miss it.

In any case, there is nothing else I want to do, nothing else I can do. If I were to be asked what I have done with my life I will have to admit that I have done nothing but look after my family, bring up my children and write. I admire versatility in others but I have learnt to accept my own narrowness. Now, after 26 years of writing I am able to define myself as a novelist and short story writer. I don't think any qualifying words are necessary—not Indian, not

Indo-English, not woman, not feminist, not third world.

Ramchandra Sharma in an article says that you cannot have poetry without faith. According to me you cannot have any writing without faith. As a writer, I believe that a moral vision exists at the heart of all literature and that without this strong faith in the moral nature of human beings, literature is worthless. I believe that writing is a calling, that it is not a craft, nor, as it seems to be becoming, a business and that the writer's integrity should be to herself/himself.

There was a time when I was scornful of what is called committed writing. I considered such writing flawed because its being message-oriented diminishes its artistic worth. But now I know that all good writing is socially committed writing, it comes out of a concern for the human predicament. I believe, as Camus says, that the greatness of an artist is measured by the balance the writer maintains between the values of creation and the values of humanity.

I find the mainstream theory of literature abhorrent. According to me, all writing that probes with honesty and artistry into the human situation is mainstream literature. The writer's race, class, caste, colour, gender—none of these matter.

I believe that English writing in this country is a part of our literatures; I consider English as one more of our '*bhashas*', as Ganesh Devy calls them. I know that our writing comes out of an involvement with this society, out of our experiences here, our readership is now here, and happily, our publishers are here as well. Yet, I am disturbed by the recent trend in English writing which in its pursuit of role models outside, is alienating itself from its roots.

I am equally disturbed by the media focus creating celebrities and superstars among writers. By this, we are bringing a sense of competition which is deadly for writers. They are insecure enough without this. For the same reason I am uneasy about awards and prizes as well. Recognition is certainly necessary for a writer—it is hard to go on without any recognition at all; but creating celebrities in the interests of sales harms writers. Most of the time, the publicity has no relation to either the output or the merit of the writer. And while such publicity may help to sell some more copies, it certainly doesn't do the author any good. Saul Bellow calls it a minor disorder—'the disease of people who live by an image of themselves created by papers, TV'. One of my favourite quotes is Virginia Woolf's line about Shakespeare: 'Now I think Shakespeare was very happy in this, that there was no impediment of fame, but his genius flowed out of him.' Yes, fame can be an impediment.

A few days back, I was asked a question: do you think you have been denied opportunity and recognition because you are a woman? Opportunity? No, I have not been denied that. I have been able to write, I have been able to write what I want, the way I want, at the pace I want. I have never had to compromise on anything in my writing. I have been lucky that both in my childhood home and my married one, I have had the full freedom to think, to live and work my way.

But recognition? Yes, I think I have been denied that. I have been put into the slot of woman writer, my writing has been categorized as 'writing about women' or feminist writing. In this process, much in it has been missed. I have been denied the place and dignity of a writer who is dealing with issues that are human issues, of interest to all humanity.

The Uneasy Mix of Tradition and Modernity: Bhattacharya's *Music for Mohini*

T.N. Dhar

Bhabani Bhattacharya, like Mulk Raj Anand, had definite views on the function of art and the role of a writer in society, though he did not write about them as extensively as Anand. In one of his well-known essays on the subject, he stressed the novelist's engagement with truth about society which, unlike the philosopher, he revealed in 'no cold statements of dogma but only in terms of life rendered through the devices of dramatization'.[1] In dramatizing this truth, Bhattacharya's novels come to grips with several social, political, cultural, and moral issues. These include his persistent concern with social change, the complex relation between tradition and modernity, and the changing status of woman in Indian society. He particularly wanted it to be known that women occupied a special position in his novels. In response to her query, he wrote to Marlene Fisher that his women characters are superior to men, because they have 'more depth, more richness in them than our menfolk', and that in adapting themselves to the transition from old to new, women have shown a deeper sense of commitment and a greater capacity for adjustment than men.[2] Using it as a basis for her essay on Bhattacharya's women, Fisher writes that in his novels 'women are either the central characters themselves, or of at least equal importance as the male characters, or provide the inspiration and meaning from which a man derives his strength'.[3] The main argument of this essay is that both Bhattacharya and Fisher are not wholly correct. In several of his novels, women have just a marginal role. Even where they have a substantial presence, Bhattacharya does not permit them the required freedom to initiate any meaningful change on their own. In fact, whatever possibilities of change his novels provide for are largely initiated by men; women only follow suit. It is true that women in his novels are brave, courageous, witty, clever, and in no way inferior to men, but they are conceived and presented within a male-dominated society, in which they are subservient to them. Even when they come out of their traditional moorings, it is only because men encourage them to do so. The limits of their freedom are set by them.

I start with examples of two novels in which women figure marginally. The first one is *So Many Hungers*! It is primarily a dramatization of one of the most traumatic experiences of the people of Bengal. Kajoli, as one of the many sufferers, has been drawn as a bold and courageous woman, who is capable of supreme sacrifice: she is prepared to sell her body for the sake of her mother and brother. Except for one or two short details, we do not get to know much about her as a woman, chiefly because the novel does not provide any scope for this. The details we get project her as a woman who is traditional in her thinking and actions. Devata considers her the very embodiment of the cultural norms of old India. When she touches Rahoul's feet, Devata remarks: 'She is a wellbred peasant girl. She has a legacy of manners as old as India. How could she give up her manners and proprieties to suit your new-fangled ideas?'[4] Kajoli's adherence to tradition has the novelist's approval, because Devata is a sympathetically-drawn character.

Kajoli's attitude towards marriage also attests to her respect for tradition. Her husband is selected for her by her father, who is in jail. Between Kajoli's first meeting with him and their wedding, we get only one small scene in a field, which confirms their attraction for each other: 'Their eyes met and forgot to withdraw. And there was such joy in his glance, such worship, that it shamed her, and she caught her breath, flushing, her eyes darting away. She stood in dumb silence, looking down.'[5] The narrator tells us that 'with her woman's instinct', Kajoli grasped the meaning of this glance: he was to relieve her of hard work and act as her protector. For shortly afterwards, he tells her: 'You will never again hold the sickle to reap. Not as long as my arm has strength. Not so long as my body has breath.'[6] Kajoli considers marriage a soul-filling experience of surrender. She tells Kishore that a 'woman wed has no hungers left to be filled'.[7]

In *He Who Rides a Tiger*, which is the most rhetorical of Bhattacharya's novels, Lekha has to go through a series of harrowing experiences, before she is rescued by her father Kalo. When he puts on the Brahminical identity of Mangal Adhikari, to avenge himself on society, Lekha is reduced to a mere adjunct. She grows into a beautiful woman, but feels that she is in prison. When she cannot bear it any longer, she tells him pointedly: 'I had enough of this gilded cage. You are content with it. How long must it hold me too?'[8] Her interest in living revives, when she meets Biten. But before their association can develop into a meaningful relationship, Kalo pushes her into the role of the Mother of Sevenfold Bliss. When she consents to marry Moti Chand to save Obhijit, she is virtually dead as a woman. Her readiness to marry, however, awakens Kalo to his real self. He makes a clean breast of his actions before a large gathering of people. The design of the novel does not allow any meaningful role for Lekha as a woman; she only provides Kalo a reason for revenge and, later on, for the realization of his true self.

In *Shadow from Ladakh*, Bhattacharya provides more space for women. By using interior monologues, he also provides access to their minds. Two main women are Satyajit's wife Suruchi and their daughter Sumita. The name-symbolism is flattering to them: the first one is an embodiment of good taste, the second of good sense, but both are in bondage to Satyajit.

In his pursuit of Gandhian ideals, Satyajit become extremely self-centred and pushes Suruchi into trying and difficult situations. When he decides to become a *brahmachari*, he gives Suruchi the freedom to remarry, but like a true Indian wife, which is Bhattacharya's ideal, she stays on with him and be 'his companion in ideas even if they are so very strange'.[9] But midway in the novel, when she is face to face with the problem of Jhanak, a spirited young woman who refuses to conform to the rigid discipline of Gandhigram, she realizes that she was no more than a stopgap: 'A stopgap—that had been her assigned role over the years. Humble, self-effacing, she had accepted that role without complaint. An ideal wife. Ideal indeed!'[10]

Suruchi is not merely conscious of what she has lacked over the years; there is also a note of regret in her voice. That is why she resolves that 'she would not stop Jhanak, who has something she herself had never possessed: courage, the resolve to grasp life between her hands; and the boldness to fight tooth and nail to secure what she deeply wanted'.[11] She also wakes up to the plight of Sumita, who, under the strong influence of Satyajit, had virtually forgotten that she was a woman. To release her from his oppressive grip, Bhattacharya develops the relationship between Sumita and Bhaskar in all its fullness. This is the only instance where the novelist allows a woman to become her own self. Fisher is far from being correct when she says that Sumita is a flat character.[12] A large part of the action of the novel shows how she grows and changes and ultimately achieves liberation from her domineering father. The interesting thing about it is that this is made possible by the love, sympathy, tenderness, and restraint that Bhaskar shows in dealing with her. The process of her change is slow, but steady. When it reaches its crescendo, 'she felt displaced, pulled from the roots of her inner self, and terribly confused. . . . She could well afford to be more concerned with her own Being. With her own becoming.'[13]

Music for Mohini is different from the novels I have already referred to. Its very title suggests that Mohini is central to its conception. It deals mainly with her girlhood, marriage, and life with her husband in a village. The novel also dramatizes the relation between tradition and modernity in very specific terms. All its characters are acutely conscious of it and discuss it in relation to actual living situations. For some, like Jayadev, it is part of an intellectual exercise, which has far-reaching social consequences. It is significant that though the problem of change has been dealt with by the novelist in relation to Mohini, two people who consciously articulate its needs and suggest ways of making it viable are her father and her husband.

Since the issue of modernity is woven into the texture of the novel, we need to see it in a perspective which is occasionally hinted in it. If tradition and modernity are seen in India in conflicting terms, it is because of its unusual history. Its civilizational past, which goes back to several hundred centuries, provided it the basis of a strong tradition. Rooted in its sociocultural ethos and heavily coloured by religion, it sanctified certain kinds of thinking, attitudes, and social practices, which did not alter much with the passage of time. But the advent of the British changed it all. Indians had to reckon with the impact of another civilization, which virtually forced them to examine critically and self-consciously the whole gamut of their tradition and the possibilities it held for making the country modern. Very broadly, modernity implies specific attitudes in which human beings relate to the world around them, such as accepting a world-view based on empirical, scientific knowledge and laying emphasis on the power of the individual to shape his/her life on the basis of a rational, secular morality. Since the basis of India's tradition and the demands of modernity looked almost incompatible, all thinking beings got involved in a cultural debate, right from the nineteenth century, to find ways and means of bridging the gap between the two. Except for a small group who upheld the strength of tradition, people proposed two major ways of resolving the tangle. The radical ones advocated a wholesale rejection of India's tradition, though this was easier said than done. The more pragmatic ones chose to retrieve whatever of value they could from the tradition, so that the transition to modernity could be less traumatic. In this transaction, the two are seen in a new spirit of accommodation, which also informs Bhattacharya's *Music for Mohini*, leading to what I have called the uneasy mix of modernity and tradition. The novel also dramatizes the changing position of woman within this synthesizing spirit.

Mohini's father and her husband Jayadev are the leading advocates of modernity in the novel; the former is a staunch opponent of tradition, but the latter does not want to dispense with it altogether. Both create space for change in woman's position and status, though they approach it from different perspectives. Mohini's father considers modernity as an attitude which can be cultivated through proper education, but its distinctive markers are to be decided by men. Discarding his mother's suggestion that Mohini be cast in the traditional mould by being taught Sanskrit and trained at home, he sends her to an 'English convent school'; this he thought would help to 'mould the girl in a modern way'.[14] He also allows her to sing on the radio and get her songs recorded. When he finds her reading a novel with a title like *The Poisoned Kiss*, he just twitches her ear, because 'he did not believe in censuring the books a young girl wanted to read' (p. 18). He dismisses his mother's plea for a horoscope for her by saying that 'in this age of microscope, who needs a horoscope?' He regards the practice no more than an amazing joke. In the same spirit, he censures two groups of people, who come to see Mohini as a prospective bride. One of them considered her a commodity, which they would have only after ascertaining that it was genuine: 'She [Mohini] had to walk a few steps . . . to prove she did not lack grace of movement. They fumbled with her prettily arranged hair and unloosed it down her back to know its length. They rubbed her face with their thumbs to make sure the fair complexion was natural, not of paint' (p. 42). The outrageous burst of Mohini's father seals his as well as the novelist's disapproval.

Mohini's father allows her all possible freedom, because of which she grows into a confident, vivacious, and sprightly woman, but he is certain that marriage is her ultimate destiny. The only concession he makes in this regard is that he seeks worthy suitors for her not through old-time go-betweens, but through matrimonial advertisements and marriage bureaus. He is so acutely conscious of his responsibility for seeing her properly married that he considers himself the sole arbiter of her destiny: 'I'll not give you away to anyone of whom I do not approve with all my heart. Better not marry at all' (p. 42). Even though he constantly censures traditional thinking and practices, he retains his belief in the custom of arranged marriages. We also find that at crucial moments of decision-making, his modernity does not work; he gives in to old practices for purely sentimental reasons, to ensure, for example, that he did not hurt his mother. This leads to the uneasy mix of tradition and modernity. The result is that in spite of Mohini's father, her marriage with Jayadev is arranged through go-betweens and even horoscopes are matched. The wedding too takes place in the traditional manner. Mohini has to go through all the tiresome rituals, including listening to her grandmother's lessons in conformism: 'Bend yourself to the customs and traditions of the village' (p. 66). The only non-traditional feature in the entire episode is that Mohini speaks in a bold and forthright manner about her proposed marriage to Jayadev and tells her father that she is willing to marry a person who lives in a village.

The episode provides another interesting insight into the novelist's attitude towards tradition and modernity. Though Mohini has education of a new kind, and is forthright in speaking her mind and defending her viewpoint, her sensibility is coloured by her traditional inheritance. The very thought of marrying Jayadev, whom she had not met till then, fills her with a desire to be lovely 'as though her body longed to be a gift, fit for offering. . . . It never occurred to her to wonder at this sudden overwhelming urge to give herself completely to a stranger. . . . A symbolic inheritance. The Hindu maiden, born and bred in the ancient starlight of Vedic civilization, washed by the running stream of the centuries, sheathing her limbs and her thoughts in a conventional dress to suit the needs of each passing age, was innately unchanged: she had retained all her ancient hunger to offer worship' (p. 55).

This significant passage makes it clear that Indian women (by which Bhattacharya all the time means Hindu women) cannot ever become modern like the Westerners. Because of occupying a particular geographical space, they would retain elements of their pristine past, their 'symbolic inheritance'. Since this inheritance forms an important part of Jayadev's project, it has implications for the place of women in society. These are suggested by the novelist through Mohini's stay with her husband in the village.

Bhattacharya places Jayadev in the category of those Indian intellectuals who seek to combine the country's political liberty with 'renascence in social life' by delving 'back into India's remote past' and not accepting ready-made Western thinking. In this exercise, his main mission was to rid the country's past of its encrustation of ritualism and superstitious faith, and taboos and inhibitions, so that it became serviceable for ushering in a new social order. This alone would ensure that India could stand up as a 'proud nation', and not as one which was 'half-slave, half-free'. Jayadev speaks of his mission much too often. When Mohini is tormented by her mother-in-law because she had not become pregnant and, therefore, according to her, posed a threat to Jayadev's life, he tells her: 'The old orthodox ways have been our yoke, have enslaved us. Let us be free' (p. 166).

As a corrective to the blind and wholesale acceptance of Westernization as a form of modernization, Jayadev's insistence on seizing on the positive aspects of his native culture, for working out a healthy synthesis between the two, is quite laudable. But his problem is that he is more of a theoretician, who writes and speaks about it, and less of a pragmatist, who can offer something in concrete terms, which could have a bearing on social practice. What is more disconcerting about him is that he is least worried by what is going on in his own home. Though he is bent upon removing superstitions and abandoning fruitless rituals, they continue to regulate the lives of the inhabitants of the Big House. Like Mohini's father, he allows their continuance for the sake of his mother. He is so much deferential towards her that he prepares Mohini to face her 'stern discipline and iron tradition'. He tells her that her new home would make heavy demands on her, some she might 'find unreasonable. Some of them will have to be met with patience and a spirit of give-and-take, other foolish demands must be resisted' (p. 78). Mohini is so much overawed and overpowered by the demands made on her that she cannot resist anything.

The novel provides elaborate details about the kind of tradition Mohini has to follow and the demands it makes on her person. Her mother-in-law provides Mohini a long account of the Big House, in which it is not a mere structure, but a veritable institution with a hoary past. Its jewellery and furniture are its precious heirlooms; the genealogy of its inhabitants goes back to seventeen generations. The family tradition had survived the onslaughts of foreign invasions and its members had succeeded in preserving its Aryan purity and values: 'meditation, self-discipline, faith, charity, renunciation, truthfulness . . .' (p. 102). What is more important, the Big House had provided leadership to the village. As the repository of this tradition, Mohini's mother-in-law wants that it should continue through Mohini; she should 'grow into the structure of the family tradition', and to become its trustee, by adopting a new way of living and thinking. The novel also details other superstitious beliefs which her mother-in-law regards with respect. She pressurizes Mohini into accepting these too.

It is not that Mohini is driven to despair only by her mother-in-law. Her sister-in-law Rooplekha impresses upon her the necessity of adjusting to her new home and to 'grow a new skin' (p. 93) for making her husband happy. Quoting her own example, she tells her that when she got married into a family which lived in the city, she had to adjust herself to a new lifestyle. She thinks that marriages between men and women of villages and cities served a worthy social cause, of working out a new synthesis between them: 'The city absorbs a little of the 'barbaric' village, the village absorbs a little of the 'West-polluted' city. . . . Our new India must rest on this foundation' (p. 94). This is how the 'Eastern view of life' would blend with 'the new semi-Western outlook' (p. 94).

Jayadev too causes problems to Mohini. Inspired by the visions of Vedic women of the past, he visualises her as a woman of his dreams. He sees her as 'no household drudge, no decorative being, but an intellectual, striding beside man in a tireless quest for knowledge' (p. 71). He wants her to become a Gargi or Maitreyi.

The multiple demands that her new home makes on Mohini, which follow both from tradition and the need for changing old ways, force her to cast herself in a new role. For the sake of her mother-in-law, she adopts an austere routine, performs newly-acquired duties, and attends to her numerous obligations as the daughter-in-law of the Big House. For her husband's sake, she decides to 'absorb new ways of thought and habit, cultivate new interests. . . . She had duties to discharge, responsibilities. How could she let herself be defeated by discomfort and desolation' (p. 106).

In the process of adapting herself to new ways, she loses her little freedoms. She cannot sing; she cannot move about the way she would have liked. The ancestors of the house and their stern demands invade her dreams. Even Jayadev she finds cold and too obsessed with traditions of a different kind. She goes through phases of unease and loneliness; in a moment of desperate rage she breaks her dilruba. She feels like revolting against her situation but she does not. Tradition comes in her way. She realises that for her 'there's no other way' (p. 109) except to play a new part, to do whatever her husband wanted: 'In the great task ahead she would play her part. She would be his true partner in feeling, in faith, and in dream' (p. 129). For this, 'she fitted herself to the rural design. Her sprightliness, her quick girlish laugh, she easily subdued' (p. 130).

It is only when Jayadev steps out of the world of his dreams into the world of action that some of Mohini's freedoms are restored to her. He gives her dilruba back to her;[15] she goes about freely, up on the trees, and plays with children. He begins to recognize her as Mohini and not as a Vedic abstraction. In the village, the forces of modernity, led by Harindra, start gaining an upper hand. But her mother-in-law's stern demands are inflexible as ever. As a strong believer in the efficacy of rituals, she forces Mohini to do a barbaric act: 'You'll cut the skin of your bosom and give her the goddess of births the blood in a lotus-leaf bowl' (p. 163).[16] Jayadev's timely intervention saves her. When it is known that she is already pregnant, even her mother-in-law becomes repentant. When she leaves the village for her father's place, the narrator tells us that Mohini felt that life was music, just because there was no discord. If there isn't any, it is because Mohini does not have many demands of her own; she would do anything to get her husband's love. This Bhattacharya sets up as an ideal—'the true quest of every woman, her deepest need' (p. 188).

NOTES

1. Bhabani Bhattacharya, 'Literature and Social Reality', in *Perspectives on Bhabani Bhattacharya*, ed. Ramesh K. Srivastava (Ghaziabad: Vimal Prakashan, 1982), p. 4.
2. Marlene Fisher, 'The Women in Bhattacharya's Novels', *Perspectives on Bhabani Bhattacharya*, p. 66.
3. Ibid.

4. Bhabani Bhatacharya, *So Many Hungers!* (New Delhi: Orient Paperbacks, 1978), p. 28.
5. Ibid., p. 90.
6. Ibid.
7. Ibid., p. 93.
8. Bhabani Bhattacharya, *He Who Rides a Tiger* (New Delhi: Orient Paperbacks, 1955), p. 174.
9. Ibid. *Shadow from Ladakh* (New Delhi: Orient Paperbacks, 1966), p. 24.
10. Ibid., p. 274.
11. Ibid.
12. Marlene Fisher, op. cit., p. 79.
13. *Shadow from Ladakh*, p. 204.
14. Bhabani Bhattacharya, *Music for Mohini* (New Delhi: Orient Paperbacks, 1975), p. 16. Subsequent references, incorporated in the text of the essay, are to this edition.
15. This, of course, also coincides with Mohini's attempts to assert herself. She speaks to her mother-in-law about the things she feels interested in.
16. It is true that Mohini's first reaction is to resist it; she would never submit to this. '*Never*', p. 163, (italics mine); she, however, succumbs to it for the sake of Jayadev, to save him from what her mother-in-law calls his impending death.

History, Change and Modernity: Markandaya's New Woman in *Nectar in a Sieve*

G.R. Taneja

For a reading of women characters and their response to the phenomenon of history, change and modernity *Nectar in a Sieve* readily lends itself as a useful if not an ideal text. Kamala Markandaya's celebrated novel provides in its narrative a variety of situations for its protagonist to confront and negotiate, and to which she responds by resisting or by allowing the circumstances to modify the pattern of her existence. Yet, one must hasten to point out, Markandaya's heroine does not project the profile of a woman who meets one's expectations contained in such vocabulary as 'identity', 'alienation', or 'fulfilment'. She sets new parameters for one's appreciation of the female self. It is only after having reconstructed such an appreciation that one can go on to adequately read the character of Markandaya's protagonist as a symbol of the triumph of the forces of modernity over those of the regressive pulls of history. A careful scrutiny of Rukmani's character would reveal Markandaya plotting a course of development in the novel that ultimately seeks to examine how the new impinges upon the old, how a female character chooses to deal with such pulls of history, and how the process of dealing with the cataclysmic changes is intertwined with a women's recognition of her own role both as a woman and as an individual. Rukmani thus fights two battles simultaneously. In one she fights to gain a heightened self-awareness in the socio-cultural context of her society; in the other she fights a battle for and on behalf of the society to deal with modernity and change.

Published in 1954, Markandaya's much acclaimed first novel was followed by a number of works which have established her ability to create a wide variety of characters and conflicts. She continually extends her range. For instance, from her focus in her first work of fiction on the poor agricultural peasant of an Indian village, she moves in her next novel, *Some Inner Fury* (1956), to an analysis of love between an educated Indian girl and her English lover in the midst of the Indian freedom movement and of conflicting Indian and Western influences on the lives of the people. *A Silence of Desire* (1960) deals with marital problems in a middle class setting. *A Handful of Rice* (1966) is the story of a poor city-dweller. *The Coffer Dams* (1969) is a perceptive study of the activities of a British engineering firm which is invited to construct a dam in India. *The Golden Honeycomb* (1977) charts the decline of British power in India and the three generations of princely fame.

What provides a firmer foundation to a number of different situations, social and historical contexts, and complex and varied authorial concerns is Markandaya's impressive skill evident in the creation of complete and credible characters. She has, as William Walsh remarks, 'the genuine novelist's gifts for fixing the exact individuality of the character' (Walsh 1990, p. 116). In Rukmani, the protagonist of *Nectar in a Sieve*, Markandaya gives us a richly delineated character whose three-dimensional quality heightens the significance of the ideological concerns that the author embodies in her.

As the daughter of a once rich head-man of a village, Rukmani grows up as a witness to the decline in family fortune, influence, prestige and power. At the age of twelve when she is going to be married, she is, therefore, without dowry and has to face the trauma of having to be married into a class of society lower than her own. What is worse, Rukmani is 'without beauty', (p. 2), the time-honoured weapon which enables women to surmount the barrier to the fortunes of the upper class. Her initiation into a new life, after her marriage to a poor peasant is fraught with unbearable pain. Her own reaction to her new moorings is one of distress and despair. 'Such a disgrace for me', she reacts. 'How shall I ever live it down?' (p. 3). The match that her family had found for her is 'below her' (p. 3). What awaits her at the home of her husband is a mud hut: This mud hut, nothing but mud and thatch, [which] was my home. My knees gave . . . and I sank down (p. 4). It is in these circumstances that she starts a new life for herself. But in Rukmani, Markandaya creates a woman who possesses strength of character, vigour of mind and sensitivity. She is endowed with fine feelings. On the river bank, Kali tells her:

> You are Rukmani, are you not? Wife of the farmer Nathan. The whole village has been curious about you—heaven knows why, one woman is like another. The fuss your husband made! Why, for weeks he was, brittle as a bamboo before he bursts into flame! He built your hut with his own hands. Yes, he would not even have my husband to help. (p. 6)

'He had made our home himself, and I had felt only fear to live in it' (p. 6). Rukmani reproaches herself. Markandaya describes her newly acquired understanding and commitment:

> While the sun shines on you and the fields are green and beautiful to the eye, and your husband sees beauty in you which no one has seen before, and you have a good store of grain laid away for hard times, a roof over you and a sweet stirring of your body, what more can a woman ask for? My heart sang and my feet were light as I went about my work getting up at sunrise and going to sleep content. Peace and quiet were ours. (p. 7)

As the narrative progresses, Markandaya shows Rukmani buffeted by the vagaries of fortunes. But she copes with the situation. As the wife of a poor peasant she accepts her fall from grace with dignity and reveals stoic acceptance of the inevitable. In her relationship with Nathan she learns the values of love, mutual respect and understanding. She shows a sense of accommodation in her reaction to her discovery of infidelity on her husband's part. She is shocked to learn of her daughter's wayward ways. It leaves her traumatized but she remains a mother who protects and nurtures her young. The intrusion of the new industrialization in the secure world of the village she strongly resents and in the long run suffers the most. But she shows an appreciation of the inevitability of change.

Young Rukmani's reactions to the world around her are motivated by a recognition that life is for living, and when the going gets tough the human mind must draw strength from an unambiguous acceptance of the inescapable. Not to breakup or destroy, but to persist with and to rebuild is what life is about. Not self-pity but self-esteem is what human existence must derive its sustenance from. Rukmani is endowed with an awareness of the possibilities of life. For her the act of living is important: life is important. And therefore the question of a woman's search for identity, meaning, alienation, or fulfilment in marriage within and without, must be part of the larger question of life and living.

Markandaya's strength lies in the fact that the female protagonist of her novel emerges as a character whose engagement with the inevitable conflicts of life do not take the form of the usual, no-holds-barred battle of the sexes so familiar from some of the more recent feminist fiction. I must illustrate this point. Shashi Deshpande's feminist heroine in her otherwise admirable, *That Long Silence*, experiences, 'differences with her husband, frustrations in their seventeen year old marriage, disappointment in her two teenage children, claustrophia [*sic*] of her childhood'. In one of the episodes the female protagonist seeks to correct the imbalance of her marital life as follows:

> 'The keys', he says, holding out his hand.
>
> But the woman, ignoring that importunate hand—it becomes that as he continues to hold it out—takes some keys out of her bag and unlocks the door. Still ignoring him she enters the flat. He continues to stand there for a moment, the hand held out, it now looks like a supplicatory gesture, and then he abruptly follows her in, closing the door firmly behind him. (pp. 7-8)

She goes on to justify her action:

> We all do it; it is part of family life. Rahul refusing to have his bath before meals, Rati refusing to tell us who it was she was talking to on the phone. Appa crushing a raw onion and eating it with relish. (p. 9)

Deshpande's female, *therefore* discontented, suffering, and oppressed, protagonist does not appear to struggle to find meaning, identity, or even escape from a context that she finds hostile. She has only contempt for human relationships. Her contempt for her husband, who is 'reconciled to failure' (p. 9) in life, is fueled by her lack of understanding that to cushion an individual's failure is what a family is all about. She is too narcissistically self-centred to appreciate the need for her contribution to stem the decline in a deteriorating relationship.

Some of the early novels of Anita Desai project women characters as obsessively self-sequestered who show almost a similar pre-occupation with their own erratic impulses rather than a recognition that a marital situation is not a personal situation but an interpersonal one. In his review of Desai's *In Custody* Salman Rushdie remarks: 'The subject of Anita Desai's fiction has thus far been solitude. Her most memorable creations [. . .] have been isolated, singular figures. And the books themselves have private universes, illuminated by the author's perceptiveness, delicacy of language and sharp wit, but remaining, in a sense, *as solitary, as separate as their characters'* (p. 71, emphasis added).

Thus, even though the universe of *Nectar in a Sieve* is dominated by a protagonist who is a woman and in which the authorial focus is on a woman's interaction—even confrontation—with the real world, that world is not artificially narrow, sequestered, or a lonely world inhabited by lonely characters. It seems to me that in their anger to destroy the wrong that the world has done to women, the feminists tend to ignore the fact that women are, and have to be, an inescapable part of the same universe. A world-view conditioned by the necessity of its having to be a feminist world-view, distorts the nature of its objective. Rukmani looks at the world around her through the eyes of a human being: for her—and for her creator—her being a woman remains incidental to her being a human being. Both Rukmani and her creator discard a narrow preoccupation and give us an incisive perception into the intricacies of living. To perceive *Nectar in a Sieve* as a statement of feminist concerns of a kind which are thought to be particularly relevant today is to minimize the significance of the contribution that Markandaya makes to our appreciation of some of the vital issues that concern us deeply, indeed.

In *That Long Silence*, Deshpande projects a situation which allows her heroine to function in a manner which is relatively earthy and quite realistic. Rukmani's responses, however, reveal a finer perception and a higher, even idealistic, level of existence. She transforms the challenge of life into a pursuit of finer values that make life worth living.

Markandaya's heroine responds to the drama of life in its entirety. She treats life as a whole in which man-woman relationship is only one of its several aspects. Failure to appreciate that life is larger than love, even sex, even man-woman relationship, and leads to an inadequate appreciation of the very nature and significance of human predicament. Therefore, Rukmani's response to the changing hues of life, that constantly emerge as forever renewing challenges, is one of greater maturity and in which reason plays a vital role.

It is in this sense that life is important, living is important and literature that deepens our faith in the fact of life is important. Major novelists, as Leavis puts it, 'not only change the possibilities of art for practitioners and readers, but that they are significant in terms of human awareness they promote: awareness of the possibilities'

(p. 10). It is in this sense that Markandaya's *Nectar in a Sieve* is not without some measure of achievement.

II

Markandaya's first novel thus establishes a major authorial concern, a concern which, as we have seen, is backed by a point of view which is carefully and consistently developed and is the foundation for the female protagonist's response to the changes that overtake her world. Rukmani's response to the phenomenon of change and the inevitable conflict between tradition and modernity within which she gets caught is deliberately plotted so as to operate simultaneously with her heightened awareness of the fact of her being a woman and her search for values that matter to her as a woman. Markandaya's essential concern then in *Nectar* is not with the feminist notions of polarity that marks man-woman relationship but with the conflict between the larger forces of time and history and the destabilization and re-organization of the social context. The inevitable march of change and dislocation had a profound impact on the mind of Markandaya's protagonist. Each move that the new and unfamiliar makes upon Rukmani's world diminishes her. But the tragic consequences of each move also at the same time make her a revitalized survivor.

A number of situations show Rukmani attempting to cope with intriguing developments in the social, personal and interpersonal contexts. For instance, the coming of the tannery to the village shatters the old world. But the tannery is too large and obvious a symbol to need detailed explanation. Markandaya uses it to explicate the nature and significance of the conflict between tradition and modernity and the role of a woman in the midst of the resultant turmoil. But there are other subtler moments which perform a more sophisticated function in the context of the novel. In the slow-time of rural India, Kenny the English doctor sounds the most disturbing note of threat to traditional beliefs, notions and ideas and the way people think, feel and behave. Rukmani narrates the incident:

> I put the rice in my sari, tuck *the precious load* [emphasis added] securely in at the waist. We turn back. On the outskirts of the village there is Kenny. His face is grim and long, his eyes are burning in his pallid face. He sees us and comes up.
>
> 'You too are starving, I suppose.'

> I tap the roll at my waist—the grains give at my touch.
>
> 'We have a little rice—it will last us until times are better.'
>
> 'Times are better, times are better,' he shouts. Times will not be better for many months. Meanwhile you will suffer and die, you meek suffering fools. Why do you keep this ghastly silence? Why do you not demand—cry out for help—do something? There is nothing in this country, oh God, there is nothing!' (pp. 43-4)

But she does not always remain a quiescent, 'meek suffering fool'. Incomprehension marks some of Rukmani's reactions to Kenny's outbursts. But her essentially earthy common sense is able to accommodate the new and the unfamiliar. The accommodation on her part is not painless. Some of Rukmani's early reactions to situations and developments around her may be easily construed as reflecting narrowly conservative and retrograde attitudes. For instance, on the birth of her daughter, Markandaya narrates:

> They placed [the baby] in my arms when I recovered a little from the birth, in silence. I uncovered the small form, beautiful, strong but quite plain, a girl's body. I turned away and despite myself the tears came, tears of weakness and disappointment: for what woman wants a girl for first-born? (p. 14)

But such reactions reflect her apprehensions of social pressures. She is a woman of finer intelligence and reveals herself as much ahead of her times. The new and the unfamiliar—as opposed to the coziness of the stability of the continuing past—raises its head in many ways. She does sound the expected note of helplessness when her daughter's husband abandons her on account of her infertility. She consoles her daughter: 'Hush! We are all in God's hands, and He is merciful' (p. 50). But she also wants to find a solution to the problem. 'My thoughts went to Kenny. He can help, I thought; surely he can do something. My crushed spirits revived a little' (p. 50).

Rukmani's attitude to the stirrings of her body is one of mature understanding of the natural urges:

> I stretched myself beside [Nathan], close to him in the darkness, and as we touched he turned abruptly towards me. Words died away, the listening air was very still, the black night waited. In the straining darkness I felt his body moving with desire, his hands on me were trembling, and I felt my senses opening like a flower to his urgency. I closed my eyes and waited, waited in the dark while my being filled with a wild ecstatic fluttering, waited for him to come to me. (p. 57)

The discovery of her husband's adulterous relationship with Kunthi stuns her: 'Disbelief', 'disillusionment', 'anger', 'reproach', 'pain', 'cruel' is the diction Markandaya employs [p. 86]. But she recovers from the shock of betrayal and responds reasonably:

> 'It is as you say a long time ago', I said wearily. 'That she is evil and powerful I know myself. Let it rest.' (p. 87)

The characteristics that mark Rukmani's personality and which help her deal with the change is her ability to absorb the otherwise highly damaging vibrations that accompany that change. Readers have sometimes found her superhuman strength unrealistically portrayed. But Markandaya's remarkable skill in creating credible characters, as I have remarked earlier, ensures against such a reading.

That Markandaya attempts to approach the threat of 'modernity' that 'tradition' suffers, not directly, but through the question of a female self's assertion of itself registers an important point. No issue of changing times can be dealt with meaningfully if the relevant feminist concerns and questions are not dealt with first. By intertwining these two strands and then resolving them in a highly satisfying manner, Markandaya reveals not only a finer awareness of the issues involved (and a degree of sensitivity particularly and noticeably absent from the feminist Indian fiction of the recent years) but also craftsmanship of a high order.

REFERENCES

Deshpande, Shashi, *That Long Silence,* 1988 (New Delhi: Penguin, 1989).

King, Adele, 'Effective Portrait' (review of *That Long Silence*), *Debonair* (June 1988, p. 97).

Leavis, F.R., *The Great Tradition,* 1948 (Harmondsworth: Penguin, 1974).

Rushdie, Salman, *Imaginary Homelands: Essays and Criticism 1981-1991* (London: Granta, 1991).

Markandaya, Kamala, *Nectar in a Sieve,* 1954 (Bombay: Jaico, 1986).

Walsh, William, *Indian Literature in English* (London: Longman, 1990).

Knocks of Modernity in Jhabvala's Novels

Neeta Gupta

Ruth Prawer Jhabvala's presence in the literary world poses an intriguing problem of classification. Being of Polish-German-Jewish origin, brought up and educated in England, she remains a foreigner, an 'outsider' for us till today. Yet, married to an Indian, having lived in India for more than twenty-four years, and by her peculiar position in the family—that of a daughter-in-law, having access to the deepest rhythms of Indian society, of Indian life—she also makes an equally valid claim for being an 'insider'. When such a writer writes about her adopted country, should her fiction not be included in line with those various Indian writers writing in Indian English? This problem baffles historians of Indian English literature and Anglo-Indian literature, alike. The result is that we find Jhabvala's name being included not only with writers like R.K. Narayan, Mulk Raj Anand, Raja Rao, Kamala Markandaya and Anita Desai (to name only a few)—Indian writers writing in Indian English, about India, but also with writers like Rudyard Kipling, E.M. Forster and Paul Scott—Europeans writing about India.

There are advantages as well as disadvantages attendant on being an outsider-insider. Jhabvala remains a detached observer in all her novels. She is never able to identify with the characters she writes about. From the first novel itself it is evident that a distance will be maintained between the observer and the observed. But even though her eyes remain consistently European, yet they are able to penetrate into the Indian household, to observe minutely all the oddities of behaviour, the nuances and the mannerisms of people, till a whole way of life is laid bare in a gently ironic, mildly satirical tone. The disadvantage however is that Jhabvala never looks beneath the surface. Her accounts may be accurate but they remain superficial. Her novels are still seen as novels of chit-chat, cross-talk, concerned with day-to-day living. The inwardness of the Indians is not touched upon. There are no heroic or larger-than-life figures in her novels, clashing with their destinies head on. We do not find any in-depth character study nor do we see any deeper, personal, emotional issues taken to depths of intensity and resolved. Jhabvala has been attacked on this score particularly by Indian readers and critics. V.A. Shahane's full length study of her work concludes on a note of dissatisfaction with her limited vision:

> The vision of Lawrence finds an objectification in his technique projecting a passionate, private world of values. But in Ruth Prawer Jhabvala the bushes are neat and green, but they do not burn. There may be writers in whose work there is burning but no bush, whereas in Jhabvala there is a bush, but it does not burn.[1]

C. Paul Verghese in his short article on 'Esmond in India', published in *The Journal of Indian Writing in English*, also criticizes Jhabvala on the same lines. He writes: 'I am certain that Mrs. Jhabvala's understanding of India is not deep and that she just skims over the surface of urban life in India . . . her preoccupations are only with the superficial concepts of Indian life.'[2]

Meenakshi Mukherjee finds fault with Jhabvala's inability to present three-dimensional characters in her novels. As she observes: 'The reader never really gets involved because of the deliberately dead-pan tone and her devices of detachment preclude all possibility of our ever-knowing the characters from inside.'[3] Even the noted Indo-Anglian poet, Nissim Ezekiel, has similarly observed that 'Jhabvala's major weakness as a novelist is her inability to create any genuinely complex or even simple inner life for her characters.'[4] The potential is there since the problems are hinted at. For example, the problem of alienation being faced by Westernized Indians or Westerners in India alike, is taken up in one novel after another, but is only skirted but not analysed by Jhabvala. Yet, even though limited in scope and vision, her novels remain skillful works of arts. In fact, M.K. Naik has called her 'a laureate of the parlour'.[5] Elaborating this personally conferred title he writes:

> The most distinctive feature of Jhabvala's novels is the subtlety and adroitness with which she unravels the gossamer threads of intricate human relationships—especially among the women in the Hindu joint family. She recreates admirably this drama of cattiness in which conversation is often a veiled battle of polite affronts, the favourite weapons being innuendoes and insinuations, left-handed compliments and deadly insults masked as innocuous generalities, while a chance word is a bomb dropped with

devilish accuracy and devastating effect. In these battles, old scores are settled and new wounds inflicted, all over a pleasant cup of tea or a glass of cool sherbet.[6]

Jhabvala's novels clearly fall under two distinct groups.[7] Her first four novels are gentle comedies of manner, having a totally Indian cast of characters, dealing with the world she was exposed to and knew best—that of the urban middle class. *To Whom She Will* (1955), *The Nature of Passion* (1956), *The Householder* (1960) and *Get Ready for Battle* (1962) comprise this first group. The second group of novels, namely, *Esmond in India* (1958), *A Backward Place* (1965), *A New Dominion* (1973) and *Heat and Dust* (1975), deals with a problem much closer to the writer's heart—that of being an alien in her adopted country. The pull of the West is felt through characters like Esmond and Etta, who yearn for one glimpse of their beloved Europe, while the East beckons through characters like Julie and Olivia, who have commitments and attachments to bind them still to this alien land. By the very nature of the theme, the second group of novels has predominantly Western/European characters. This paper, which attempts to look at the picture of the Indian woman in Jhabvala's novels, from the point of view of tradition and modernity, consequently restricts itself to a detailed study of two novels belonging to the first group, namely *The Nature of Passion* and *Get Ready for Battle*.

As with the rest of the issues, however, even Indian womanhood is not discussed or revealed in its totality in Jhabvala. If we desire a three-dimensional or multifaceted picture of the Indian woman, covering all aspects of her personality, ranging from Annapoorna the provider to Kali the destroyer, then Jhabvala's novels fall sadly short of it. But even in her chosen limited scope, she succeeds in giving us an astonishingly true picture of some aspects of the average Indian women, especially women of Hindu households still upholding the joint family system. On the one hand we witness how even in their constricted world, which is carefully segmented from the male world, these women carry on their day-to-day living with nothing else to occupy their minds except matters like food, clothing, marriages, childbirth and deaths. On the other hand there are indications that things will not remain so for long. Faint stirrings are felt of a rebellion against the life that Indian society has so far chalked out for its members of the fairer sex. Jhabvala, with her Western background, has perceptively noticed that issues like that of identity, equality of the sexes, recognition as individuals—issues that have made the feminists stand up in arms against the male-dominated world, have not yet reached the average Indian household. Modernity in its true sense of a redefinition of roles and rules is still a far cry. Yet what we do see in Jhabvala's novels are the first indications of a desire to overthrow the bondage, to be independent, to revolt even though it may materialize in something as inconsequential as having one's long hair cut short.

Like her first novel *To Whom She Will, The Nature of Passion* is also a gentle social comedy, a comedy of manners almost in Jane Austen's style. The story revolves around a beautiful young girl, fortunately placed in life, having a fair share of intelligence and awareness. To some extent the novel traces the development of this female protagonist. Yet at the same time, the novel is also an astute study of a typical Hindu joint family with the two worlds of men and women carefully compartmentalized. There is an abundance of drab and dreary details of daily living, yet amidst all this Jhabvala skillfully unravels the complex web of human relationships—fathers and sons, fathers and daughters, brothers and sisters, sisters and sisters, aunts and uncles, mothers-in-law and daughters-in-law, husbands and wives—and so on. Lala Narayan Das Verma, a self-made affluent Punjabi businessman of Delhi, is the head of this family. From the first paragraph itself, the tension between tradition and modernity is established. Lalaji, in spite of having a number of bedrooms in his house, prefers to sleep in the open; there are five marble bathrooms, but he is used to brushing his teeth outside; the sitting room idea is still alien to him. Everything is 'very different from what he had grown up with and got used to'.[8] Lalaji is obviously an old-fashioned man, trying to keep pace with the changing world, cluttering up his house with expensive things yet not really liking it all one bit. But what about changing his outlook? Does 'being modern' mean merely changing one's physical surroundings, acquisition of modern furniture, modern gadgets? Or does 'being modern' also include a modification of one's conservative attitude, especially one's attitude towards women? It is obvious that for Lalaji this latter and more important part of the business of becoming modern, does not figure anywhere in the picture. There is an indication of this in his attitude to his wife. He misses her once she is away at the nursing home at Shanta's confinement. But he misses her not because of any deep emotional bond but because 'she was part of his routine' (p. 2). He feels that she will not be there to perform her wifely duties. His food would not be cooked properly, he would be served by servants, even his pyjama cord had not been knotted the way she knotted it. In other words she is more of a habit than an individual in her own right. But as nothing could be done about it, he just made up his mind and was reconciled and Jhabvala hastens to add—'If his wife had died, he would have made up his mind to it just like that, and been reconciled' (p. 3). Is Lalaji's wife merely like a comfortable chair which if broken one misses but is reconciled to the loss soon enough? In other words, is she being treated merely as another possession that Lalaji has acquired? This immediately poses the question of the position of women in households like these. Their role is well defined and restricted to the home. As Lala Narayan Das muses about the marriage of his most beloved daughter Nimmi, Jhabvala forcefully underlines the subservient position of women in Indian society: ' . . . a woman is a woman and her duties in life very different from the duties of a man . . . it is a woman's fate to leave the house of her father and go to a husband's house, to bear his children, to look to the comforts of his family' (p. 112). Whether a household is rich or poor, the life of women is always the same.

> . . . The women lived a life apart. They got together in the inner courtyard and saw to the cooking and the children. This was right. This was right as it should be. A family was not a family, a home not a home, unless there was a women's quarter in which the women could lead their own lives. Demure daughters-in-law, stern mothers-in-law, widowed aunts, all pounding spices, sifting rice, scolding servants, washing babies; the stone jars of rice and lentils, the vat of boiling milk, the barbecue, the pump in the courtyard; quarrels and recriminations and occasional songs, nostalgic peasant songs or plaintive hymns winding round the ceaseless kitchen noises, these constituted the necessary—if unconsidered, background to a man's life' (p. 112)

In such a world, marriage becomes the sole aim of a woman's life. We see an ironic, humorous treatment of this aspect of Indian women when Jhabvala describes the event of the birth of Om's third child—a baby girl. The moment Lalaji receives the good news from the hospital, he is beside himself with joy and brushes aside Nimmi's doubts of a good life for her with a triumphant outline of his own: 'The life of a queen she will have. . . . Such a wedding we will make for her, the best husband in the whole of Hindustan we will get for her, the richest, the fairest. . . . ' He continues thinking in the same vein: 'All the rich men in Delhi will run after her with their sons. The dowry I will give with her, no one will believe the figure' (p. 15). Clearly, another item has been added in Lalaji's long list of expensive possessions. Om, though belonging to a generation ahead of his father is no different in defining an exactly similar role for his daughters. Pointing to his six-year-old child he says:

> When she is seven, I will find a good husband and betroth her. Then she can come back to the house and learn from her mother and aunts to make chapatis and mango pickle. When she has learnt that well, and also how to manage servants and children, she can go to her husband's house and be credit to us there. (p. 16)

All this talk, all these plans for children, one of whom is barely six years old and another who has probably not even had its first glimpse of the world: it is humorous yet appalling. Can there be questions of identity and equality of the sexes in such a stifling and socially predetermined world? Not if all daughters are like Usha. She is complacent and docile, refusing to look beyond the four walls of the house and closing her mind to all other things except thoughts of her approaching marriage. It is girls like Usha who conform to the traditional roles laid out for women and who justify Om's objections to educating the girls of the house: 'This college', said Om, talking more loudly, 'it is only a waste of time and of good money, and will perhaps even give her wrong ideas. Look at that one there', he said, thrusting his chin towards Usha massaging her father's legs· 'How much money was spent on her education, and what has it all led to now? A betrothal today, a marriage tomorrow, children the day after. Only with her we were lucky: She is too stupid to get any harm out of education' (pp. 16-17).

It is not Usha but Nimmi who trembles with fury at this affront. Nimmi, almost a reincarnation of Amrita (*To Whom She Will*) is Lalaji's favourite daughter and stands apart from the crowd. She goes to college, has a number of friends from the upper circles of society, is exposed to the club culture and at the same time is aware of the difference between their sophisticated world and hers—a difference which she realizes, money alone cannot bridge. She is quite critical and disapproving of all the women in her household except Kanta, her sister-in-law whom she tries to emulate. At the nursing home, when Nimmi has tired herself with appreciating the new baby, she sits and looks around her at the women in the room: 'How fat they all are!' she thought with disdain; and if not fat, then thin and dry and meagre like Phuphiji. And how badly dressed they were; of course they were old women but, Nimmi thought, even if she were old, she would still take care to be always beautifully dressed. . . . And what bad manners they all have, she thought, looking at her female relations' (p. 27). One by one she observes all of them and each is brushed aside as being too traditional and conservative. Only Kanta, the younger daughter-in-law of Lalaji stands as distinctly apart from the crowd as Nimmi does.

Kanta, wife of Chandra Prakash, younger son of Lalaji, is a girl from a different community, and gives enough cause to the women of the household to raise their eyebrows at her disapprovingly. The England-returned Chandra Prakash, employed as a gazetted officer in a government office, has broken free from the joint family system and lives separately in a house of his own. Yet, a complete severance of the bonds is not possible since Kanta and Chandra Prakash look to Lalaji for financial help now and then, taking it as their right. This modern idea of a nuclear family is therefore only half-formed and quite hypocritical. But in Kanta's household Nimmi is able to get all that she finds lacking in her father's house. Kanta maintains and carries herself well, speaks good English, sends her children to an English school, throws parties at her house, is member of a club and even smokes and drinks at times. Instead of bearing a baby every year of her married life, she prefers to practise family planning. She is thus poles apart from Shanta, the other daughter-in-law of Lalaji, who is docile and subservient. Kanta can be called modern in the restricted sense that Indian society was interpreting modernity at that transitional stage—a mere aping of the West. The other women of Lalaji's household are however not ready even for this onslaught of superficial modernity and Kanta causes quite a flutter whenever she is around. At the nursing home, she gives enough anxious moments to her mother-in-law by coming late. As the latter sits there she muses about her:

> . . . it was not often that she could understand her daughter-in-law Kanta. The girl had very strange ways . . . Surely even in other communities, even in Kanta's community, daughters-in-law were expected to honour their

mothers-in-law, respect and submit to their husbands' family. Kanta neither honoured nor respected nor submitted, she did not behave like a daughter-in-law at all. (p. 26)

Finally when Kanta does arrive with her family, more eyebrows are raised since: 'All the women of Shanta's family noticed that Kanta did not touch her mother-in-law's feet, nor her elder sister-in-law's. They were pleasantly horrified at such disrespectfulness . . .' (p. 48). She is branded as bold, self-confident, fashionable.

A peep into Kanta's house and her life confirms Jhabvala's accusation when she says that Indians see 'modernity' as a blind aping of the West. Kanta, and other women like her who profess to be modern, painstakingly try their best to become as anglicized as possible, deriving hints from magazines on how to conduct oneself socially. The writer outlines some of these pretensions for us while describing Kanta's life style:

She lavished much care on the furnishing of her house, studied copies of Bombay women's magazines and learnt how to arrange armchairs and settees round a fireplace, place little doilies on occasional tables, serve drinks from a cocktail cabinet, polish her dining-table and decorate it with cork mats and a candelabra. (p. 51)

It is also from the magazines that she learns 'to style her hair, take care of her skin and make casual conversation' (p. 51). She wears nylon lingerie, joins the best club and does ballroom dance and gives informal dinners. It we compare her life with Shanta's, who is content to sift rice and pound spices and rear babies in the women's quarters of Lalaji's house, we cannot fail to notice the wide gap between the two. From all existing standards, Kanta is 'modern'. But this modernity is only skin deep for when it comes to bickering and cattiness, the emancipated Kanta has an equally narrow mind. She enjoys bitching about and criticizing Mr. Ghosh and Mrs. Shankar Lingam to Nimmi. Also, she does not hesitate to demand her right from Lalaji in the form of occasional monetary gifts, even though she may not do anything for her in-laws in return. The only member of that family, whom she likes and appreciates, is Nimmi, who is another one fast falling in line with such modern women of India.

Almost every aspect of Nimmi's behaviour and personality mark her as different from the other womenfolk in the family. We can dismiss her mother and Phuphiji as being a whole generation behind and hence being old-fashioned. But what about the others? Shanta conforms to the traditional image of an ideal daughter-in-law. But Nimmi's own sisters Rani and Usha have none of the characteristics which differentiate Nimmi from them. Rani, married and well settled in life, considers herself very modern and fashionable but is found to be too vulgar and pompous by Nimmi. Usha, the other sister, thinks day and night about her forthcoming marriage. While Nimmi delights in her college education, Usha has failed repeatedly. While Nimmi is curious about the meaning of the words 'sensuous' and 'sensual' and wonders which one would describe Pheroze Batliwala best, Usha even refuses to think about, let alone discuss, the process which makes babies come. Nimmi is contemptuous of and angry with her for marrying a man whom she hardly knows. But Usha's placid reply is: 'Afterwards there will be plenty of time to know him' (p. 154).

Nimmi revolts and rebels against the confines of this tradition-bound society. She cuts her hair causing an uproar in the house. The foremost worry in the women's quarters is how a husband would be found for her now. They all blame Lalaji for having been too indulgent and lenient with her. But there is no stopping the bold strides of this girl. She goes to the club with her friends and plays tennis dressed in shorts, drinks sherry 'even though it tastes like petrol', has a Parsi boy friend and even allows him to kiss her in the moonlight! In addition to all these rebellious acts of hers, Jhabvala notices some other effects that this desire for emancipation has on her mind. She questions the battle of cattiness which is for ever raging in the women's quarters: 'Nimmi, listening, wondered why her mother and her sister and her aunt should feel so bitterly towards Shanta's family. She had heard the women of that family abused by the women of hers for almost as long as she could remember, but lately she had begun to question this' (p. 46). For her part, she decides to do away with hypocrisy and be friendly to only those people who she wanted to be friends with. Thus she turns a cold shoulder towards Lakshmi, whom she does not like.

Though naïve and innocent, Nimmi is quite firm in her likes and dislikes and decides for herself rather than be led by others. So it is, when Kanta tries to prejudice her mind against Mrs. Ghosh and Mrs. Shankar Lingam, Nimmi finds out for herself that they are rather nice and pleasant company. She notices the difference between Kanta's household and her mother's. While they have dinner, she is surprised to find the atmosphere quite informal. The men did their bit in passing the dishes around and Nimmi muses to herself: 'It was nice for men to be domesticated; not like her father and her brothers and all the other men in her family, except Chandra, who were rough and clumsy and had no idea how to be polite to ladies' (p. 57). The picture is diametrically opposed to the one in Lalaji's house where women are even forbidden to sit with the men, required only to serve the food. When Om questions her presence at the dinning table while the men are eating, Nimmi screams in exasperation: 'I am not in purdah' (p. 78).

Nimmi's defiant attitude and unconventional behaviour is labelled as disrespect and immodesty and has the whole women quarter up in arms against her. Their patience boils over when Shanta's mother comes and reports that Nimmi had been seen going around with a Parsi boy in a night club. Lalaji is at once summoned from his office along with Om. One can almost recall a similar incident in *To Whom She Will* when Amrita's father is made to intervene by Radha, to stop the former's affair with Hari. Disgrace had fallen on Lalaji's family because Nimmi had been 'allowed to become eighteen years old and no husband found for her'. And she has been to college. A verdict is passed: '. . . take the girl away from this college. . . . She must stay at home here with us and not move out of the women's quarters' (p. 164). Lalaji, who all along had been dreading this moment of separation from his beloved daughter, is rather sad at the thought though not once does he blame her. All along Jhabvala has successfully described him as a man accustomed to old ways yet trying to make way for the new. Even now he had no doubt that Nimmi was blameless. 'The possibility that she might have done everything beyond going out to restaurants and dancing did not occur to him, as indeed it did not occur to others. Such a possibility lay too far outside the orbit of their society' (p. 165). But there was the other danger of the news spreading and her name being maligned. 'So the only thing to do when there was a threat to the reputation was to find the husband, quickly, at once, before the canker spread' (p. 165).

A husband is found and a marriage is fixed and Nimmi agrees to it after a few initial fanciful bursts of ideas like running away and becoming a teacher. It is a bit difficult to believe this of a girl who had defiantly stated that if her marriage were arranged like that of Usha's she would spurn it aside. Describing how she would do this she had said: 'I will never say yes if they come to me with a husband they have kindly found for me. On the contrary I will tell them:

Thank you, I am grateful to you for your trouble, but if you do not mind I will find my own husband. This is a work I will do for myself' (p. 154). Quite ironically the reverse of what she has stated, actually happens. There are two reasons for the change in Nimmi's behaviour. The first is her disappointment with Pheroze, who sends his congratulations on her engagement. She is unable to comprehend his behaviour: 'She found it hard to believe that he—he who had kissed her—should be willing to lose her altogether; and harder still to believe that the escape she had been expecting almost confidently should after all be denied to her' (p. 179). Nimmi is no romantic fool. In spite of all her flighty behaviour she has a level head on her shoulders. Unlike Shakuntala in *Esmond in India*, who is overcome by passion and consequently tarnishes her life for ever, Nimmi takes a practical view of everything. Right from the beginning she herself has treated her affair with Pheroze in a detached and ironic manner—an experience to be had. She goes out with him not because she loves him but because it is fashionable to have a boy-friend. Even while she is being kissed, her mind is busy recording the experience—'so this is how a man kisses—and next: what would they say at home? — and next: How excited Rajen will be when she hears' (p. 104). Pheroze is equally uninvolved. So it does not come as a surprise when Nimmi gets over her initial disappointment. She had thought of Pheroze as he was the most logical way out of the impending doom. But when that is denied Nimmi tries to explore other avenues open to her. She finds there are none. She has no money to run away and no place to go to. Even the thought of going and earning her own living as a teacher is appalling to her ears. But the thought of getting married and becoming like Shanta and sitting all day in the womens' quarters, feeding babies, is equally appalling. Nimmi's friend Rajen is unable to understand how Nimmi's family can do such a thing and Nimmi is unable to explain. With a rare touch of insight Jhabvala writes:

> Perhaps until now she had not fully understood herself how much, how completely, she belonged to her family. She had wondered how Usha could submit so meekly to the marriage they had arranged for her; now she understood that there was nothing for it but to submit. The independence on which she has prided herself, her differentness from the other women in the family, were only an illusion. In reality, her position was no different from Usha's and, ultimately, from Shanta's. (p. 182)

It is a no-win situation; Nimmi's wishes are overruled and she bows to the family. But the end is a happy one since the novel is in the genre of a social comedy.

Nimmi's little escapade succeeds in pulling the mask off from the professed modernists in the novel. Kanta does nothing to help the poor girl in her predicament, except labelling her as another victim of society. Rani, with her face flushed, declares she would not return to her husband's house until something is done about Nimmi, and the disgrace that she has brought to her family. Viddi, another one in the long line of Jhabvala's modern, effete pseudo-intellectual, fashionable, placid and complacent, good-for-nothing male figures, also accepts Nimmi's match with Kuku weakly. It is only Rajen, Nimmi's friend, who lends voice to some of the most feminist utterances in the novel. Quite indignantly she asks: 'How can your family do such a thing? It is like selling you as a slave. Daddy always says arranged marriage is a primitive custom and should not be allowed' (p. 182). Throughout the novel, quite indirectly, Jhabvala has been giving us glimpses of a parallel process which is taking shape in a few families, where women are recognized as individuals in their own rights. Rajen's mother belongs to one such family and is an indication of the shape of things to come. Of course, since the focus of the novel is on Nimmi, and since Nimmi represents a girl from an average Indian family, one cannot generalize and say that most modern Indian girls are as progressive in their outlook and behaviour as Rajen is.

Once Nimmi's marriage is fixed, a picnic is arranged to let the boy and girl meet. Nimmi draws consolation from this: 'For it was almost as good as having a proposal of marriage; almost as good as choosing one's own husband' (p. 188). But during the meeting, even Nimmi's ideas of modernity stand qualified. She agrees with Kuku when he says that college would be of no use to her:

> what, in the end, had she to do with English literature and John Keats? They did very well to pass away the time till one could begin to live in earnest, but beyond that there was nothing in them. Pretty girls from rich families did not have to bother themselves with such things. They were of value only to plain girls from poorer families who had to think of making a living by teaching. She feels sorry for such girls. (p. 189)

Finally, for Nimmi, too, marriage has become the ultimate goal in life.

Though Nimmi may not have proved to be enough of a radical, yet she does succeed in creating ripples in the serene, sedate, predetermined lives of the tradition-bound women of her family. Jhabvala allows us a glimpse of the stirrings within the Indian woman, of having an independent say in important matters, of desires which leap beyond the confining walls of her home, of longings for a share in the world beyond, of an identity of her own. Though in the end the male factor threatens to swamp her identity, yet she succeeds in making an indelible impression on the readers' minds. We remember her as a fresh breath of spring—as Nimmi—and not as Lalaji's daughter or Kuku's wife. With her personality, she has managed to shake off at least some of the labels. As she stands on the threshold of matrimony, there are strong indications that she will find her fulfilment in marriage.

Only one novel, *The Householder,* intervenes between *The Nature of Passion* and *Get Ready for Battle,* but we find a completely different set of characters in a changed kind of atmosphere, with a new and radically different set of relationships. Though the setting chosen this time is once again a familiar one, that of a rich Punjabi businessman and his family, yet many differences set it far apart from the story of Lala Narayan Das Verma. Society seems to have taken a number of progressive steps as far as the household of Gulzari Lal goes. We do not have a women's quarter here, nor do we have subservient wives who are content to sift rice, pound spices and rear babies. Instead, the three women that we meet in this novel, namely Sarla Devi, Kusum Mehra and Mala, are far from being subservient to their male counterparts. In fact, divorce and separation are in the air. If a husband's way of life does not suit his wife, it is not necessary for her to stay with him; if a widow, even though a grandmother, happens to like a man, there is nothing to stop her from marrying him; if a husband neglects his wife and expects her to sit passively at home, it is too much to ask and revolt is not far behind. This is the scenario that Jhabvala unfolds for us in her fourth novel *Get Ready for Battle*.

After reading the first two paragraphs of the novel, it becomes evident that social norms here are quite different from what they were in *The Nature of Passion*. Gulzari Lal, though a rich and successful businessman like Lalaji, is several steps ahead of him in attitude and outlook. While Lalaji struggles hard to accommodate the changing ideas of a progressively modern society, Gulzari Lal has already acquired some of these ideas. The business party going on at his residence, could never even have been possible at Lalaji's house, let alone a mistress who has usurped the place of Gulzari Lal's lawfully wedded wife. At every step we are conscious of the differences and Jhabvala seems to be in a hurry to underline the fact that these are modern times now. She writes: 'These being modern times, many people had brought their wives who sat in a semicircle at one end of the room and sipped pineapple juice.'[9] But this modernity is very new for most of them. Jhabvala adds that among this group of strangers 'even those who had met before did not feel easy enough in these overwhelmingly social circumstances, to make any kind of conversation' (p. 8). The process of transition is obviously a slow and painstaking one for women who have lived passive and sheltered lives till now. The only person who seems to be at ease is Kusum Mehra, whose status in the household is clearly stated at the outset. Lest we should be misled into thinking that she is Gulzari Lal's wife, Jhabvala quickly reveals her to be his mistress. A widow, a mother, even a grandmother, but here she is, feeling quite comfortable in the house of a man with whom her relationship has no legal, social or moral sanction. It is later disclosed that she has been maintaining this position for the past eight years. But now it is clear that things are changing. 'Kusum had now become modern and decided that mistresses were no longer socially feasible and that remarried widows were' (p. 35). She refuses to become like Phuphiji in *The Nature of Passion*, old, wrinkled and haggard. Therefore we find her to be the strongest advocate of the idea of divorce in the novel. As she tells Mala on one occasion: 'We are all modern now, we have a Hindu Code Bill, we have divorce' (p. 11), and later to Brij Mohan: 'We are living in modern times, divorce now with us is only something legal, it is nothing more than signing some kind of agreement' (p. 139). She repeatedly carries on her onslaughts of these 'modern' ideas even on Gulzari Lal, and enviously tries to make him miss her so he would agree to divorce his wife Sarla Devi.

Sarla Devi refuses 'ever to be a wife such as [Gulzari Lal] wanted and thought he had a right to expect' (p. 38). Her intensely spiritual and other-worldly nature comes in direct conflict with her husband's thoroughly materialistic outlook. So they decide to part ways, Sarla Devi free to follow her interests and Gulzari Lal his.

Sarla Devi is a character who stands separate and isolated in the long gallery of Jhabvala's women. In her battle for the poor and the oppressed, in her routine full of political meetings, demonstrations, processions, hymn singing and communal spinning, in her simple life style shorn of everything except the bare necessities, and in her visionary outlook, she has all the potential to be developed into a strong and credible representative of all the women who had come forward during the independence struggle. But quite characteristically Jhabvala does not develop even this character fully, with the result that she remains 'a paper revolutionary, too saintly a figure to make any positive impact'.[10] However, she is convincingly modern in her outlook as she willingly accepts divorce so that her husband can marry his mistress with a free conscience. She fights a losing battle for the dwellers of Bundi Basti who are being threatened with eviction under the pretext of slum clearance and provision of better environment. Ironically it is Gulzari Lal who is hoping to acquire the land and profit by it. Sarla Devi's requests of help from her son Vishnu fall on deaf ears. It is a final twist of irony when Ramchandran, the leader from Bundi Busti, who had all along been imploring Sarla Devi for her help, is won over by the moneyed group and her cause is lost. Even so, she resolves to continue working for the poor and the downtrodden. Unlike other women who find their fulfilment in marriage, home and children, Sarla Devi's quest continues. Only by helping the poor and the needy does she hope to find spiritual freedom, which is the ultimate goal in her life.

Mala, the daughter-in-law of Sarla Devi is diametrically opposed to her. Her possessiveness about her husband stands in sharp contrast with Sarla Devi's detached and indifferent attitude towards Gulzari Lal. To some extent Mala can be seen as the prototype of traditional Indian wives. At least Gulzari Lal thought so when he chose her for his son:

> She was as the woman of a house should be: tall, stately, slow, broad-hipped; she was neat and did exquisite needlework, she hardly ever left the house and had no interests outside it. All these qualities ideally fitted her to be the mother of children and the centre of a happy household. . . . She was everything that his own wife had not been. But, all the same, things had not turned out as he had anticipated them. (p. 111)

It is clear that marital disharmony has struck Mala and Vishnu as each is discontented with the other. Vishnu wants to break free from the shackles of his father's business which makes him a restless wanderer, frequenting parties and clubs in order to stay away from home and office. Mala resents this. Shanta in *The Nature of Passion*, had accepted Om's visits to the prostitutes unquestioningly. Not so Màla. She frets and fumes at being neglected and turns into a virtual tigress with biting teeth and clawing nails. She complains angrily to Vishnu: 'You have the office, you have your friends. You drive off in your car and do what you like, while I sit here only and wait for the day to be finished'. In exasperation he cries at her: 'We are living in modern times . . . go and be modern' (p. 28).

Vishnu has obviously been influenced by Toto and Ushi's smart, fashionable, Westernized set, as far as his concepts of modernity go. Sumi is visibly impressed by one member of the set. 'I have never met anyone so modern (p. 58), she whispers to Mala as she watches Gogo move freely among the boys, cigarette dangling from his fingers. Toto and Ushi are leaders of the young married set, 'Very sociable, very up-to-date'. Writing about Ushi Jhabvala says:

> She was an excellent hostess and took a lot of trouble over her parties, always serving something original like chicken with mushroom and banana, or trifle a la mode, which she made with her own hands while the cook looked on and learnt. She also had a lot of conversation, for she kept up on things: She read a lot—*The Illustrated Weekly* and *Femina* and *Time* magazine (which kept her up on international affairs)—and she went to local art exhibitions, and she and Toto always bought tickets for the production of the UK High Commission or the Army Headquarters Dramatic groups. (p. 60)

These shallow, pretentious, pseudo-intellectual Westernized, young socialites, increasingly becoming a part of modern India, expose the narrow and restricted sense in which modernity was being interpreted by such people. It is they and their likes who have prompted Jhabvala to describe the modern Indian woman in obliquely satirical terms:

> She has been to Oxford or Cambridge or some smart American College. She speaks flawless, easy colloquial English with a charming lilt of an accent. She has a degree in Economics or political science or English literature. She comes from a good family. They have always lived a Western-style life, with Western food and an admiration for Western culture. The daughter now tends to frown on this. She feels one should be more deeply Indian, and with this end in view she wears handloom saries and traditional jewellery. . . . She is interested in a great variety of topics and can hold her own in any discussion. She loves to excercise her mind, and whatever the subject of conversation—economics or politics or literature or film—she has a well formulated opinion on it and knows how to express herself. . . .[11]

All this affected behaviour, all this eulogising of Western life and Western culture, serves only to delink them from their own country, from their own society and culture. Such people,

> while they are fully aware of India's problems and are up on all the statistics and all the arguments for and against nationalization and a socialistic pattern of society, all the time it is as if they were talking about some other place—as if it were a subject for debate—an abstract subject—and not a live animal actually moving under their feet. ('Myself in India')[12]

Mala, clearly out of tune with this circle of friends in Vishnu's life, wants him away from it and totally for herself. The rift between husband and wife is finally patched up by the prospects of a move to Chandnipet.

All along the narrative we find dual standards of modernity being upheld by various people. While on the one hand they profess to be modern, on the other they reveal themselves to be still not quite free from the shackles of tradition. Kusum wants to keep up with the times, not be declared an old fogey, upholds the idea of divorce and yet demands a legal, social and moral sanction for her relationship with Gulzari Lal. Mala, is modern enough to demand her right but conservative enough to even suspect the innocent relationship between Vishnu and Sumi. Sumi, another one who professes to be modern in outlook, sees nothing wrong in going out with another woman's husband. As she tells Mala: 'What is wrong? We are not in purdah, we are free like Western women. I can go when I like with my friends' (p. 77). Yet it is this same Sumi who is happily and willingly ready to marry a man chosen by her parents and whom she has never seen before in her life. Even Gogo, the most Westernized of the lot, is obviously nervous as she sits with Vishnu in his car after the party. He has offered to drop her home and Jhabvala gives a subtle hint of the mask slipping away. She writes: 'Gogo talked about the party and all the people who had been there. She talked fast and sat quite a long way away from him.' (p. 63). Except Sarla Devi, almost all other characters in the novel display this tension between the old and the new.

The Nature of Passion and *Get Ready for Battle* are not the alpha and omega of Jhabvala's fiction. Yet one fact which emerges from them as well as from her other novels is the dominating aspect of the Indian woman's personality. She may be confined to the women's quarters like Lalaji's wife or she may be playing the role of an assured hostess at a social gathering like Kanta or Kusum or she may even be acting as a crusader for the poor like Sarla Devi; in fact she may be either traditional or modern but with a few exceptions like Shanta (*The Nature of Passion*) and Ritu (*Heat and Dust*) she distinctly dominates over her male counterparts. Yolantana May, while interviewing Jhabvala questioned her about this aspect of her characterization of the Indian women:

> One tends to associate Indian women with meekness and submissiveness. But they all seem strong characters in your books, even the apparently repressed wife in the *Householder* finds enough courage to defy her husband's wishes: She does exactly as she pleases. It's the men who seem weak and vulnerable.

To this Jhabvala replied:

> Oh yes, it is like that in India. Women are much more dominant characters, they know all the tricks, and they are not certainly slow to use them.[13]

Gone are the days of unquestioned wifely devotion of which the number of suttee shrines speak quite eloquently in *Heat and Dust.* In the same novel we are given the other side of the picture when the narrator calls Inder Lal's mother and Maji 'Merry widows'[14] (p. 55), for whom life seems to have begun only after the death of their husbands. The modern widows of Satipur refuse to either whine and pine for their husbands or throw themselves on their funeral pyre. Instead they choose to live on and live their life as they wish to. In fact even in the earlier novels in characters like Phuphiji (*The Nature of Passion*), Radha (*To Whom She Will*) and Kusum Mehra (*Get Ready for Battle*), the change was evident. The transition from the old to the new, from past to present, from traditional to modern has almost been completed as far as this aspect of a woman's position in Indian society, after her husband's death, is concerned. The long, laborious and painful process which ought to have filled the gap between the suttee shrines and the merry widows is however not discussed at all. But one can have a fair idea that here as in other aspects of Indian life, the transition has not been smooth and effortless. For a society which has slumbered for so long in its tradition-oriented set-up, it is obviously difficult to change itself. But changes are knocking at the door as Jhabvala has skillfully shown—

in matters of women's desire for independence, their education, their individuality and assertiveness. It is now only a matter of time for Indian society to imbibe all these changes. At the same time one should not forget Jhabvala's warning that though it may be easy to become Westernized in the name of modernity, it is not enough.

NOTES

1. V.A. Shahane, *Ruth Prawer Jhabvala* (New Delhi: Arnold-Heinemann, 1976), p. 192.
2. C. Paul Verghese, 'A Note on *Esmond in India*', *Journal of Indian Writing in English*, July 1976, pp. 33-7.
3. Meenakshi Mukherjee, 'The Ruthless Jhabvala Touch', review of *How I Became a Holy Mother, The Times of India*, 12 September 1976, p. 10.
4. Nissim Ezekiel, 'Distorting Mirror', review of *Heat and Dust, The Times of India,* 4 January 1976, p. 10.
5. M.K. Naik, *A History of Indian English Literature* (New Delhi: Sahitya Akademi, 1982), p. 235.
6. Ibid., p. 235.
7. Ibid., p. 234.
8. Ruth Prawer Jhabvala, *The Nature of Passion* (London: Penguin Books, 1956), p. 11. All subsequent page references to the novel are from the same edition.
9. Ruth Prawer Jhabvala, *Get Ready for Battle* (London: Penguin Books, 1962), p. 7. All subsequent page references to the novel are from the same edition.
10. Shanta Krishnaswami, *The Woman in Indian Fiction in English* (New Delhi: Ashish Publishing House, 1984), p. 304.
11. Ruth Prawer Jhabvala, 'Myself in India', *Out of India* (New York: William Morrow and Company, Inc., 1986), p. 16.
12. Ibid., p. 17.
13. Yolantana May, 'Conversation with Jhabvala', *The New Review*, December 1975, p. 56.
14. Ruth Prawer Jhabvala, *Heat and Dust* (London: John Murray, 1976), p. 55.

Looking the World in the Face: The Changed Woman in Anand's *Gauri*

T.N. Dhar

Mulk Raj Anand grew up amidst fast-changing developments in the political and social life of India. People's movement against the British had gathered momentum and acquired a sharp and purposeful direction under the banner of the Congress led by Gandhi; massive programmes against social oppression and baneful customs had also begun alongside. It is to Anand's credit as a writer that he responded to the call of his times with courage, conviction, and commendable commitment. He not only endorsed political and social change, but also analysed India's cultural tradition with a critical insight, to uncover its blind spots and inadequacies. This he thought necessary for incorporating new values into it, to make it relevant to the changing needs of the times. Going to the very root of the degraded social and political system, Anand found that his countrymen had lost faith in themselves because they had relied far too long on the theories of *kala, karma,* and *kismet*; they had believed that change was divine-ordained and that history was governed by forces beyond human control. This was the prime cause of their apathy and of their abject servility towards the British. It was also responsible for the tame surrender of the poor and suffering masses to the tyrannies of the exploitative, stratified, and hierarchical social order. Anand was convinced that nothing short of a 'total reorientation of one's outlook on history' could help improve matters. This meant that all Indians had to learn to oppose 'all theories of fatalistic acceptance of God, predestination and determinism', and to recognize that 'every man is a master of his own destiny'.[1] Anand dramatized all these vital issues in his fiction, to promote people's understanding of the complexity of their situation and to help them face up to their problems with a clear and healthy awareness of their potential.

Anand was keen that along with men women too should learn to master their destiny. Like the heroine of *Gauri*, he wanted them to look the world in the face. She fought the age-old and outmoded traditions of her village and strove for her rightful place in the social order as a dignified and respected human being. But before I discuss the novel in detail to show how Gauri negotiates the difficult terrain between tradition and modernity, I shall make a brief comment on Anand's artistic involvement with the concerns of his day to build a perspective on women in his earlier novels.

Before *Gauri* was published in 1960 under a different title *The Old Woman and the Cow*, Anand had produced more than half a dozen novels. All of them are suffused with his deep social and political awareness about which he made significant formulations in *Apology for Heroism*. He believes that art has to have social relevance and artists have a prominent role to play in the cultural reorientation of societies. They are most suited and therefore effective in helping people for working out a proper climate of change and for promoting new values. As a literary intellectual with a critical consciousness, Anand successfully located himself in history, strove towards attaining higher awareness, and shared it with his fellow beings through his writings.[2] His sense of commitment is so strong that quite often his fiction comes dangerously close to propaganda.

Projecting the idea of novel as a revolutionary form of writing,[3] Anand specifies the areas of social experience which dominate his writings: 'I am conscious of the need to help raise the untouchables, the peasants, serfs, the coolies and other suppressed members of society, to human dignity and self-awareness in view of the abjectness, apathy and despair to which they have been condemned'.[4] Since his first efforts at writing were devoted mostly to the poor and the downtrodden classes, exclusive attention to women had to wait, but not for long. In the 'Postscript' to a later edition of the *Apology*, the suffering people who claimed Anand's love and attention included 'the eternally wronged woman'.[5]

On account of Anand's preoccupation with untouchables and coolies and the political ferment in India, women figure marginally in his earlier novels. Most of them are victims: either of the oppressive political system or of the lust of British and Indian men. Berry has provided a detailed catalogue of women who have to put up with abuse and atrocities in these novels.[6] From amongst them, two deserve our attention: Maya in *The Sword and the Sickle* and Janki in *The Big Heart*, who share some interesting qualities. They live with their male companions Lalu and Ananta respectively because they love them. They cannot be married to them because they are widows. Their relationship with their lovers is therefore outside the normal social framework.[7] (Very late in the novel, Lalu marries Maya according to Arya Samaj rites to avoid embarrassment.) In spite of their lack of formal education, they are fairly intelligent and participate in the political activism of their lovers. Of the two Janki is more impressive, because she helps Ananta to sort out his confusions. Through discussion, argument and sustained interrogation, in a spirit of critical sympathy, she enables him to clarify himself to himself on the issue of the use of machines in his trade and of his projected solutions to the problems arising out of the intricate relationship between tradition and modernity.[8]

Although he does not deal specifically with the problems of women in the novels published before *Gauri*, Anand sharpens our awareness of the injustice done to them as a part of his overall strategy of censuring all that is evil in the system. He is also conscious of their problems as women in a set-up which is tradition-bound, fixed, and overwhelmingly male-dominated. During the course of one of her several debates with Ananta, Janki refers to her situation as that of a person who is denied freedom by society. This is how she orders her complaint: 'First of all, my parents, who created me not because they loved each other but because they considered it a duty, and who regarded me, when I was born, as a curse because I was a girl. Then my husband and his relations, who were more concerned with the dowry I brought them with me. Later, when the owner of my house had died, society considered me as one who should be dead to all impulses and live only to worship the memory of my dead lord and master.'[9] It is a fairly comprehensive picture of the traditional status of a woman in our society. She is considered inferior to men. She is a curse because she has to be provided with a dowry at the time of her marriage so that she is accepted by her husband and his parents. She hardly has a life of her own. It virtually ends with the death of her husband. Once a widow, always a widow. If she challenges her destiny, she is treated with contempt. Although Ananta accepts and loves Janki, his relatives and associates talk to her slightingly. When she lived with him in Bombay, even the followers of the Mahatma who believed in and fought for freedom despised her because she was a widow and not married to him. Some even called her a prostitute.

When Anand finally wrote his heroine-centred novel in *Gauri*, he put into it all the tenderness and sympathy which he felt for women, evidence of which can be found in his later autobiographical novels.[10] Two significant details about *Gauri* need to be stated right in the beginning. First, it is located in a village, which is very backward and steeped in orthodoxy and dead customs. Since it has been written in the realistic mode, many of its scenes and episodes may appear even exaggerated, when compared with novels about women which are located in urban or metropolitan centres. Second, Gauri comes from a poor family. Economic hardships impinge heavily on her life and account largely for her misery. Gauri is also without any formal education. In the atmosphere of rigidity and fixity and indigence and need which characterizes the village, change of any kind is not merely difficult, it is virtually inconceivable. But Gauri does change in a major way, after she experiences the different environment of a city where, through a happy chance, she meets people who provide her the new light of education. This helps her to conceive of new alignments in her life, which culminate in her revolutionary decision to live away from her husband. The novel also clarifies that in her first attempts at changing her situation Gauri uses tradition itself as a resource of change and hope, confirming that 'the assumption that modernity and tradition are radically contradictory rests on a misdiagnosis of tradition as it is found in traditional societies, a misunderstanding of modernity as it is found in modern societies, and a misapprehension of the relationship between them'.[11]

The novel opens with Gauri's marriage to Panchi. The marriage is a negotiated one with a strained history: 'The relationship had been broken off three times and renewed again'.[12] Details about her 'comely and innocent' looks and her being a 'cow, very gentle and very good' (p. 11) are made available to us through Panchi. He even considers her a 'prize of a girl—a girl whom he could fold in his arms at night and kick during the day' (p. 11). The sentence sums up her destiny: she has to submit to her husband for his pleasure and also for providing him an outlet for his rage. The parting advice of her mother 'Be like Sita' (p. 30) is meant to remind her that she has to pay unqualified obeisance to her husband.

Gauri has had no say in the choice of her husband. She does not know him and is not even aware if he has anything to live on. Since he had been living with his uncle and aunt, he continues to do so even after his marriage. His aunt Kesaro treats Gauri as her daughter-in-law and asserts herself as a proverbial mother-in-law would. She becomes the cause of friction between Gauri and Panchi which results in his beating her invariably. Kesaro constantly draws his attention to her lapses and complains to him that the economic hardships of the family are because of her inauspicious presence. At one point, she provokes Panchi's ire against her by telling him that she had spoken to one of his friends without covering her head and had not cared to tell her about her menstruation periods. She had moved about freely when she should have been like 'an untouchable' and 'isolated and given food away from the kitchen, and not allowed to contaminate anything' (p. 41). In a fit of violence Panchi beats Gauri and tells her to be patient with Kesaro. This produces Gauri's first bout of temper: 'Patience, how long can I go on being patient against the nagging of that woman and your shoe beatings on her behalf? (p. 44) Panchi is taken aback by her outburst and wakes up to the fact that she was 'not the mere innocent she was reputed to be, but had an uncanny grasp of things' (p. 49). He is so demoralized that he has to invoke *dharma* to justify his punitive actions: 'the husband has to chastise his wife if she goes wrong' (p. 51). But it is he who has to decide when that would be.

Anand carefully brings out the difference between Gauri's relationship with her mother-in-law and her husband. Gauri strongly disapproves of the actions and behaviour of Kesaro, but hardly says anythings against her husband's attitude, especially after he moves out of his uncle's house to set up a separate home with her. She is soft and submissive toward him, and pays him his due, traditional respect. When he is in need of money, she willingly gives him the only gift he had given her, and in ritual submission, 'she bent down and symbolically touching his feet, got away' (p. 64). Panchi is moved by her devotion and considerateness and acknowledges 'to himself that he had bullied her since she had come to his home, first at the instigation of Kesaro and then through habit' (p. 77). When he is frustrated in his efforts to do well and gives himself up to despair, she cheers him up and urges him to keep trying. In contrast to this, when Kesaro visits them in their new home, she becomes furious and snubs her with vehemence: 'Get out of my house, witch' (p. 95). Her changed visage alarms both Kesaro and Panchi. He is 'overwhelmed by the sudden flashing power that had come into the gentle Gauri, turning her into her other incarnation, Kali, the divine destroyer herself' (p. 95).

As a village-bred girl, Gauri's conception of the relationship between husband and wife within the framework of marriage is largely based on what she has observed and heard from people. Later events in the novel confirm that her thinking has been influenced by her knowledge of her heritage: the stories of gods and goddesses, Puranic *kathas*, and the lives of saints. She firmly believes that her husband, no matter how harsh he is to her, is her lord and has to be won through devotion: she 'believed in the worship of her lord and master, and wanted ultimately to conquer him, with her devotion. . . . For, in her inner being, she believed that he, who was capable of tenderness once, had an inexhaustible well of love in him, if only the shell of suspicion could be removed and the heart-source could be cleansed' (pp. 100-1). She thinks that if Mira Bai could melt the heart of her God, she too could do it. The significant thing to note here is that in accordance with the dictates of tradition she persists in believing that her husband is her lord. Nevertheless, she wants to change his attitude towards her. For this too the resource comes from her own tradition: from the examples of Savitri and Mira Bai.

Gauri's efforts to change Panchi prove effective for a while. But when she tells him about her pregnancy, Panchi one again becomes violent towards her. It seems that Kesaro's words have sunk deep into him and he is not sure if the child Gauri is carrying is his. He tells her to leave their place, but she stays on stubbornly. It is only when he becomes unbearably violent because of the 'resurgence of demoniac hate in him', and slaps her all over her body and kicks her behind that she leaves the place. She is determined to 'protect her womb against any further violence from him' (p. 103). But she still does not give him up. At her mother's place, she feels that she should have persisted in her efforts to win him over; she even thinks of a different strategy: to combat his violence with her own kind of violence. She considers it the only course available to her to awaken him to the new reality he was afraid of facing: '. . . she should have turned on him and hit him with both her hands, and all her strength, to make him realize the cry of that innocent spark in her womb which he was frightened to see' (p. 113).

The reason for emphasizing these details is to underline the point that Gauri is not asking for any radical change in her relationship with her husband. Given the conditions in which she has been living and the kind of exposure she has had, such a change is inconceivable. She accepts her position, but wants a slight adjustment in it: that her husband should love her, treat her with respect, and not be violent to her. She uses her tenderness, tact, and patience to effect a change in him—the change of heart, as Anand would have called it. When her mother tells her that 'he [Panchi] is not the only husband' to suggest the possibility of her remarriage, Gauri tells her clearly that she is already married. A change of husband would obviously not solve her problem; she wants and needs to effect a change in the husband. But before she can even attempt that, she has to reckon with other problems.

Gauri's problems in her mother's place arise out of poverty and desperation, which are a part of the village scene. Her uncle is an unscrupulous exploiter and her mother is his desperate victim. He also represents 'the malignant power of . . . man's physical authority. Gauri can see and feel its evil and demon-like power, but she cannot match it. Therefore, she prays for strength from within the possibilities of her own tradition: 'Oh Mother, you who are enshrined in our home and who gave me her name, come into me, so that I have strength to bear this. And give me wings to fly away from here' (p. 124). But prayers do not work with Amru. Like Draupadi, he drags her out of his house by her hair. Her mother watches helplessly while he assaults her body and forcibly sends her to Hoshiarpur to be virtually sold to a rich, widowed businessman.

At this point, Anand widens the scope of the novel. A woman has not only to face problems within her family, where she has to reckon with her husband and her in-laws, but also outside it, in a male-dominated society, which threatens her very existence. At every turn, she has to conform to the wishes of male exploiters and suffer agony and pain. Gauri's playmate Paro sums up her situation succinctly: 'Suffering for us sister, suffering, only suffering for us women' (p. 116).

In Seth Jai Ram Das's house, Gauri understands how religion is exploited by people for base, personal gains. Before her marriage, the village priest had tried to seduce her; now the Seth was 'sanctifying rape with holy verses' (p. 134). She is outraged by his behaviour; in a fit of desperation she curses even the gods: 'May the gods die if they favour these dogs' (p. 134). But because the gods are also her only source of hope, she cannot help seeking their protection: 'Hey Devi Parvati, Gauri, spare me, spare me'. When the Seth attempts to violate her sexually, she warns him menacingly: 'I am guarded by the goddess! So do not come near me. Or you will burn' (p. 145).

Gauri succeeds in getting out of the clutches of the Seth because she is sick and has to be admitted to the nursing home run by Dr. Mahindra and Dr. Batra. She refuses to go back to his place and the doctors allow her to stay with them. There Gauri gets a taste of independent existence, but that is not her goal. She still thinks of going back to Panchi, of proving her devotion for him and winning his love: 'A spasm of ambition arose in her and told her that if she could, indeed, invoke the Goddess, become possessed of her spirit, and perform the heroic feat of walking to her husband's village, he would be impressed by her devotion and at once take her in, for she was convinced that her suffering would ultimately redeem her position, as good *karma* always improved one's prospects for the future' (p. 161). The important thing to note here is not merely her desire to go back to Panchi and accept his lordship, but also her belief that gods are going to help her in her efforts for a better future. But because she has no knowledge of how to reach him and is not sure that she would not be waylaid by 'raksha demons', she fails to make up her mind. She little knew that a demon was waiting for her in the nursing home itself. Taking advantage of her situation, Dr. Batra, who is a philanderer of sorts, tries to assault her. Once again, she summons the energy with which she fought the overtures of the Seth: 'From some unplumbed depth there arose in her, however, Kali, the energy of sheer negation, the harness of whom she had brought against Seth Jai Ram Das' (p. 142). The attack strengthens her resolution to go back to her husband, who would be her protector.

Before Gauri's wish can materialize, Anand twists the plot of the novel to bring her mother Laxmi and Adam Singh to the newly-established clinic of Mahindra, who has parted company with Batra. He is used specifically by Anand to fire his guns at the society of his day. He speaks vehemently against the new exploitative class of 'brown sahibs' and other unscrupulous classes and the poisonous effect of the race for wealth and property on his compatriots. Finally, he chastises Gauri's mother for her callousness towards her and speaks of the need of dedicated young men and women who would work with honesty of purpose to inject health into the system: 'There will have to come young men and women who will take vows of dedication, who will be like Essai missionaries who go into the wilds and serve the lepers. You folk must hang on to your turbans! I don't mind, so long as you can avoid being cruel and can pause to consider the feelings of a girl like Gauri before casting her to the wolves . . .' (pp. 228-9).

This sermon is a blemish in the novel because the bitterness of Mahindra is not adequately dramatized. Mahindra's censure touches upon concerns which have not been dealt with in the novel. Even without it the novel would have made its point. What is of crucial importance in the context of Gauri is that in Mahindra's company she has become self-reliant, free, and frank, and has overcome her inhibitions. She returns to Panchi along with her mother as an altered person, but there is no indication of any startling change in her relationship with him. She loves him as she loved him earlier; since he has been injured in a scuffle, she serves him with vigour and competence, because she has learnt the art of nursing. However, there is a marked change in her appearance, bearing, and manners; she also exudes confidence. She no longer covers her face before her elders and other men and goes about without any self-consciousness about her. She talks to everybody with assurance, and does not hesitate to point out to people their weaknesses and deficiencies. Although Panchi looks quite happy with her, he is somewhat awed by her new appearance and her forthright manner of talking.

Gauri's transformation raises eyebrows and provides grist for the mills of gossip and rumour. Their loudness brings her happy days with Panchi to an end. Everybody tells him that she is impure; she had been in the house of the Seth for several days and had also been attacked by Dr. Batra. Since Panchi cannot bear the taunts of his villagers, he gives Gauri a chance to clarify her position. When she says, 'I have come back to him—as pure as I went away', Panchi asks for proof. When he starts beating her again, she tells him that she would go away: 'She was defiant and her face knit together with a terrible strength, even though the tears were in her eyes' (p. 263). But before she goes away, she tells him that he is a coward: 'He pretended to be a lion among the men of the village. But really he is a coward! They are telling him that Ram turned out Sita because everyone doubted her chastity during her stay with Ravana! . . . I am not Sita that the earth will open up and swallow me. I shall just go out and be forgotten of him' (p. 263). The statement also testifies that Gauri has matured to be able to understand that traditions should not be accepted blindly; they can cause unhappiness and pain.

When Gauri makes the crucial decision to leave Panchi, she becomes what Anand would like every woman to be: a confident being with a will of her own, who has the strength and courage to look the world in the face. Anand writes that at this moment, Gauri's face 'transfigured from the gentle cow's acquiescent visage of the time when she had arrived in Panchi's house, to that of a woman—with a will of her own, though her heart palpitated with every step' (p. 264). She takes this extreme step because within the home she shared with her husband she could not live with respect and dignity. In her altered view of a man-woman relationship, she gives importance to faith and mutual trust. Since Panchi has no faith and trust in her, she has to take the extreme step of coming out of the marital bond. But it does not leave out the possibility of their reunion, that is, once Panchi is able to see the point of view of Gauri.

In conclusion, one could say that Anand wants women to be bold, courageous, and capable of taking extreme decisions, if they find that their lives have become dwarfed by the burdens of obsolete traditions. However, *Gauri* ends with a nagging doubt in the mind of a reader. We see that Gauri's anger against Panchi is approved by Anand because she has been able to maintain her 'purity'. What if Gauri had not succeeded in defending her virtue? Would Panchi have had the freedom to abandon her? Anand's modernity too is hemmed in by tradition.

NOTES

1. M.R. Anand, *Is There a Contemporary Indian Civilization?* (Bombay: Asia Publishing House, 1963), p. 159.
2. Anand's concern with culture is similar to that of Gramsci's. Gramsci states that culture is 'organization, discipline of one's inner life, a coming to terms with one's own personality; it is the attainment of a higher awareness, with the aid of which one succeeds in understanding one's own historical value, one's function in life, one's own rights and obligations'. Antonio Gramsci, *Selections From Political Writings: 1910-20*, selected and edited by Quintin Hare and translated by John Mathews (London: Lawrence and Wishart, 1977), p. 11.

3. For Anand's views on the novel, see *Apology for Heroism* (New Delhi: Arnold-Heinemann, 1986), pp. 127-34.
4. Ibid., p. 137.
5. Ibid., p. 198.
6. Margaret Berry, *Mulk Raj Anand: The Man and the Novelist* (Amsterdam: Oriental Press, 1971), pp. 56-7.
7. It is interesting to note that Anand's strategy of associating romantic love with widows closely resembles the efforts of the early writers of realistic novels in India. See Meenakshi Mukherjee, *Realism and Reality* (New Delhi: 1985), pp. 69-70.
8. For more details on this, see my '*The Big Heart*: Anand's Novel of Ideas', *The Indian Literary Review*, Vol. V, No. 3 (October 1987).
9. M.R. Anand, *The Big Heart* (New Delhi: Arnold-Heinemann, 1980), p. 74.
10. Anand's sympathy for his mother and aunt Devaki is very clear in his autobiographical novels.
11. Lloyd Rudolph and Susanne Rudolph, *The Modernity of Tradition: Political Development in India* (Chicago: The University of Chicago Press, 1967), p. 3.
12. M.R. Anand, *Gauri* (New Delhi: Arnold-Heinemann, 1981), p. 11. Subsequent references to the novel in the text are to this edition.

The Politics of Gender in Raja Rao's *The Serpent and the Rope*

Sarla Palkar

'In the complex fabric of contemporary Indian civilization', remarks Meenakshi Mukherjee in *The Twice Born Fiction*, 'the two most easily discerned strands are the indigenous Indian traditions and the imported European conceptions. Almost every educated Indian today is the product of the conflicts and reconciliations of two cultures, although the consciousness of this tension varies from individual to individual'. She further goes on to observe: 'This cultural conflict—or synthesis, as the case may be—has for some reason always assumed a vital significance for the Indian novelist who writes in English' (p. 65). As most of Raja Rao's critics including Meenakshi Mukherjee have pointed out, the East-West encounter and its consequences on the minds and lives of the characters is a major theme of *The Serpent and the Rope*. As often happens in this kind of encounter, it is very difficult to keep one's sense of proportion and the reactions are likely to be very strong or extreme. When a Naipaul or a Nirad Chaudhari denigrates or rejects his native tradition and culture, it is easy enough to note the impact of the Western thought on him. But when someone like Raja Rao goes into ecstasies while recalling the greatness of the ancient Indian tradition it is not easily recognized that his 'rather aggressively metaphysical definition of India' (S. Nagarajan, p. 84) may owe a great deal to the. Western Orientalist's construction of the classical Orient in general and India in particular.

When the English language was introduced by the British rulers in India, the new language did not disturb the existing hierarchies in the country. Those who had previously been learning Sanskrit—whether they were the Brahmins of Bengal, Maharashtra or the south—maintained their hegemony over others by mastering the

*The article was published in the first issue of *Indian Panorama*.

colonizers' language for political and material gains without necessarily giving up the study of Sanskrit whose prestige had been enhanced a great deal by the work done by the Orientalist philologists. English and Sanskrit often co-existed peacefully as the two belonged to the Indo-European family of languages and as both the languages had become the symbol of intellectual, moral and spiritual superiority. This happy marriage between English and Sanskrit is very much in evidence in Raja Rao's handling of English in *The Serpent and the Rope.* The following remarks of Raja Rao also bear out that he sees no opposition between English and Sanskrit:

> Now, some languages have history and, according to some, all languages have history. It would be better to say just as Indian civilization is the making of the *Rishis* (the sages), and the Western, of heroes and prophets, that some languages seem to have this breath of eternity in them and have attained then to the status of what A.E. called 'the language of the gods'; others are mere vernaculars.
>
> The Sanscrit language is such a 'language of the gods' and through Sanscrit all Indo-European languages participate in this, including the much abused English language. After all, remember, Shakespeare used the English language. ('The Writer and the Word', p. 4)

The conflict, then, is not so much between English and Sanskrit as between 'the languages of the gods' and 'mere vernaculars'—between high culture and low culture. The English of the novel is supposedly adapted to the rhythm of Sanskrit and not to any modern Indian language spoken by the masses. Also, in his text, Raja Rao praises the classical tradition, whether Indian or European, and either ignores or criticizes the contemporary Indian reality. His chief enemy is history as it threatens his politics of the *status quo* with the forces of change that it has ushered in. This conservative ideology in the last analysis affects the treatment and the fate of women characters in the novel, which is my chief concern here.

Though in Raja Rao's own words, *The Serpent and the Rope,* is 'a "Pauranic" recreation of Indian story telling' (quoted by Naik, p. 259) and though, as M.K. Naik points out, it is a conscious attempt to create a truly 'Indian' novel with its roots firmly embedded in native tradition (p. 259), it shows strong affinities with the Western modernist tradition in literature. Actually the parallels in Raja Rao's work and that of the modernist writers are so many that they would require a separate treatment. Here I will emphasize only those aspects which have a bearing on the hypothesis I am trying to advance. As the old bourgeois order and culture appeared to be crumbling, many great artists in the first half of the century went back to myths and archetypes in their search for roots and permanent values. There was also a tendency to valorize the inner self, the inner reality, at the expense of the social and historical reality. In his recourse to the Indian myths and archetypes Raja Rao is trying, among other things, to preserve the values of the ancient Brahminical tradition. With his insistence on the primacy of the subject over the object, of the perceiver to what is perceived—the outer world—and his construction of an India that is beyond time and history, Raja Rao too, like the modern artists in the West, seeks to divorce himself from history.

A brief outline of the story of *The Serpent and the Rope* would be of help in the discussion of the novel: Ramaswamy, who hails from an ancient Brahmin family of the south, goes to France to do his doctorate on the Albigensian heresy. There he meets a French woman, Madeleine, who is five years his senior and who teaches history at a college in Aix. Ramaswamy marries her. Their first child Pierre Krishna dies in infancy. Rama comes on a visit to India to meet his sick father and after the death of the latter, he takes his stepmother to Benares in order to perform the death rites there. His sojourn in north India makes him keenly conscious of his spiritual roots in India. It is on this trip to the north that he meets Savithri, who later on plays the role of a nurturer or a spiritual guide in his life. On his return to France, in spite of their best efforts, things do not go smoothly with Rama and his wife, and the rift between the two widens. While Madeleine is expecting for the second time, Rama makes another trip to India to attend his stepsister Saroja's marriage. Before he can leave the country, however, he gets the news of the death of his new-born son. When Rama returns to France he discovers that Madeleine has taken to Buddhism. They are ultimately divorced and the novel ends with Rama's resolve to go to his Guru at Travancore who will show him the path to the Absolute Truth.

As David McCutchion has observed, there is very little story. 'Of the more than four hundred pages, few are narrative, most are meditation—an unhurrying philosophical soliloquy on the nature of reality: serpent or rope' (p. 91). The story is narrated by Rama in the first person and therefore all the incidents and characters—including women—are filtered through his consciousness. Now what sort of a person is Rama? Because his portrayal of things and people is likely to be coloured by his own preoccupations and biases. Even sympathetic critics like M.K. Naik have to admit—albeit grudgingly—that 'Rama has his share—who does not—of certain rather uninviting traits of character also. It is possible to be irritated, as some have been, at his insistence on his own Brahminical purity, his fits of intellectual arrogance, snobbery and intolerance, and his tendency to make capital out of his "romantic" illness' (p. 290). Rama often projects himself and his own obsessions on the world around him and therefore his picture of it is partial and exclusive. Take for example his definition of India. 'India is an idea, a metaphysic' (p. 380), he declares. Naturally since India is an abstract concept for him, 'India has no history, for Truth cannot have history' (p. 104). India has to be straitjacketed into his Brahminical and Vedantic conception of it. And this nostalgia for the origins makes him ignore the long history of India which went on accommodating various cultures, religions and philosophies in its chequered career.

Like most of the heroes in the modernist fiction Rama is in flight from the nightmare of history and therefore he refuses to take cognizance of the historical process through which his Vedantic and Brahminical India has been transformed into an urban, industrial, modern nation. For him

> India would never be made by our politicians and professors of political science, but by these isolate existences of India, in which India is rememorated, *experienced* and communicated; beyond history, as tradition, as the Truth. Anybody can have the geographic—even the political—India; it matters little. But this India of Coomaraswamy, who will take it away, I ask you, who? Not Tamerlane or even Joseph Stalin. (*The Serpent and the Rope*, p. 357)

Alas! foreign invaders—though not Tamurlane and Stalin—have changed the course of India's destiny throughout the ages and though we do not question the great contributions the expatriates like Coomaraswamy have made to enhance India's prestige, the fate of modern India does lie in the hands of its self-serving politicians and industrialists. But then it is typical of Rama to turn his back upon the present political realities of India and cling to an immanent image of it that is pliable and soothing.

Rama has a sentimental attachment to cities like Benares, Paris, London, Cambridge, etc., which have been sanctified by tradition and seem to possess an inner reality for him. Even Marseille, though 'certainly horrible' (p. 46), is singled out for praise by the virtue of its sea which reminds him of the Greek conquest and the first Christians. But an urban and metropolitan growth like Bombay is denounced. To his mind 'this barbaric city simply had no meaning for a Brahmin like me. It spoke a language so alien, had a structure so improper, made a demand so vehement and secondary, that one had no business to be there. Bombay had no right to exist' (p. 46). Rama, like the Orientalists, overvalues the classical India and undervalues its contemporary realities. Like them too his is a male conception of the world. As Edward Said has pointed out:

> . . . the male conception of the world, in its effect upon the practicing Orientalist, tends to be static, frozen, fixed eternally. The very possibility of development, transformation, human movement—in the deepest sense of the word—is denied the Orient and the Oriental. As a known and ultimately an immobilized or unproductive quality, they come to be identified with a bad sort of eternality: hence, when the Orient is being approved, such phrases as 'the wisdom of the East'. (*Orientalism*, p. 208)

One wonders whether Rama has not fallen into this Orientalist trap when he equates India with Truth, with tradition or with wisdom, all of which are one and the same to his mind. He also bears out with vengeance Hegel's view that Indians have no sense of history by his insistence that India 'has no history, for Truth cannot have history' (p. 104).

The Serpent and the Rope may be described as a discourse on the doctrine of Advaita Vedanta. It narrates its hero Ramaswamy's quest for the one in the play of the many, for the Absolute Truth in the world of illusion or *maya*, for the Timeless and the Unchanging in the flux of history and temporality. The paradox at the heart of the novel lies in the fact that it is trying to convey something that is beyond time and space through the medium of a form which is basically rooted in these two elements. That is why Rama's symbolic tutelage to the discipline of history during the course of the novel and his marriage to a woman who teaches history. As S. Nagarajan observes, 'In the marriage of Rama and Madeleine, two contrary world-views, two contrary epistemologies, come together, and the novel is a study of that encounter' (p. 85). Since various critics have studied the complex symbolism of the novel and attributed different symbolic roles to its characters, there would be no harm, I suppose, in saying that Madeleine, Rama's French wife, represents history here. The novel recounts not only the sad consequences of an encounter between the East and the West through the marriage of Rama and Madeleine, but also underlines the incompatibility between Truth and history, between Being and Becoming, between essence and existence. With Rama's parting of the ways with Madeleine, the linear movement of the novel comes to its conclusion.

Considerable praise has been showered on Raja Rao and *The Serpent and the Rope* by a section of critics who, significantly enough, hail from south India and who share the author's background and his ideology. But they too fail to trace the exact reasons for the dissolution of the marriage between Rama and Madeleine. C.D. Narasimhaiah, for instance, admits that 'The novel relates no sufficient or immediate cause for the breakdown of relationship between Rama and his wife, and the reader can only guess at it' (*Raja Rao*, p. 105). But at the same time he and M.K. Naik are quick to put the onus of the blame on Madeleine. In this context Raja Rao's own remarks in his letter to M.K. Naik are illuminating:

> Man finds life natural with a woman; that is human destiny. But a woman can only find her God through man. But the 'modern woman' thinks she can reach the Ultimate directly. This is heresy . . . Denis de Rougemont's famous book *Passion and Society* . . . influenced me to think seriously of the problem. Modern love, according to de Rougemont, is a heresy. . . . Revolution too, so history tells us, is heresy—in the sense that revolution (like the Cathar or Albigensian revolt against Catholic dharma) is beautiful and noble like modern love, yet is heretical—tradition being wisdom. Wisdom (that is Tradition) as history is anti-history. Hence India refused to have history—just as Sita accepted Rama (and all his doings) and did not revolt against her 'cruel' husband. Thus marriage as history (Rama-Madeleine) fails, but love as Savithri-Rama succeeds, for in one Madeleine seeks her own God but Savithri her Rama (through whom she sees the whole human experience and beyond). . . . India is classical, that is traditional, in which the woman being in her true and own place inherits the world (as queen, hence the coronation of the Queen of England, etc.). The man who seeks, the pilgrim of the Absolute, is lonely, man is ever lonely. Woman seeks her man for her own fulfilment and for her inheritance, the world. The Devi swings because Shiva dances in the crematorium. And that is civilization. (quoted by M.K. Naik, p. 264)

The patriarchal bias here is so blatantly obvious that it needs no further comment. Though I would not go to the extent of identifying Rama with his author, the pronouncements made in the above excerpt—like many other comments made by Raja Rao from time to time—clearly indicate that Rama not only enjoys his creator's approval and sympathy but also carries the burden of the latter's philosophy and prejudices. The passage also underlines the binary conflict between wisdom and history.

Raja Rao has assigned definite places and functions to men and women and he disapproves of any deviation from the assigned gender roles. The greatest heresy on the part of Madeleine, therefore, seems to be that she has had the audacity or foolhardiness to seek her God on her own instead of seeing the Ultimate in her husband or through her husband. One of the interesting ironies of the novel arises from the implication that Rama is a modern Siddhartha. Rama in fact makes several references to Kanthaka, Siddhartha's horse, with the help of whom Siddhartha first set out on his quest of the Absolute Truth. But then Madeleine almost snatches this prerogative of Rama's from him and literally follows in the footsteps of the Buddha, and without Kanthaka too. This also is a transgression on her part, as Raja Rao pronounces in the same letter: 'Madeleine through her own Catholicism (by going back to it, through it and beyond it) would have reached Rama better. To be true to one's background is to be true to all backgrounds' (quoted by Naik, p. 263). This kind of orthodoxy cannot stomach any change, any evolutionary process, that threatens the supremacy of the privileged few and that is why revolution and history are banned as heretical. According to this logic there is no scope for human effort, for human struggle, and you are saved or damned by your birth. The following dialogue between Madeleine and Rama confirms this impression:

> 'What is it separated us, Rama?'
> 'India.'
> 'India? But I am a Buddhist.'
> 'That is why Buddhism left India. India is *impitoyable*.'
> 'But one can become a Buddhist?'
> 'Yes, and a Christian and a Muslim as well.'
> 'Then'?
> 'One can never be converted to Hinduism.'
> 'You mean one can only be born a Brahmin?'
> 'That is—an Indian', I added, as an explanation of India.
> (*The Serpent and the Rope*, p. 336)

This is not so much an explanation of India as of Rama's own stand on the nature of reality in general and India in particular. It is in the course of this crucial exchange, which seals the fate of their marriage, that Rama cites the famous disquisition on the serpent and the rope on which concept the whole of the novel is based. It again underlines the irreconcilable conflict between his position and that of Madeleine: 'There can be only two attitudes to life', he declares. 'Either you believe the world exists and so—you. Or you believe that you exist—and so the world. There is no compromise possible' (p. 337). That is why he believes in his subjective abstract construction of India and not in the material and historical India that exists out there: 'India has, I always repeat, no history. To integrate India into history—is like trying to marry Madeleine' (p. 337). After listening to such pronouncements it is not surprising that Madeleine is led to exhort him to 'Find then, my friend, an Indian Maitreyi. Let me be the woman of the marches' (p. 341). At the end of this scene, which may be described as the climax of the novel, Rama heaves a sigh of relief with the observation that 'The battle at last had ended' (p. 341). The divorce that comes at the end is then a foregone conclusion.

The serious lapse on the part of Madeleine, according to the male Brahminical value system propounded in *The Serpent and the Rope* is her inability or unwillingness to play the role of *Prakriti*, the creative power of *Purusha*, with the help of which man can achieve self-realization. She, therefore, does not fit into the ideal of 'Feminine Principle' that is extolled in the novel. As M.K. Naik observes, 'the fact that the marriage of Rama and Madeleine ultimately proves barren, both their children dying in infancy, may be considered symbolic of Madeleine's failure to be the true Feminine Principle' (Naik, p. 283). But one cannot understand why the woman should be held responsible for the barrenness of a marriage, and not the man. The same critic also condemns Madeleine for her inability to recover from the trauma of the death of her children and praises Rama for the detached objectivity he shows in the face of death. On my part I find Rama's reaction, on whatever grand and noble philosophy it may be based, unnatural and callous—in short, inhuman. When he learns of the death of his second son, Rama informs us, 'In the bathroom, later, when I stepped on the wash-slab I laughed. I was neither in pain, nor was I relieved; I felt above both, like a child looking at a kite in the sky' (p. 287); and this description of his response to death continues till the end of the section:

> I laughed hilariously the whole afternoon, playing country chess, first with Little Mother, and then with Saroja when she woke from her siesta. In the evening I took them all to the cinema. (*The Serpent and the Rope*, p. 288)

Now if this is to be interpreted as a defence mechanism that the human mind sometimes builds up against the sudden onrush of the acute, unbearable pain, one can understand it. But if it is supposed to denote some kind of spiritual strength, my sympathies are with the persons who fail in the spiritual test, as Madeleine does. As far as Madeleine is concerned, the death of the children no doubt hastens the disintegration of the marriage. The experience of death drives Madeleine, as it had led her Guru, the Buddha, to renounce the world and reject her body as 'the eighteen aggregates'.

If Madeleine is the obstacle in the path of the hero in his quest for Absolute Truth and therefore according to the patriarchal terminology plays the role of a destructive woman—one thinks of the famous Madeleine of Saul Bellow's *Herzog*—or a death-dealing mother—the woman who is made to represent *Prakriti*, Feminine Principle, the nurturer or the life-giving mother in the novel is Savithri. The symbolic significance of the name of Savithri in Indian myths and tradition is yet again highlighted by the novelist. Savithri of the novel is mostly a creation of the male fantasy and desire and therefore has to carry the burden of the symbolic role that is literally thrust upon her by the hero. Still, as Meenakshi Mukherjee remarks:

> Savithri may be the ideal of Indian womanhood for Ramaswamy, but as a character she comes alive most vividly when she is her own self—the argumentative, rebellious, cigarette-smoking undergraduate fascinated by the wisdom and philosophy of a South Indian Brahmin who for her has the additional glamour of possessing a French education and a French wife—rather than when she is enacting the representative role of Radha. (*The Twice Born Fiction*, p. 93)

Whatever spirit of rebellion and modernity that Savithri may possess is effectively smothered by the intervention and entry of Rama into her life, who joins forces with the demands made upon her by her orthodox family. Savithri is the daughter of a small Raja in north India. Savithri may have been given an European education, but this is in no way expected to come in the way of her marrying according to the royal customs. It appears that Savithri had got interested in a young Muslim boy in London and perhaps this is the reason why she has developed an aversion to Pratap, the boy chosen for her by her family. Her attachment to the Muslim boy is not allowed to surface except on an occasion or two, and one wonders whether her final resignation to the role that Rama has carved out for her is not due to her frustrated feelings. It is significant that she gives the appellation of the Turk to Pratap, her future Hindu husband, and not to her Muslim lover. Rama with his impressive personality and erudition, however, weans her away from her foray into modernity and fits her into the traditional role of an Indian woman, who moreover like Radha or Mira may dance to the tune of her Lord and Master, the modern Krishna that Rama imagines himself to be.

When she is about to be married to Pratap, Savithri almost loses her nerve and appeals to Rama for help: 'No Hindu woman would wed a Turk. I feel besieged—the Turk is at the door. Help me to jump into the pyre, Lord my Master, of this life and of all the lives to come. Help me' (p. 295). And how does her Lord and Master react to her desperate cry for help? He who had gone through a sentimental ritual with her in London when he offered her the toe-rings, *kumkum, choli* and *sari* and thereby conferred on her the symbolic honour of a Hindu wife, now when he sees the mark of kumkum that Savithri has stuck beneath her signature, smugly observes, 'What sentimental people we Indians are!' and further reflects, 'Of course, there was a charger waiting for me. It would not take me to the Turks. Its name would be Kanthaka . . .' (p. 295). The struggle, the fight for earthly goals, Rama leaves to the lesser mortals. His path is that of passive renunciation. Though earlier he was angry with Savithri for her resigned attitude to her marriage, now it is he who abandons her to her fate in the pursuit of his metaphysical ideal.

Though Raja Rao has evoked the authority of Denis de Rougemont for the support of his arguments on the subject of the traditional concept of marriage as opposed to modern love, one must not forget that after all Rougemont and Madeleine share the same Western episteme. If we apply Rougemont's theory to Rama's relationship with Savithri, which is out of marriage, then it becomes a romantic attachment to something that is distant and unattainable. By the same standard the failure of the marriage of Rama and Madeleine can be attributed to their self-destructive romantic yearnings and their inability to come to terms with what is near and accessible to them—their inability to respect their partner as 'the other', as the neighbour.

Savithri is not only Rama's Radha or Mira but also his Maitreyi—a willing and receptive pupil who absorbs the wisdom that is doled out to her by this modern Yajnyavalkya, the great sage from whom Rama claims his lineage. Rama, like a parrot, is very fond of preaching his philosophical platitudes on all occasions and in all sorts of unlikely places. Though Madeleine playfully addresses him as 'Monsieur le Professor', being a teacher herself and moreover a Westerner, she cannot play the role of a pupil successfully and satisfy Rama's male ego. When Madeleine admonishes Rama to find out an Indian Maitreyi she does not know that he has already found one. The following dialogue, which is just one of the many such scattered throughout the novel, bears out how deftly Savithri can play Maitreyi to Rama's Yajnyavalkya:

> 'What is truth?' I asked.
> 'Is-ness is the Truth,' she answered.
> 'And is-ness is what?'
> 'Who asks that question?'
> 'Myself.'
> 'Who?'
> 'I.'
> 'Of whom?'
> 'No one.'
> 'Then "I am" is.' (*The Serpent and the Rope*, p. 132)

Because Savithri can play the game according to the patriarchal rules and can accept the place that is allotted to her by the tradition, we may assume that she is crowned as the Queen who 'inherits the world' as the Queen of England is crowned in the novel. But like the Queen of England too Savithri remains a titular head with no actual powers. The individual in Savithri is squeezed out in the service of an abstract ideal. She is made to marry a man she does not love and to offer her obeisance to her husband as well as Rama, her Lord and Master.

Poor Saroja, Rama's stepsister, is also sacrificed at the same altar of marriage. The novel attempts to cover up the institutional nature of marriage by valorizing it as an impersonal principle. When Rama meets Savithri for the first time she strikes him as being too modern for his taste and he starts reflecting on the difference between the north and the south:

> I could not understand these Northerners going from strict purdah to this extreme modernism with unholy haste. We in the South were more sober,

and very distant. We lived by tradition—shameful though it might look. We did not mind quoting Sankaracharya in law courts or marrying our girls in the old way, even if they had gone abroad. The elder brother still commanded respect, and my sisters would never speak to me as Savithri spoke to her father. . . . (*The Serpent and the Rope*, p. 34)

Yes, why should Rama not swear by the tradition which has conferred on him all the benefits, while other people are made to suffer on account of it? As the patriarch of the family he can command respect from all the members without ever lifting a finger for any of them. The tradition does not come in his way when he decides to go to Europe or marry a European woman. But it does come in the way of his sister and her aspirations. Saroja in one of her letters to Rama expresses her desire to join her brother in Europe and study medicine there. Rama informs us that though he was happy at the thought, 'I knew she would never come. In any case we could not afford it' (p. 108). Why not? The family could afford to send Rama to France to work on an abstruse subject like the Albigensian heresy, but Saroja is denied the opportunity of visiting Europe or pursuing a useful profession like medicine.

One of the important matters on which the novel is significantly silent is the monetary aspect. Who is supporting Rama for his research in Europe? His family or his French wife? And are not his lofty spiritual and intellectual pursuits a luxury granted to him by a sound economic base? David McCutchion draws our attention to this vital point when he remarks:

The realist, who may not have so much money as Rama (shortage of money makes one realist just as lack of it or too much of it makes one transcendentalist) might remark somewhat testily that it is all very fine dissolving into the tender gratifications of 'intellectual sadness', when you can travel first class on French trains, fly to and fro between India and Europe, and even take a taxi from Marignanne to Aix-en-Provence. (When Madeleine one day persuades him to take the bus to Marseilles, he objects because it is smelly—at any rate his nose is in contact with reality!) ('The Novel as Sastra' in *Considerations*, p. 95)

And yet this Rama who does not deny any material comfort to himself smugly and selfishly tramples upon the just aspirations of his sister and rationalizes his cruel treatment of her in the name of an eternal, frozen image of Indian woman as a mysterious essence: 'What a deep and reverential mystery womanhood is. I could bow before Saroja and call her Queen' (p. 52). Saroja, being a sensitive and tender-hearted person, lacks the strength to resist the ideal construction that is put upon her and has to go through the agonising ordeal of marrying according to the tradition that her brother so highly respects.

As the hour of marriage approaches, Saroja in her anguish protests against the way women are treated in India:

> She wished she had been a European woman; it would have given her so much freedom, so much brightness.
>
> 'What freedom?' I exclaimed. 'The freedom of foolishness. In what way, Saroja, do you think Catherine or Madeleine is better off than you?'
>
> 'They know how to love.'
>
> 'And you?'
>
> 'And we know how to bear children. We are just like a motor-car or a bank account. Or, better still, we are like a comfortable salary paid by a benign and eternal British Government. Our joy is a treasury receipt.'
>
> . . . .
>
> 'Times have changed, Saroja.'
>
> 'Not in India yet—and certainly not among Brahmins. You had better wait till you see my in-laws. They already think I'm a cloth in their washbasket: they'll know when to beat me against the stone, to make me white as milk. We girls are thrown to other families as the most intimate, the most private of our clothes are thrown to the dhobi on Saturday morning. Like cotton, we women must have grown on trees . . .'
>
> There was no answer to give. (*The Serpent and the Rope*, p. 259)

'There was no answer to give' because Rama actually approves of the view of woman as a passive accessory to man, of which Saroja is so critical here. His position regarding women is the same as his position on India. Like India, woman as an abstract, static and timeless ideal is valorized whereas the flesh and blood woman, woman as history, who, like modern political India, is likely to challenge the Brahminical male hegemony is given no quarter in the value system of the novel.

Rama's two other sisters provide interesting contrasts to Saroja and to each other. Kapila, the eldest sister, is married according to the custom and is still a blot upon it. Rama's Little Mother on the contrary has unconsciously absorbed all the patriarchal values and is therefore portrayed with sympathy and affection. Little Mother's upbringing in a poor family of seven children where her father regularly used to beat her has taught her not to expect much from life. She is content enough to marry in a family which is better off, socially and financially, than her father's. The winds of modernity have never touched her and raised the conflicts and the storms that rage in Saroja's heart and, to some extent, in Savithri's. Little Mother is happy in her ignorance, though her situation perhaps is the most pathetic of all in the novel.

Sukumari, the youngest sister, is full of joy and vitality. In this respect she provides a contrast to Rama and Saroja, both of whom are given to low spirits and sadness. Sukumari, a bold girl, shapes her life the way she wants to. She settles down in Bombay, the city that Rama abhors most, and joins the Communist Party, which is another anathema to her brother. It is no wonder that she hates her brother as the arch-reactionary. The example of Sukumari goes on to prove that whatever may be Rama's views regarding history and modernity, he cannot stop the inevitable historical process and that the future is more likely to throw up Sukumaris than Savithris or Sarojas.

The most ironical thing about *The Serpent and the Rope* is that while it advocates the noble doctrine of non-dualism, it also clings to the orthodox prejudices which divide people on the basis of birth, class and gender. The novel perpetuates the traditional gender differences when it insists that the spiritual and intellectual life is man's monopoly whereas women should not look beyond their material and earthly domain. It also lacks the awareness that even a factory worker, a peasant, or a fisherwoman may be capable of reaching the highest truth, that even a daily commuter on a local Bombay train may have the experience of *stasis* while he/she is being hurled through the space. The timeless and the temporal do not exclude each other, but each complements the other. To divest human life of any of these dimensions is necessarily to impoverish it, which is what the novel attempts to do in its denigration of historicity.

The Serpent and the Rope also lacks a dynamic conception of tradition. What is new and modern today may be a part of the orthodoxy tomorrow. In the passage that is quoted at the beginning of this study, Raja Rao has appealed to the authority of Shakespeare to strengthen his case for the English language. And yet the same Shakespeare, who has become part of the English tradition, was looked upon as a rough modern in his own time and was taken to task for not observing the rules of the ancient classical tradition in literature. Similarly, the prestige that the English language enjoys today is not derived from its divine origin, but from the political power that it exercises in the temporal world. Raja Rao seems to believe that tradition is divine and, therefore, beyond history, whereas in actual fact tradition is a human creation and is created in the temporal dimension. The practices that become irrelevant or harmful have to be discarded from time to time so that the tradition remains a living and sustaining force and not a dead weight on the people. The same holds true in the case of women. They do not have to conform to the definitions that were imposed upon them by an old order which was created to serve the interests of a particular group, even when that old order, as in *The Serpent and the Rope*, makes its appeal in the name of a divine and sacrosanct tradition.

REFERENCES

McCutchion, David, 'The Novel as Sastra', in *Considerations*, ed. Meenakshi Mukherjee (New Delhi: Allied, 1977).

Mukherjee, Meenakshi, *The Twice Born Fiction: Themes and Techniques of the Indian Novel in English* (New Delhi and London: Heinemann Educational Books, 1971).

Nagarajan, S., 'An Indian Novel' in *Considerations*.

Naik, M.K., '*The Serpent and the Rope*: The Indo-Anglian Novel as Epic Legend', in *Critical Essays on Indian Writing in English*, ed. M.K. Naik, S.K. Desai, G.S. Amur (Dharwar: Karnataka University, 1972).

Narasimhaiah, C.D., *Raja Rao* (New Delhi and London: Arnold-Heinemann, n.d.).

Rao, Raja, *The Serpent and the Rope* (London: John Murray, 1960).

———, 'The Writer and the Word', in *Critical Essays on Indian Writing in English*.

Said, Edward, *Orientalism* (London: Penguin Books, 1985).

Validating the Self: The Female Hero in R.K. Narayan's *The Painter of Signs*

Usha Bande

I was, being human, born alone;
I am, being woman, hard beset;
I live by squeezing from a stone
The little nourishment I get.

—*Elinor Wylie*

I have gone out, a possessed witch,
haunting the black air, braver at night;
. . . .
A woman like that is not a woman, quite.
I have been her kind.

—*Anne Sexton*

My God died young. Theolatry I found
Degrading, and its premises unsound.
No free man needs a God; but was I free?

—*Vladimir Nobokov*

The above three quotations—one by a male and two by female poets—sound the keynote to the attitudes and assumptions manifest in R.K. Narayan's portrayal of the three main characters in *The Painter of Signs,*[1] namely, aunt Laxmi, Daisy and Raman. The novel, first serialized in *The Illustrated Weekly of India* in the mid-seventies, raises several pertinent issues about Indian womanhood *vis-a-vis* the changing social environs and the fast-approaching feminist trends. The author seems to dread the fate of the male in the new social order based on 'rejections'—Raman's aunt rejects the new, liberated woman and opts for freedom to pursue her God; Raman rejects his aunt's God in his quest for a rational approach to life; and finally, there is Daisy, rejecting everything for her freedom as an individual. Comically, Raman shrugs off all ties when he paddles toward the so-called stability of the 'Boardless', proclaiming it to be the only 'solid, real world of sublime souls' (p. 143). But one wonders: will the 'Boardless' ever substitute the 'solid, real' security of a home? Hasn't the 'Boardless' obliterated its own identity by being nameless? I shall attempt to answer these and several other questions in the following discussion which will primarily focus on Narayan's portrayal of women.

Critics of R.K. Narayan often contend that he is an acute observer of life and a storyteller, *par excellence*, but not a social commentator in the sense Mulk Raj Anand, Bhabani Bhattacharya and Kamala Markandaya are. In order to substantiate their thesis, these critics and scholars refer to Narayan's views expressed in the *Reluctant Guru*, that 'a novel is about an individual living his life in a world imagined by the author, performing a set of actions (up to a limit) contrived by the author. But to take a work of fiction as a sociological study or a social document could be very misleading'.[2] Most critical studies focus on his comic vision in portraying eccentric characters and remain silent on his depiction of the lived social reality. Though the novelist appears to be unmindful of the socioeconomic changes sweeping across the country, it would be unfair to conclude that he and his Malgudi are impervious to changes. The world of Narayan, the storyteller is, as a reader observes, 'composite and organic'[3] in which 'each forms a part and parcel of total life and is indispensable for the attainment of a four-square understanding of existence'.[4] A close study of the novels from *The Dark Room* (1938) to *The Painter of Signs* (1976) reveals that the novelist draws his creative sustenance from his cultural past and shows a subtle understanding of the present. Syd Harrex spots 'the issues of sexual politics, romantic love, marriage, family planning and women's liberation' in *The Painter of Signs*, in 'relation to a conflict of values—of traditional customs challenged by an activist sociology'.[5] Social issues are, thus, not side-tracked. Rather, we see in his novels progressively, the caste barriers breaking, joint families disintegrating and women raising their voice against social injustice. In an interview, Narayan counters his critics:

> Sometimes I hear them say that I do not reflect the great urge of the nation, whatever that may be. I don't understand what they're saying. No one can express the urge of a nation. Such a big nation as ours, 200 languages, 700 million people, so diverse. But compare my new novel *The Painter of Signs* with *The Dark Room*, that's a contrast. The new liberated woman, and the traditional housewife completely suppressed. You see a whole social change.[6]

He portrays the new trends with deft touches. Most of his women may not fit into the Western feminist frame, but some of them certainly refuse to toe the line drawn by the Sati-Savitri-Sita stereotype.

I

In order to make an assessment of R.K. Narayan's portrayal of women in *The Painter of Signs*, we must throw a quick glance at his two earlier major works depicting woman's predicament—*The Dark Room* and *The Guide*. The time gap between these two works accounts for much contrast between Savitri, Shanta Bai and Rosie. *The Dark Room* was written in 1938 and *The Guide* in 1958. Socially, in these twenty years, the position of women changed considerably though the hold of tradition on the social psyche remained tight. Another eighteen years, and *The Painter of Signs* appears in 1976 wherein the Malgudi society is considerably transformed. The male protagonist in this novel is no longer an infidel husband, nor is he the possessive, self-willed male, he is a lover ready to accept his woman on her terms. Malgudi still has its wagging tongues and its moral conscience keepers, but it has learnt to tolerate, to an extent, a woman in authority.

In *The Dark Room*,[7] Narayan is conscious of the discomforts experienced by women in a male-dominated society. By juxtaposing two women—Savitri, Ramani's submissive wife and Shanta Bai, his educated mistress—the novelist visualizes two alternatives and seems to reject them both as unsatisfactory. Savitri is an epitome of womanly virtues. She embodies the cultural ideals of devotion, submission and faithfulness. Her world centres round her home, husband and children. But that does not redeem her. Ramani extols her traditional virtues: 'What a dutiful wife! Would rather starve than precede her husband. You are really like some of the women in our ancient books' (p. 16). Ramani's words remind one of Anita Desai's Monisha. One can note the contrast between the approach of a male writer and that of a female writer here. Anita Desai's disgust at traditional Bengali women walking 'five steps behind' their husbands is expressed through Monisha in *Voices in the City*.[8] Coming back to *The Dark Room*, we see that while Ramani appreciates his wife's dutifulness, he himself gets involved with Shanta Bai and neglects Savitri. Savitri reacts sharply, leaves her home, makes an abortive attempt at suicide and finally comes back home. But now something within her has withered away. 'A part of me is dead' (p. 177), she reflects, refusing to submit when her husband approaches her at night.

What Ramani does is not new. Dandekar, in Kamala Markandaya's *Silence of Desire* suspects his wife of infidelity but he himself visits prostitutes when under tension. Savitri attributes her trouble to the fact that she is uneducated and economically dependent. She resolves to remedy it in the case of her daughters whom she wishes to educate. On the contrary, Shanta Bai though educated avers that 'it is all nonsense to say that women's salvation lies in education. It doesn't improve her lot a bit . . . (p. 61). Without social reorientation, woman's liberation is meaningless. Theoretically, man agrees to give women freedom; practically, it is fake because it is conditional. What Ramani says about women's freedom is relevant to quote here:

> Of course . . . there was some sense in the women's movement: let them by all means read English novels, play tennis, have their All-India Conference and go to the pictures occasionally; but that should not blind them to their primary duties of being wives and mothers . . . . (pp. 122-3)

Ramani's words are reminiscent of Gandhi's views on the position of women in the new social order of his dreams. Gandhi encouraged women to join the national struggle for freedom but restricted their major field to their homes: 'In the new order of my imagination . . . women will be part-time workers, their primary function being to look after the home'. Not that we blame Gandhi or Ramani for their restrictive views. This was the general condition of women's life in the early decades of the present century and it was accepted by both men and women. Savitri and Shanta Bai are representatives of a sad, lonely, friendless world. It takes two more decades before Narayan could uplift Rosie from that 'low-key' position and grant her the right to self-determination.

In *The Guide*,[9] the author places Rosie between Marco and Raju to afford us an opportunity to see her from two angles. But, since the narrators are male, we get only a one-sided picture. We, therefore, must understand Rosie as she appears to us through her actions and reactions. In this novel, too, the conventional and the unconventional women are placed side by side. Raju's mother represents tradition. For her a woman's salvation lies in being meek, mild, gentle. Conquering the husband not by powder or lipstick, but by self-sacrifice, is a woman's primary task. She resents Rosie because the young dancer stands nowhere near her concept of a woman. Rosie is too assertive, independent and self-reliant to be acceptable to the mother.

Trouble begins for Rosie because the society is not yet ready to look sympathetically at an independent woman, seeking her own identity through her personal excellence. It never occurs to Marco that his wife needs his attention. For him, it should be enough for a woman to merge her name, identity and her dream in her husband's and live vicariously shining under his glow. The situation presented in Ibsen's *The Doll's House* is re-enacted here. Raju shows some understanding of her creative urge but his main motive is to 'keep her in a citadel' as his possession. Neither Marco, nor Raju loves her for her own sake.. Rosie shows to the two men that she can stand alone. If she can leave Marco to pursue her art, she can discard Raju too. Mapping her success, Raju acknowledges her spirit, and though jealous of her self-reliance, he appreciates her ability to 'manage' her life. 'Neither Marco nor I had any place in her life which had its own sustaining vitality . . .' (p. 199). Rosie is not the passive, self-effacing, helpless victim of male fancy. She is an awakened woman who paves the way for Daisy.

II

Daisy, the family planning worker in *The Painter of Signs* is a liberated woman in many respects—as a spirited adolescent she has rebelled against the suffocating joint family norms; now she has carved out a career for herself; established her identity; and gained economic security and emotional strength. With these resources, she can reject male support. 'Not only is she not dependent on men, she actually has no use for them as an integral part of her life.'[10] As for social sanction, she does not let it hinder her decisions. The traditional Malgudi society has learnt, it seems, to let such freaks as Daisy go by without disturbing it unduly. Raman's aunt is troubled but she avoids conflict by going away to Kashi to seek salvation on the banks of the Ganga. Once Gaffur's taxi rattles through the old streets, carrying Daisy and her coworkers, called the 'three witches', and Raman throws away the key in the dry fountain, all is quiet in Malgudi. Does it indicate that underneath the veneer of change, the India society is immutable? Or is it a pointer toward the damage fiery and unthoughtful woman's liberation may do to the society? Since the woman question is closely linked with the sociocultural context, we must study Daisy-Raman affair in the light of social exigencies.

Narayan juxtaposes the conventional and the unconventional characters to highlight the emerging social trends. Raman's aunt Laxmi is the traditional woman, dependent on her nephew, living for his welfare. Complacent and undemanding, the aunt is an epitome of Indian motherhood—unselfish, ever-protective and ever-forgiving. Raman is often flippant with her, but she never bothers about it. They follow their respective life-patterns—he, painting, earning, reading and whiling away his free time with friends; she, cooking, managing the house, meeting her friends and attending the sessions of Puranas in the temple. They take each other so much for granted that they never pause to gauge the depth of attachment each has for the other. Raman is usually irritated by her questions, counter-questions and her endless, repetitive narrations. 'How could the Age of Reason be established if people were like this' (p. 19), he broods. These minor irritants apart, he acknowledges gratefully her care and concern and feels pity for her. 'Morning till night, planning something for his delectation—for years, unwavering attention to his needs. She rarely asked him for anything in return, no demands, whatever . . .' (p. 25). She is indeed a mother for him, 'the giver of blessings, the giver and protector of life. She is the . . . goddess to be respected and worshipped.'[11] Raman is deeply attached to her. When she decides to go away to Kashi, he weeps bitterly, like a child.

The aunt's departure shows the sagacity of the traditional Indian philosophy. By withdrawing in good time, the old woman avoids conflicts—interpersonal with Daisy (if she were to marry Raman) and intra-psychic (since the old aunt could not have accepted her). When Raman wails over her departure, Daisy takes a cool rational view: the old woman had every right to 'seek her life's pattern as she likes'. For Daisy separation is the law of life. Commensurate with her philosophy, she leaves Raman toward the end of the novel without any qualms.

In Daisy, Narayan presents an Indian woman far ahead of the times. Not only does she have an unconventional name, she also has an outrageous profession—advocating family planning contrary to the prevailing notions. We admit that by mid-seventies India was fairly influenced by Western feminism and that women were becoming aware of their rights but Daisy's type of radical feminism was unheard of even in the large cities of India.

Malgudi was certainly not the place to welcome a Daisy. That is the reason why the author gives her a 'non-denominational name' making her almost nameless; also he lets her go away from Malgudi. He does this because he probably does not wish to defeat Daisy by letting an able and fiery woman fall into the traditional rut.

Obviously, Daisy is a curious figure in Malgudi, awe-inspiring yet comic. Raman variously calls her 'the siren', 'the stern mentor', 'the ruthless dictator', 'the tight-lipped-monomaniac', 'Mohini', 'the general planning a campaign', 'a despotic queen' and so on. These remarks, derogatory or otherwise, sum up the male view. In the traditional small-town society, many things go against Daisy—her dubious identity, her background as a runaway from home (which is a sin in a woman), her unusual work and her non-conformist way of living. But Daisy is a force to reckon with. She is not 'just a suave bureaucrat who got sign-boards written and files completed and properly knotted with red tape', she has 'a furnace of conviction' (p. 47) and so she could not be trifled with.

In the beginning of their acquaintance Raman assesses Daisy with the conventional male attitude. He is drawn to her because she is unapproachable. She evokes his sense of wonder and curiosity: her slightly masculine voice, and her strong profession enthrall him. 'Daisy! what a name for someone who looked so very Indian, traditional and gentle' (p. 28), he broods. Soon he realises that she is 'firm and gentle', a woman who 'seemed to know her mind and its limits' (p. 31). After his third encounter with her he recognizes her strength. She looks 'frail' but she is not gentle. He tries to expel her from his thoughts. Comically, he uses the funny dark glasses to see the charming 'temptress' as an ugly Surpanakha. Daisy removes his glasses so that he could see her as she is—a human being with physical hunger and mental strength. He—'an edifice of self-discipline laboriously raised' (p. 38)—crumbles down. Feeling powerless, nervous and cheated by his near 'complete surrender' before the 'goddess' he makes one last effort to feel strong by asserting his masculine superiority. 'When I need a wife, I will know how to set about it, all in good time. I don't have to succumb to the first female brushing against me. . .' (p. 42). Interestingly, two pages later, Raman accompanies Daisy on a tour to select sites for family planning slogans.

Daisy's energy, zeal and dogged persistence evoke admiration from the readers and earn her the respect of the villagers. According to a critic, her 'absolute conviction, untrammelled modern-mindedness, steel will and practicality, make her a superb missionary in this cause'.[12] She is almost a masculine female, most 'undaisy-like', as Raman sees her. She pursues her 'steel-framed itinerary'; unmindful of sniggering men and giggling women, she explains to them the pros and cons of family planning, she commands the villagers with authority and intimidates them by her knowledge. In her personal life, she has reduced her wants to the bare minimum. She could sit anywhere, adjust to any type of food without taboo, and sleep anywhere spreading her little role of carpet. Her 'astonishing adaptability' is chosen by herself. It is not imposed in her by social conditioning. In her dress, she is unassuming. She wears 'a sari of the drabbest shade' she 'never used any powder or make-up, and did her hair indifferently . . .' (p. 50). Thus ready to meet the male on their own terrain Daisy, unsmiling, serious and efficient, challenges male society.

Beside Daisy, Raman fades into insignificance. He appears unheroic, weak-minded and often a comic figure. The author enjoys poking fun at him—the celibate bachelor becomes 'sex obsessed', behaves like a teenager, then indulges in flights of fancy and finally lands from where he had taken off. It is amusing to see him think of himself as a 'considerate husband' both 'charmed and frightened' by Daisy's imperious manner while she sits in authority like Queen Victoria or Rani Jhansi (p. 65). Enthralled and yet confused, Raman is bewildered, unable to decide what to accept and what to reject. His male superiority is exercised only at the level of imagination—he could rape her, impregnate her, foil her family planning programme, make her his dependent wife by being 'an aggressive lover'. When he cannot possess her, he enjoys her discomfiture in the presence of the village priest beyond Mempi Hills, he is happy in the end when she 'humbles herself' by asking his pardon before leaving.

Whatever Raman's imaginary superiority, in reality, he cannot keep pace with her. This is symbolically presented during their tour to a distant village. He tires out and she climbs up, way ahead of him. In real life situations, Daisy is the decision-making authority. Raman accepts her on her terms: they would have no regular marriage but only *Gandharva* wedding which amounts to the modern Western concept of living together, she would not be a housekeeper or a cook, she would not change her name, they would have no children and he would not question her ever. Raman dreads such a marriage but his traditional Brahminical mind gropes for role-models in the Indian epic: there was Rukmani and Krishna eloping to get married, there was Mohini, the enchantress, there was Shantanu accepting Ganga on her terms. These stories of the heroes of yore prove psychological props.

The reversal of roles is clearly indicated here. Raman is gripped by uncertainty because of his approaching marriage. 'She was indeed a great puzzle at every turn. Sometimes he paused to wonder how he was going to carry on with her a whole lifetime, without any knowledge or understanding of her at all. He was perhaps making a fool of himself by this marriage' (p. 32). In *The Guide*, Raju's mother tells Rosie, 'Living with a husband is no joke' and she recounts how husbands could be unreasonable, obstinate and moody. This can well be repeated for Raman with some modification. While Raman plans to decorate the house, Daisy doses off and he wistfully waits for her to speak.

Feminists have, over they years, identified areas which define male and female precincts. Upholding culture and its values, looking after home and children, having respect for the contingent order are female fields. Since housekeeping and child-rearing are women's responsibility, their experience is home-bound and one of repetition and waiting. This is termed as 'statis'. Statis is 'different from the assertive striving more typical of masculine temporal mode, questing'.[13] Man is the quester, the conqueror. Folk stories, fairy tales and legends recount man's quest for the holy grail, the golden fleece and the golden apple. The prince or the knight goes out while the princess waits.

In *The Painter of Signs*, Daisy is the quester, the conqueror. She goes on a tour and Raman tags along; in the end, she leaves Malgudi and he is left behind to await her return, she is his provider, as she gives him the job of painting boards; he respects culture, despite being a self-appointed crusader for the establishment of the Age of Reason, she breaks all cultural ties as binding tags. Interestingly, she is in the driver's seat, Raman is willing to let her drive because 'two drivers cannot be at the steering wheel of a motor car . . . . He was quite prepared to surrender himself completely to her way of thinking, and do nothing that might leave him in the plight of

Santhanu. No questioning and the wife stays, but any slight doubt expressed, she flies away forever' (p. 131). After getting Raman to toe her line, Daisy drops him as unceremoniously as she had once accepted him. 'Let us face the fact', she tells him categorically. 'Married life is not for me' (p. 139). He pleads with her to let him accompany her. 'I'll in no way interfere with you, live as you live, in the open or in a hut, walk barefoot in the forest paths, seek nothing, demand nothing, I will not mind any hardship if I can be with you' (p. 139). It is almost reminiscent of Sita pleading with Rama to take her along with him. Only the roles are reversed.

Daisy is not only unlike the traditional Indian woman, she is different from any other woman portrayed so far in Indian English fiction. She is both cold and warm, feminine and masculine. She has a 'smiling side to her and a non-smiling one: a talkative and non-speaking' (pp. 48-9). Discussing Daisy, the novelist tells one of his interviewers that Daisy is 'a very strong character. All the same when you read the novel you will find she is very feminine also. There is the conflict. That is the whole point.'[14] There is, however, no conflict in Daisy's psyche. She is at peace with herself because she is sure of herself. In Indian English fiction we come across a large number portraits of women—mostly Indian and a couple of them Westerners, but none is so fully liberated as Daisy is. She does not whine or whimper, nor does she sulk or rebel. Sentiments have no place in her life, though she has sufficient human warmth. She has indeed crossed the stage of sulking, rebelling, whining and has trained herself to stand for her 'self'. As a critic points out, in Narayan's fiction the 'Indian woman growing up through Savitri, Suseela, Bharathi, Ambika and Rosie, into Daisy, has now come of age. She is an image of social revolt and knows the world for what it is. She fights, manages, endures, but never whines or sulks in the dark room. She is a radically new role model. . . .'[15] Daisy has not achieved her liberation all of a sudden. She has suffered innumerable hardships since she broke away from her home in her teenage.

Literature, both Indian and Western portrays the urge of women to escape from family ties in search of their 'selves'. Kate Chopin's Edna, D.H. Lawrence's heroine who rode away, Atwood's heroine of *Surfacing* are a few examples from Western literature. Nearer home, Shashi Deshpande's Saru, Anand's Gauri, Anita Desai's Sita and Narayan's Savitri, aunt Laxmi and grandmother leave home when disillusioned. But what these women do so at a later stage in life,

Daisy has already experienced early; some of these women return to their protective homes, Daisy does not; some renounce the world but Daisy jumps into life. It is almost a Chekovian escape *into* life or it is like Arjuna's jump into the Kurukshetra—the field of action and duty. She has overcome self-pity and vulnerability. By deconstructing the dependent character structure, she has developed strength to oppose abuse. In the words of psychologist Marcia Westkott, she is the 'female hero' who has learnt to 'fight back as a responsibility to herself'.[16]

Narayan, despite his remarkable portrayal of Daisy as a liberated woman, is too astute a writer to disregard the social psyche. One is constantly aware, while reading the story, that the author lets Daisy live in Malgudi on the periphery of the real town. She is tolerated because she is not one of the various Laxmis, Savitris or Gauris, the daughters of the town, but a 'foreigner' with a strange Christian name, implanted amid them. Her going away does not matter even as her coming had not been taken much note of.

With all her fire, Daisy appears dry and unemotional. There is nothing tender about her. She rejects love, substitutes it with sex and terms it 'moments of weakening'. No wonder, Raman is reminded of the 'Three Witches' of *Macbeth*—masculine, bearded females, dry, untender and misleading. The author also seems to be wary of Daisy's kind of liberation. If gender divisions are obliterated by transgression into each others' boundaries, the result is going to be social chaos. One cannot break away from the old traditions symbolized by Laxmi, Raman's aunt. If we dig the roots, the tree on which we plan to build our 'nest' will fall. What happens to Raman may happen to the society. The 'Boardless' cannot be one's destination. With traditions allowed to go awry and the new ideas unwilling to stay man will be rudderless.

Not only man, even woman suffers when new concepts are stretched too far. Narayan is aware of the sacrifice a woman has to make. Daisy cannot marry because marriage may hinder her activities. Daisy is not the only example of unmarried woman in literature. Anita Desai's Bim stays single and so does Nayantara Sahgal's Sonali. Bim is helpless, burdened by family responsibilities, Sonali is self-willed, fired by an urge to be different. But both Sonali and Bim have tenderness. They long for love. Bim finds it in her brothers and sisters and Sonali feels satisfied to know that Ravi

Kachru still loves her. Narayan does not give this advantage to Daisy. She does not need affection. She has lost that fountain in her pursuit of duty which Wordsworth calls the 'Stern Daughter'.

Symbolically too, the fountain is 'dry' into which Raman throws the key. Narayan, it seems, admires a strong woman, but would prefer some via-media between traditional and modern concepts so that woman does not suffer as Savitri does in *The Dark Room*, and man does not make a fool of himself as Raman does. Daisy mirrors the author's own predicament as a man—his insecurity, isolation, bewilderment and emotional vulnerability.

NOTES

1. R.K. Narayan, *The Painter of Signs* (Harmondsworth: Penguin, 1976). All references hereafter are to this edition.
2. R.K. Narayan, *The Reluctant Guru* (New Delhi: Orient Paperbacks, 1974), pp. 9-10.
3. V.V.N. Rajendra Prasad, *The Self, The Family and Society in Five Indian Novelists* (New Delhi: Prestige, 1990), p. 73.
4. R.K. Narayan, *Gods, Demons and Others* (Mysore: Indian Thought Publication, 1979), p. 4. According to Narayan the legends and myths contained in the Puranas are illustrations of the moral and spiritual truths contained in the Vedas. 'Everything is inter-related, stories, scriptures, ethics, philosophy, grammar, astrology, astronomy, semantics, mysticism and moral codes—each forms part and parcel of total life and is indispensable for the attainment of a four-square understanding of existence'.
5. Syd Harrex, 'R.K. Narayan—Painter of Signs', in *Commonwealth Literature: Themes and Techniques*, eds. P.K. Rajan *et al.* (New Delhi: Prestige, 1993), p. 36.
6. R.K. Narayan's Conversation with Alex Hamilton, *The Guardian*, 12 Sept. 1971, p. 16.
7. R.K. Narayan, *The Dark Room* (New Delhi: Hind Pocket Books, 1972).
8. Anita Desai, *Voices in the City* (New Delhi: Hind Pocket Books, 1965), p. 120.
9. R.K. Narayan, *The Guide* (Mysore: Indian Thought Publications, 1963).
10. 'A Day with R.K. Narayan', *Span*, April 1975, p. 42.
11. Meena Shirwadkar, *Image of Woman in the Indo-Anglian Novel* (New Delhi: Sterling, 1979), p. 79.
12. William Walsh, *R.K. Narayan—A Critical Appreciation* (London: Heinemann, 1982), p. 158.

13. Kathryn Allenl Rabuzzi, *The Sacred and the Feminine: Toward a Theology of Housework* (New York: Seabury, 1982), p. 151.
14. *Span*, April 1975, p. 42.
15. Shantha Krishnaswamy, *The Woman in Indian Fiction in English* (New Delhi: Ashish Publishing House, 1984), p. 134.
16. Marcia Westkott, *The Feminist Legacy of Karen Horney* (New Haren: Yale University Press, 1986), p. 201.

From Modernity to 'Purdah': Geeta's Acculturation in Rama Mehta's *Inside the Haveli*

Kamal Bhasin

The article is divided into two sections. Section I deals briefly with Rama Mehta's other two novels: *Ramu: A Story of India* (1966) and *The Life of Keshav: A Family Story from India* (1969). The purpose is dual. First, to say a few words about these two novels, which have somehow escaped notice of critics in India, and second, to bring out the link between *The Life of Keshav* and *Inside the Haveli* (1977). In the former, the beneficent nature of the inmates of Jeewan Singhji's haveli is highlighted. It is the same haveli which is the centre of action in the latter, where Ajay, Keshav's childhood friend from the haveli, brings Geeta, the protagonist, home after their marriage in Bombay.

Rama Mehta wrote an article entitled 'Purdah to Modernity'[1] dealing with the changing social manners and mores of the women of Oswal community in Udaipur. Conversely, this article has been named 'Modernity to "Purdah": Geeta's Acculturation in *Inside the Haveli*', where the protagonist, Geeta, moves from Bombay, a 'modern' city, to a haveli in Udaipur—which is a symbol of old traditions and values. Section II aims at showing how *Inside the Haveli*, at one level, deals with the process of Geeta's assimilation into an orthodox culture.

I

Rama Mehta the sociologist-cum-novelist's first novel *Ramu: A Story of India* was intended to be a children's book—rather as an introduction to India for 10-12 year olds. It was written almost on request when the Mehtas were in Germany on a diplomatic assignment.[2] Santha Rama Rau rightly states in the foreword to the novel that it 'captures the atmosphere of a small Indian town with authenticity'.[3] *Ramu*, however, can at best be called an episodic novella spread over five days, dealing with the childhood pranks and excitement of Ramu a few days before Diwali.

Mehta's second novel *The Life of Keshav* is a more comprehensive and credible account of a village family which is possessed with a mission to help its son, Keshav, complete his education even at the cost of starving other members of the family. Her account of the travails of the family in this mission is graphic in details and universal in its implication for the small landowning families of Rajasthan. The novel also shows how each additional pair of hands in a poor farming family is an insurance against economic backwardness and, further, how denial of even a meagre contribution to the family income can push the family into a deeper financial crisis. Keshav the protagonist—a promising child going to night classes—is picked up by the teacher Narayanji for a merit scholarship and is put in Vidya Bhawan School in Udaipur where children like Ajay from the rich havelis like Jeewan Singhji's also study. The scholarship is instituted by Jeewan Singhji on the birth of a boy child to his son Ajit Singh. Jeewan Singhji's haveli in *Keshav* assumes the name of Jeewan Niwas in *Inside the Haveli*. *The Life of Keshav* deals with the period when the families of Ajay's great-grandfather and his three brothers, Ram Singh, Akhe Singhji, and Jeewan Singhji—'Ba Saheb used to live in this haveli'.[4] The haveli which was in the background in *The Life of Keshav* comes to occupy centre stage in *Inside the Haveli*. Rama Mehta seems to be picking up the thread from where she left it in *Keshav*. If it was a poor village boy's education in *Keshav*, it is girls' education and child marriage, among other issues taken up by her in *Inside the Haveli*, which are debated and projected in all their facets by Geeta.

Rama Mehta has in these two novels dealt with these common themes unconventionally, and with a greater degree of perception and insight. In *Keshav*, education, which should ordinarily help equip a family overcome its poverty, on the contrary, brings upon it more suffering and economic backwardness during the period of Keshav's education. It brings only an illusory hope of happy days thereafter, i.e. after the child has completed his education. Ajay of *Keshav* has grown and become a Professor of Science. He gets married to Geeta, a Bombay girl, and brings her to Jeewan Niwas, in Udaipur which is the scene of action in *Inside the Haveli*.

II

Rama Mehta's experiences during her sociological study of the status of women of the Oswal community in the State of Mewar as recounted in her article 'From Purdah to Modernity' seem to have impelled her to write the novel *Inside the Haveli.* This novel is a realistic and authentic account of the status of women in the erstwhile State of Mewar. It is a sociological study recollected aesthetically by the novelist. Talking about the works of Balzac, Dostoyevsky and Proust, Michel Zeraffa in his essay, 'The Novel as Literary Form and as Social Institution' says that their novels are 'both aesthetic analyses and syntheses of a reality which the novelist had already analysed and synthesized before he started to write'.[5] Zeraffa's statement about the three Western novelists can very aptly be applied to Rama Mehta. She has both 'analysed and synthesized' the socio-cultural realities of the haveli tradition and projected a balanced synthesis of tradition and modernity in the novel, with the former yielding ground to the latter gradually but surely. As K.R. Srinivasa Iyengar rightly says it is 'a sensitive piece of realistic fiction, even an authentic sociological study'.[6]

Geeta, the protagonist, a girl brought up and educated in Bombay, gets married to Ajay, a Professor of Science from Udaipur. Immediately after her marriage she sets out on a journey to Udaipur to join her in-laws there. Metaphorically speaking, Geeta's journey from Bombay to Udaipur is a journey from an open society to a cloistered one. It is the story of her own acculturation and assimilation into a more traditional society, where she embarks on yet another journey to throw open the gates of the haveli to things hitherto forbidden. Living in the haveli herself she liberates many young women from socio-economic shackles, by imparting to them education, or vocational skill in tailoring so that they can become more self-reliant and acceptable in better families than their own, as has been the case with Sita, the daughter of one of the haveli servants.

How has Geeta's assimilation into the haveli culture come about? Has she lost her individuality completely? Has she obliterated her self? What role have the people of the haveli played in bringing about the change in her personality? Or, is it that people have changed themselves to change her? Finally, and more importantly, what kind of a society does Rama Mehta envision? And how does she achieve transformation of an 'outsider' into a willing 'insider' of the haveli?

A close analysis of Geeta's character and of her relationship with other men and women of Jeewan Niwas will provide answers to these questions.

> Keep your head covered; never argue with your elders; respect your mother-in-law and do as she tells you. Don't talk too much. (p. 14)

These prescriptive exhortations by Geeta's mother, before she left Bombay for Udaipur after her marriage with Ajay, echo in her ears two years later as she lies on her bed a few days after the birth of her daughter Vijay, reminiscing about them. Underneath these exhortations lie genuine and natural apprehensions of the mother of a newly married girl before she leaves for her in-laws' house after her marriage. Geeta's mother is aware of the cultural gap that exists between the two families. Her daughter, having studied in a co-educational college, is accustomed to an atmosphere of free-mixing of the opposite sexes whereas, in Udaipur the women of the upper class, among them Ajay's mother too, have remained in purdah. Immediately after arriving in Udaipur Geeta is isolated from her husband, the only person she knows in this new place, and is thrown into the company of unfamiliar women. The young couple was expected not to mix up openly in the presence of the elders of the family. They were supposed to show some restraint and reservations. The division of the havelis into two parts—one for the men and other for the women—was a part of the tradition aimed at segregating them, at least during the daytime. These women, on their part, are shocked by her (Geeta's) readiness to show her face even to the members of her own sex. With one, apparently retrograde, step of marrying into a conservative feudal family she is pushed into the world of purdah, and is, subsequently, cooped up in the constricted atmosphere of the haveli for the rest of her life, where, at times she feels herself trapped, and finds its atmosphere oppressive.

While in Udaipur, soon after her arrival there, Geeta hears her women relatives repeat the exhortations of her mother. Besides, they also express serious apprehensions about Geeta adjusting to the atmosphere of the haveli. Kanwar Sa, her mother-in-law too administers her own dose of do's and don'ts:

> Do not talk too much to your cousins-in-law, it's not becoming. You know, the women are critical because you are still clumsy. (p. 26)

Geeta vividly remembers one of the women expressing doubts about her ability to adjust in the haveli culture:

> She has good strong features but she is dark. Let us see how she adjusts. After all she is educated and on top of that she is not from Udaipur. What a risk to get an outsider, especially when there is only one son. (p. 15)

There is, obviously, a commonality of attitude shared by women all around towards a girl as soon as she gets married. She is expected to shed her impetuosity, a certain degree of her freedom of thought and action, and her naturalness overnight, and became more reserved, more cautious about her responses to her in-laws and also more tolerant of their whimsical behaviour. Such a change in a newly married girl is expected and considered necessary both by her own parents and her in-laws. Such expectations, and fears probably lie deep more in the psyche of women—be they from Bombay or Udaipur.

Anxieties and apprehensions mentioned above notwithstanding, Kanwar Sa is determined to show her relatives that even 'an educated girl can be *moulded*' (p. 26, emphasis added). Happily enough, seven years later Geeta's aunt-in-law, Nandu Bua, appreciatively and with a sense of pride exclaims to her:

> Looking at you now child, who could say you were not one of us! You have become a real Rajasthani. (p. 92)

Kanwar Sa who had her own way of prevailing over others is a blend of maturity and tenacity. She all along maintains decorum and dignity of her status as the mistress of the haveli. She is, herself, both a daughter-in-law and a mother-in-law. In her dual capacity she is an understanding woman representing the middle generation between the old Bhabha Sa, and the young Geeta. Kanwar Sa is also a very tactful woman who exercises her 'authority' very judiciously. She is ever willing to give some elbow room to Geeta whenever the situation so demands, though she simultaneously keeps up the public image of being the ruling matriarch of Jeewan Niwas. Geeta too very discreetly does not contradict her mother-in-law publicly so long as it only boosts her ego without interfering with her own rights in the family, both as a wife and as a mother.

Kanwar Sa has ever enjoyed the confidence and support of her husband which has earned her the status of a respectable mistress of the haveli. Having enjoyed this wifely privilege herself she happily grants the same to her daughter-in-law. And as a mother Kanwar Sa does not keep her only son Ajay, tied to her apron string. Unlike the mother in Masti Venkata Iyengar's story *The Curds Seller*[7] she does not arrogate to herself the role of the saviour of her son against her daughter-in-law. She has mentally demarcated the area of her jurisdiction as a mother which she does not transgress. When she comes to know of the possibility of Ajay joining Delhi University, she leaves it to the young couple to decide things for themselves. She would not like their love for the Haveli or their consideration for the aging parents stand in the way of Ajay's personal satisfaction and fulfilment. She willingly gives up every control and lets the two of them decide, though as she tells Geeta, she also knows that,

> . . . he would rather sacrifice his happiness than cause us a moment's pain. The men in the haveli are like that. Your father-in-law refused the Prime Ministership of Bikaner because he knew I would not be happy living outside Udaipur. (p. 140)

Kanwar Sa projects herself as a fine example of mother's unselfishness and self-abnegation, when she tells her,

> We are old and our work in the world is over. But you both are young and the future is open to you. . . . I am a mother. I want to see my children happy and fulfilled. You alone can make him see this. You must not let him give up something that will bring him respect and satisfaction. There are times when you must not think of the haveli. (p. 140)

Kanwar Sa thereby completely wins over Geeta, who puts her head in her lap, the idea of shifting to Delhi out of it, and sobs like a child. There is irresistible tenderness and maternal warmth in Kanwar Sa's bearing.

In this woman-centred novel one does not have frequent male-female or female-female encounters giving rise to familial tensions in their relationship as man-wife, daughter-in-law—mother-in-law, etc. Also, there is hardly any chance for daily husband-wife skirmish, with husband usually visiting the wife only at night. Moreover, men in the haveli do not interfere in the day-to-day running of the household. By and large, they conform to the dictum: 'Woman for the hearth and man for the field'. Most of the time it is women folk of the haveli who solve all the household problems. So much so that one does not hear menfolk of the haveli having come to know of the running away of Laxmi—a maid-servant. Most of the time it is Kanwar Sa or Geeta or Parijiji dealing with the servants or interacting with women from other havelis.

Two issues, that of sending Sita, Laxmi's daughter, to school, and marriage proposal for Geeta's daughter Vijay from Daulat Singhji's haveli, however, threaten to bring about a confrontation between Geeta and Kanwar Sa. In such critical situations they mostly oppose each other by proxy. In both the cases it is the menfolk of the haveli who show a lot of understanding of Geeta's viewpoint and do not impose any decision on her. Of the two issues the former concerns Geeta on a more general level while the latter touches her more intimately. Personally, as a mother she should have the right to decide about her daughter's future. For her, women's education is a first essential step towards self-reliance. Her classes have helped girls from the havelis to earn money and thus be released from the drudgery of menial jobs. Socially, being a witness to the life of childhood-widow Parijiji, and child-bride Sita, she just would not allow her daughter to be pushed into marriage until such time she has completed her education.

About women's education in general and Sita's in particular, Geeta is supported by her father-in-law, Bhagwat Singhji and her husband Ajay. Bhagwat Singhji not only consents to Sita being sent to school, but he also encourages Geeta in her endeavour to educate and train women from other havelis, too, in tailoring by giving her two sewing machines, and by meeting all the expenses of the classes from his personal account. Ajay too lends his unambiguous support in her attempt to bring about this social change.

The women's attitude towards woman's education is, however, quite ambivalent. Kanwar Sa thinks that Sita's education will deprive the haveli of a potential domestic help but Manji Bua Sa tells her,

> . . . we should not be selfish if we can help the poor to improve their lot. (p. 96)

She too, like the two men, encourages Geeta in this. 'I am glad you are bringing new ideas into the haveli', said Manji. Geeta, however, is not sure about the ultimate outcome of her efforts, and says without hesitation,

> I do not know, Bua Sa whether it is right to disturb the life within the haveli'. (p. 94)

She is, however, not sure whether education is good for the poor. 'They stand together in their poverty. Education could even be harmful if it separated them from one another', she feels, as is the case in *The Life of Keshav.* It is in such situations that Geeta acts as Rama Mehta's alter ego and looks at education for the poor in all its ramifications. Geeta is, however, goaded on by Manji Bua Sa:

Do not be afraid. It is time things changed. Once we, the old, are dead, the havelis will no longer survive. It is no good living on in the past; for the sake of our children, we must look to the future. (p. 94)

Later on, however, Manji changes her stand when Nandu and Kanta come with her to the haveli to complain against the maids who are not doing their jobs properly. The three women too apprehend complete deprivation of domestic help in case these maid-servants are educated by Geeta, as had been feared by Kanwar Sa initially. Giving education to the maids is 'undermining the dignity of the havelis' (pp. 34-5) they concur. Earlier Manji had questioned, 'Can education harm anyone child?' and asserted, 'Our sacred writings say that to educate the poor is the highest form of charity. If Sita can learn to read and write, she will never feel helpless' (p. 94). But she too, is confused about the present situation as she attempts to distinguish between regular schooling and private coaching by Geeta. She approves of Sita going to a proper school, but maids coming to Geeta's classes is 'just a wonderful excuse to get away from work. And this will harm them in the long run' (p. 134) she feels. Such an accusation causes consternation to Geeta and Kanwar Sa too feels hurt. But this time Kanwar Sa sets at rest all her (Geeta's) anxieties. 'Once your father-in-law gives his approval to something then I am not afraid what the world says' (p. 139).

On the issue of Vijay's marriage to Vir Sigh of Daulat Singhji's haveli, though no definite viewpoint is expressed, there is a perceptible softening of Geeta's initially rigid attitude towards the end. This is projected by the inner conflict between Geeta, the woman, and Geeta, the mother of a marriageable daughter.

Initially, when Geeta learns of the purpose of the visit by women from Daulat Singhji's haveli, her reaction is an angry disapproval. She, for the first time, speaks to her mother-in-law in a raised voice: 'Bhabhi, whatever happens, Vijay can't get engaged at this age' (p. 164). Kanwar Sa remains silent as Geeta's face turns hard and stern. Later, she expresses her feelings more furiously to her husband, Ajay.

I have put up with enough in your family, and I am not prepared to bend any more. I won't ever agree to this criminal act of deciding who Vijay will marry when she is still a child. I know exactly how things work in this place. . . . You are all a bunch of hypocrites. In order to get the girl you want you make any promise, agree to anything. Don't I know the smooth velvety language of the havelis. Well, Ajay, let me tell you that I don't care what family Vir Singh comes from or how much money he has buried in the ground. I will never agree to engage Vijay to a boy who is still in college. Who knows what he will be like when he is a man? (pp. 164-5)

Ajay's response to this fiery outburst of his wife is very sedate and complacent. Speaking matter-of-factly and with poise, he says,

I haven't even given it a thought. . . . When you have a girl like Vijay, hundreds of proposals come, otherwise her parents send out a hundred proposals and wait and see which family accepts their daughter. How did your parents find a husband for you? Have you forgotten? I don't understand why you have made yourself sick over this visit. (pp. 165-6)

Having been addressed in a rash manner by Geeta about Vijay's engagement, Kanwar Sa is too proud to broach the issue again to her herself. She leaves it to Bhagwat Singhji to settle it with Geeta. Even during the visit by the women of Jeewan Niwas to Daulat Singhji's haveli the subject is not touched upon. Rather, the visit is spent in showering encomia on each other's family. The ladies' behaviour towards each other is very dignified. Towards the end of their visit when Vir Singh is asked to seek the elders' blessings, Geeta notices a 'certain dignity in his demeanour' (p. 174). Her fears are proved false. She does not find any affectation. She finds herself completely confused and distracted. A glimpse of the tall handsome Vir Singh who showed 'the reticence and shyness of a well-bred young man' only adds to her confusion and pushes her into a state of indecisiveness. Yet she is determined not to agree to the engagement in the present situation.

To Daulat Singhji's wife Geeta was the best ornament of Bhagwat Singhji's haveli. Hence, their eagerness to seek Vijay's hand in marriage for Vir Singh. Daulat Singhji himself visits Jeewan Niwas along with his brother to show their earnestness about the match after the horoscopes of Vijay and Vir Singh have been tallied. The matter has come to a head. Now is the time for Bhagwat Singhji to talk to Geeta about the subject. He, on his part, wanted to be 'sure about' his own feelings before he spoke to her. He dwells on all the aspects of the issue and comes to the most potent objection from Geeta's point of view, and speaks with unusual vehemence, and preemptingly says,

I have told Daulat Singhji that under no circumstances would I permit Vijay to be taken out of school. I am against early marriages. Girls must study; they cannot be kept ignorant. (p. 198)

Geeta realizes the wisdom of his words. She is no longer sure of herself. She is in a real dilemma. Bhagwat Singhji's praises of Vir Singh's personal qualities and their own responsibility as parents of Vijay echo in her ears. She thinks of her own marriage. 'Her parents had chosen the right man for her; she was happy; she had not gone on to higher studies' (p. 201).

Bhagwat Singhji has handled the situation very adroitly and has driven home to Geeta the positive aspects of the proposal. This compels her to brood over the proposal less apprehensively than she had done before. His personality has 'a natural simple elegance which commanded respect. A wonderful calm seemed to radiate from his reserved personality. . . . There was an aloof reticence in his bearing that did not permit frivolity' (p. 82).

The most significant thing to note in both the episodes, namely women's education and marriage proposal for Vijay, is that each of the persons involved exhibits a great degree of flexibility and patience. No idea or opinion, however radical or unconventional it may be, is rejected out of hand. This is even more true of the male members. There is in them a certain degree of placidity which comes of self-assurance. There is always an attempt to understand the rationale behind Geeta's viewpoint. Most importantly, none of the members at any time creates an 'either-or' situation, which invariably leads to a breaking point. Mutual adjustment is the key word. The haveli may be constricting in atmosphere, but men living therein show open mindedness.

Living in the company of such people Geeta is imbued with the spirit of the haveli and its heritage.

In the haveli culture, the masters and their menials cut across socioeconomic barriers during festivities and bereavements. Writing about the position of the maid-servants in the havelis, Rama Mehta says:

> These maid-servants and their children were brought up and integrated into the family. Their position was not that of menials. Depending on age, they were required to be given respect by younger family members . . . a daughter-in-law was expected to touch the feet of the old maid-servant of the husband's family, and refer to her with respect and show her courtesy in form and manner.[8]

Geeta also observes such courtesies in her behaviour with the maids of the haveli and shows them due regard. When Kanwar Sa goes to look up her ailing brother, Geeta finds the haveli quite 'empty' without her. On the full moon night the Goddess of wealth must be worshipped suggests Parijiji to her. Geeta is guided by Dhapu and Parijiji about the rituals and after the *pooja* has been performed she touches the feet of Parijiji, the eldest woman present during the absence of her mother-in-law. Geeta has internalized the proprieties and decorum of the haveli slowly but definitely. She, thus, becomes a carrier forward of the traditions of the haveli, which have, of course, been diluted over the years. They together form the warp and woof of the haveli. Geeta found that life with all its suffering,

> . . . was never unbearable. They shared each others' joy and wept together in sorrow. They were strong and even ruthless, when it came to upholding family customs and ties. Tradition was like a fortress protecting them from the outside world, giving them security and a sense of superiority. (p. 93)

It is this capacity of one and all to empathize with others which has very subtly instilled in Geeta a liking for the haveli.

Earlier on two occasions, once, when seeing the portraits of the ancestors Geeta had thought with pride, 'these must have been the kind of men who fought and won battles against the Moghuls' (p. 17). And, secondly, watching the males celebrating Vijay's birth, she is filled with a sense of pride.

> These were good people, gentle, kind and chivalrous . . . she forgot her daily irritations; she felt proud to be young mistress of the haveli. How could she allow little discomforts to blind her to the great traditions of the family? (pp. 34-5)

Such thoughts help her transcend her insignificant, petty irritations. She considers herself to be a part of the glory of Mewar and its history. Haveli too at such moments doesn't remain a symbol of oppressive tradition and customs, but becomes an inseparable part of the glorious history of Mewar.

Writing about the sociologist and his interest in the social beings, Michel Zeraffa says, 'For the sociologist, a good deal of interest attaches to . . . efforts of the self to somehow create its own social destiny. . . .'[9] Rama Mehta, the sociologist, knows fully well that in the Indian situation a woman's place ultimately is in her husband's house. This is more so in case of Rajasthan where people are far more deeply rooted in their tradition. Writing about woman and society in *The Divorced Hindu Woman*, she finds that 'on the whole the growth of feminine awareness is far more rapid than the liberalization of the society itself and that this imbalance can be very ominous for the women who break away from social restraints, both psychological and social'.[10] Geeta is fully aware as to where her destiny lies. She does not break away from psychological and social restraints. She rather enchains herself with certain traditions, customs and taboos. Lakshmi, the maid, who acts as a foil to her, on the contrary, leaves her husband's house. This impulsive decision only tosses her from one man to another in search of security of a home, and leads to her ultimate disintegration. Savitri, in R.K. Narayan's *The Dark Room*[11] also revolts against her husband Ramani's overbearing demeanour. Ignited into action by Ramani's adulterous relationship with Shantabai, she leaves her home in protest but ultimately returns to the security of the hearth and love of her children. Geeta too once, in a fit of anger, threatens to leave Ajay's house but immediately realizes its futility. She thinks that it is better to come to grips with a problem to be able to solve it rather than run away from it. This, however, involves some compromise on the part of the protagonist.

Geeta's assimilation into the traditional atmosphere of the haveli is made easy by the reasonableness of her in-laws. They are ever willing to change themselves, but within the parameters of their sociocultural milieu and are also willing to relinquish the material possessions both for their own posterity and also for their servants. They are fully conscious of the inexorable law of nature that the 'Old order changeth yielding place to new'.

Besides, their innate humaneness and generosity have coalesced in them to make them good human beings. Kanwar Sa's concern for the seemingly insignificant matters like those pertaining to the breakfast or tiffin which Sita takes to school reflects her basic humanism.

Bhagwat Singhji and his wife, though rooted in the tradition of Mewar, are modern in their sensibility. Distinguishing between contemporary and modern, Irwing Howe writes, 'where the contemporary refers to time, the modern refers to sensibility and style, and where the contemporary is a term of neutral reference the modern is a term of critical placement and judgement'.[12] Both, the husband and wife, display modern sensibility in crucial and critical situations in the novel. They not only give their consent to but also encourage Geeta in training women of the havelis. Bhagwat Singhji further relaxes the etiquettes of the haveli by allowing Geeta to sit in his presence and discuss matters, such as women's education and Vijay's engagement when no outsiders are present, and even talk to him directly. So '. . . the more she [Geeta] saw him the more she admired him. He saw more than the ordinary eye and felt more than the normal heart' (p. 143). She is given a great deal of latitude to fulfill her ideas. Support from Bhagwat Singhji and Ajay in this regard is explicit and unambiguous. Kanwar Sa, on the other hand, can only keep the pretence of being fully in control of things, and in spite of being the mainstay of the traditions of the haveli, she too, ultimately yields ground.

In his conception of dialectical development Marx, according to M. Brewster Smith, held that 'people work upon the world and in shaping their world, by the same token, people are shaped by it. The process is interactive, but it is also cumulative.'[13] Similarly if Geeta has brought in new ideas into the haveli, she too, on her part, has imbibed the spirit of the haveli. Though the haveli is the embodiment of feudal tradition, Bhagwat Singhji the patriarch is generous and liberal in his ideas. He does not live in the dead past. His flexibility evokes reverence for him in Geeta.

The elders of the haveli believe in giving away things, and they hold material possessions in a spirit of trusteeship. Significantly both Bhabha Sa and Bhagwat Singhji give away gold and money from their sick beds, to their servants and relatives. The former gives a gold bangle each to Bhatianiji and Parijiji—the maids of long standing with her and another to Geeta, while Bhagwat Singhji defrays the entire loan Ganga Ram, Sita's father, had incurred on the marriage of his daughter. Kanwar Sa, too, hands over the keys of the household to Geeta to run it herself when Bhagwat Singhji falls ill a few days before his death. Immediately after the death of Bhagwat Singhji, even in a moment of personal bereavement Kanwar Sa does not forget the haveli tradition and urges upon Geeta 'to keep this haveli as a trust for your children' (p. 208) as she and Bhagwat Singhji had done on their part.

The haveli, though a symbol of tradition, is inhabited by people who have human warmth and concern, camaraderie, generosity, willingness to relinquish control over people and property—people who hold material possessions as a trust for younger generation and above all, who are willing to change with the changing times. Their giving away of material and financial help to their servants with a view to enabling them to be self-reliant exhibits these two traits of their personality. They are the people who always maintain their mental equanimity and seldom lose temper. They ever observe decorous formality in their behaviour. In the company of such people Geeta cannot but carry forward the proprieties and decorum of the haveli, where simultaneously with her education she would be, to use Betty Friedan's words, 'a cultural leaven of her family and community'[14] and thus usher in an era of more open and more liberal society.

NOTES

* The author acknowledges with gratitude the help rendered by late Rama Mehta's husband Mr. Jagat S. Mehta in supplying to him two novels: *Ramu: A Story of India* and *The Life of Keshav: A Family Story of India*, which were not available locally, as also important information about circumstances leading to the writing of the former.

1. Rama Mehta, 'From Purdah to Modernity' in *Indian Women: From Purdah to Modernity*, ed. B.R. Nanda (New Delhi: Vikas, 1976).
2. Information contained in the correspondence between Jagat S. Mehta and the author.
3. Santha Rama Rau, Foreword to *Ramu: A Story of India* (New York: McGraw Hill Co., 1966), p. 4.
4. Rama Mehta, *Inside the Haveli* (1977; rpt. New Delhi: Arnold-Heinemann, 1981), p. 21. Subsequent citations from *Inside the Haveli* are identified by page numbers enclosed in parentheses following the citations in the text of the essay.
5. Michel Zeraffa, 'The Novel as Literary Form and as Social Institution', in *Sociology of Literature and Drama*, ed. Elizableth & Tom Burns (Harmondsworth: Penguin Books, 1973), p. 46.
6. K.R. Srinivasa Iyengar, *Indian Writing in English* (Delhi: Sterling, 1985), p. 753.
7. Masti Venkata Iyengar, 'The Curds Seller', in *A Book of Short Stories*, eds. A. Bhattacharya and K. Essauloff (Calcutta. Indian Press Pvt. Ltd., 1968), pp. 67-80.
8. Rama Mehta, 'From Purdah to Modernity', p. 120.
9. Michel Zeraffa, p. 46.
10. Rama Mehta, *The Divorced Hindu Woman* (Delhi: Vikas, 1975), p. 159.
11. R.K. Narayan, *The Dark Room* (New Delhi: Orient Paperbacks, 1976).
12. Irwing Howe, 'Introduction: The Idea of Modern', in *Literary Modernism*, ed. Irwing Howe (New York: Fawcett, 1967), pp. 12-13.
13. Brewster M. Smith, 'Perspectives on Selfhood', in *American Psychologist* (December 1978), p. 1059.
14. Betty Friedan, *The Feminine Mystique* (rpt. 1963; New York: Dell Publishing Co., 1964), p. 124.

Arun Joshi's Women: An Esoteric Experience

Usha Bande

Speaking of the works of Galsworthy and Kipling, Virginia Woolf remarks in a famous passage in *A Room of One's Own*, 'Do what she will a woman cannot find in them that fountain of perpetual life which critics assure her is there. It is not only that they celebrate male virtues, enforce male values and describe the world of men; it is that the emotion with which these books are permeated is to a woman incomprehensible.'[1] This statement even though it concerns women readers and smacks of feminism, can well be applied to Arun Joshi, who writes, as it were, 'with the male side of [his] brain',[2] of man's world, his successes, frustrations and existential problems, relegating women to a secondary position. At the centre of all his novels is the male experience which largely determines his themes, choice of characters and also his technique.

Thematically, Joshi's works are about modern man's struggle to find a meaning in life. His 'conscience-torn'[3] characters, as a critic calls them, are almost always trapped in the human predicament. Structurally, his novels follow the quest-motifs and are linear in design, except *The Last Labyrinth* and *The City and the River*[4] which are circular in design. In this scheme of things women characters are but appendages to their male counterparts and are meant to be passive. Moreover, the central consciousness in these novels is that of man, which does not afford much scope for an understanding of the female psyche. The rhetoric is built round the men, and it is *their* life that the author seeks to explore. That could probably be the reason why critics and scholars have not focused on Joshi's women. Whereas a large number of papers have appeared on the *angst*-ridden, self-alienated male questers,[5] no paper exclusively examining the women has appeared so far. For some critics, female characters are almost non-existent in Joshi's fiction, for others they are non-entities, and for quite a few they exist only to fulfil the men.

However, my quarrel is neither with Joshi nor with the critics, for my purpose here is not to build a feminist perspective but to study the feminine experience in *The Last Labyrinth*, in the light of tradition and modernity. With the help of his other works, viz., *The Foreigner, The Strange Case of Billy Biswas, The Apprentice,* and *The City and The River*, I shall examine his treatment of women, evolve my thesis and then analyse *The Last Labyrinth*.

It would help, I think, to approach Arun Joshi's women characters through his men, and the milieu they are placed in, in order to recognize their cultural characteristics. The milieu of Joshi's novels is unmistakably modern Indian urban society with its fast changing values, rapid Westernization and the resultant materialism. It is a society 'without norms, without direction, without even, perhaps, a purpose', where frustrated men sail about in confusion, as Ratan Rathore, the protagonist of *The Apprentice* puts it (p. 77). Through the personal tragedy of a hero, who embodies most but not all of his culture's values, the author projects the tragedy of dehumanization and degradation and its corroding effect on the individual psyche, which leads each of his male characters toward an existential quest. Be it Sindi Oberoi, Ratan Rathore, Billy Biswas or Som Bhaskar, each is disillusioned ultimately by materialism and seeks to grapple with spiritual realities. Thus, the novels about individual struggle in the classical tradition of Western fiction, become a saga of twentieth-century man's efforts to heave himself out of a nullity thrust upon him by a materialistic culture. In fictionalizing this struggle, Joshi achieves two things: first, he offers us a critique of modern society by exposing its ills, and second, he reveals the primitive urges in man lying hidden underneath the 'glossy surfaces',[6] which he terms as the 'mysterious underworld'[7] of the human soul. But, whatever be a protagonist's demand on life, his female counterpart is always with him, and she has attributes matching his demands though significantly, she is denied individuality. Thus, we get a gallery of women without flesh and blood. It is this gallery of portraits that we shall examine now in the ensuing paragraphs.

The Foreigner, Arun Joshi's first novel, presents several women in the life of Sindi Oberoi. Broadly, they fall under three categories or types—Kathy, Anna, Judy, Christine seek a man for pleasure, make no demands on him and walk out of his life without leaving much to fall back on; they are the non-conformists; June is the one to move the soul; and Shiela is the typical Indian woman, childlike, passive and vulnerable. The same trio we meet again in *The Strange Case of Billy Biswas*, and *The Last Labyrinth*. In Billy's life the females are Tuula and Rima, his friends, Meena, his wife, and Bilasia, the eternal female. While with Tuula there is 'no male-female tangle' (p. 175), he has a fleeting affair with Rima. Rima loves him but he is not emotionally attached to her; his relationship is one of friendship, not love. Meena is good enough as a wife—a social symbol—but she holds no fascination for him. He disregards her feelings and goes to Bilasia. Bilasia, 'the embodiment of that primal and invulnerable force that had ruled these hills, perhaps this earth, since time began . . .' (p. 226), moves him and confuses him. Billy marries her but is punished, as it were, for his transgression and he pays for it with his life. In Som Bhasker's life in *The Last Labyrinth* it is Leela Sabnis, the modern Indian free woman subscribing to free sex; Geeta, his wife, and the *femme fatale*, Anuradha. The lives of these men in Arun Joshi's novels move round and within the charm spread by these women. It is significant to note the attitude of the three men, viz., Sindi, Billy and Som—toward their women. None of the three respects or loves the free, frivolous type but each has a sense of pride and ownership for the Indian prototype, and an irresistible and incomprehensible attraction for the soul mates (June, Bilasia and Anuradha).

The picture changes with *The Apprentice*. Here, we find Ratan Rathore so engulfed in his confessional narration that he does not have much inclination to talk of his women. We learn of his wife whom he married as a 'deal' in return for his promotion and career advancement. Like his predecessors, Ratan is a great womanizer and has had mistresses whom he used to visit in his heydays, partly to relieve tension and partly because it was the 'in' thing in his moneyed social circle. But, unlike his predecessors no woman moves him to dizzy heights or thrusts him down unfathomable depths of the labyrinth of the soul. He lacks that esoteric experience with the mysterious women which Som, Billy and even Sindi, have.

In Sindi's case, however, the experience is tragic and his awareness of it is belated. His tendency to escape responsibility behind the facade of 'detachment' leads June to desperation and death. Truly enough June does not possess the primitive force of Bilasia or the spiritual aura of Anuradha, but she has a disarming sincerity etched against which Sindi's harangue about 'non-involvement' sounds phoney. June affects Sindi 'in an unusual way' (p. 24) and gives him 'a strange world of intense pleasure and almost equally intense pain' (p. 82). June has all those female traits that hold a man—she nurses Sindi, almost mothers him, feeds his vanity, yet is frank enough to show him his shortcomings. It is through June that Sindi understands himself and we understand Sindi. June fascinates him by her beauty, love and humane approach to life, but Sheila, demure and petite, draws him out of his alienation. She is respectable and Sindi knows 'one just didn't talk like that to a girl like Sheila', when he makes a loose remark. And then, isn't it for Sheila that Sindi reverses his decision to leave the Khemka office and decides to stay on 'as long as I'm needed' (p. 230)? What with all her qualities of head and heart, one doubts if Sindi would really have accepted June the way he accepts Sheila. Instinctively, he adopts a protective attitude toward Sheila. Her dutifulness fills him with 'a sense of sympathy for all Indian women who always had their back arched, stooping to someone's service' (p. 218). And, neither Joshi nor his protagonist resents this servility; on the contrary, both seem to relish it. Sindi concludes his narration with a telling remark, 'I had a feeling we were just beginning to understand each other' (p. 230) and celebrates it with a cup of tea with Sheila. The author creates two more proto-typical Indian wives in Meena and Geeta to fill in the gaps left by Sheila.

The archetypal pattern the author had been building up takes shape in *The City and the River*, culminating in the portrayal of women as archetypal figures. Here Joshi transcreates the archetypal female in all her power and strength. Shailaja, though not a 'palpable presence'[8] is none the less a representative of that docile, demure and soft woman whom Joshi has celebrated in his earlier works. The 'headman' of the fishermen is the strong woman who can hold and direct all—men, women and children. The most memorable figure is the Eternal Mother—the River. She protects, destroys and sustains. She is the embodiment of all that a woman stands for. A *Yajna* is performed to purify her as if the 'impure' image of Ratan Rathore's mother is being cleansed. It may be mentioned here that mother figures do not have much role to perform in Joshi's fiction. Sindi and Billy do not seem to be influenced by their mothers; Som is, but to him we shall turn later. Ratan Rathore's mother was a 'loose' woman, a 'whore' and he has unpleasant memories of her materialistic approach to life. Joshi's presentation of Ratan Rathore's mother can well be contrasted with Anita Desai's portrayal of mothers in *Voices in the City* and *Cry, the Peacock*. Ratan is not sentimental about his mother's character, he simply records it, whereas Anita Desai's Nirode in *Voices* raves and rants over his mother's supposed affair with Major Chadha. Likewise, Ratan's mother, a freedom fighter's wife, has no aura about her that Gautam's mother, also a freedom fighter's wife, has in *Cry, the Peacock*. She is a revered presence in the house and a respectable figure in society. Joshi misses out on these subtle touches which Desai lends to her female characters.

This brief survey of the treatment of women in Arun Joshi's novels reveals certain significant facts. First, the novelist depicts his women as types and sees them exclusively from a male angle. Second, like his protagonists, he too is puzzled by the mystery called 'woman' and does not know whether he would like to see his women as traditional, modern or primitive. Making this the basis, I shall now concentrate on *The Last Labyrinth*, his Sahitya Akademi Award winning work.

II

In *The Last Labyrinth*, we come across five women: Som Bhaskar's mother, Geeta (his wife), Leela (his mistress or let us say, his friend), Anuradha (his soul-mate), and Gargi (his spiritual prop). Each exercises an influence on Som and he requires each at different stages of his mental life. Som's mother is tender, loving, lonely, vulnerable and patient—endowed with qualities which Som finds so endearing in his wife Geeta, later. The mother is a woman of great faith as Geeta is a woman of great trust. Likewise, when mother's body suffers due to her illness, she turns to Lord Krishna for strength of soul; and when Geeta 'had every right to the adulteries of the body she had only taken to the cleansing of the soul' (p. 63). Som's relations with his mother are tender if one could surmise from the way he combs her hair, paints her nails and pleads with her to go to the hospital instead of languishing in her room with her blind faith in Krishna's healing power. An embittered Som recounts at a later stage in his life how his mother 'believed Krishna would cure her and flushed her capsules down the toilet' (p. 57). Here, we recall Kamala Markandaya's Sarojini in *A Silence of Desire* with her conviction that faith and not medicine would cure her ulcer. She tells her rationalist husband, '. . . faith and reason do not go together and without faith I shall not be healed'.[9] Ultimately, Dandekar and Sarojini meet half way through and Markandaya succeeds in showing us how faith and reason can join hands toward human wellbeing. Sarojini is cured without damage to her faith, Dandekar develops faith without giving up his reason. But not so with Joshi. Som suffers the trauma of shattered faith and can never reconcile himself with this existential loss. It seems to me that the mother's faith is ingrained in Som's unconscious, but since God could not cure his mother, He becomes a malevolent force. This generates conflict between his conscious and unconscious minds; between the modern attitude of distrust toward spiritual truth and the archetypal pressures to have faith. The voice 'I want, I want' (pp. 11-12), his 'orchestra of discontent' (p. 12), is indeed the cry of his soul to find an anchor in faith he has lost after his mother's death. He wants a spiritual prop to replace his mother and Gargi takes her place.

Som is a strife-torn man in his thirties, a successful businessman rolling in wealth, buying shares greedily, when he meets Gargi. His first thought on seeing her is '. . . I had met her before somewhere' (p. 60). Later, he tells us that he has seen 'her before, walking silently about the darkness of my dreams' (p. 99). Her smile is reassuring and he wants to 'hug' her when she smiles. He is at home with her and pours his heart out to her as he would have done with his mother. He is sure she is the 'only one who understands' him (p. 117). He turns to her again and again despite his apparent lack of faith in the spiritual values Gargi upholds. She brings Som and Anuradha together when she exhorts him 'Don't quarrel. She is your *Shakti*' (p. 121), but weans him away from her when she senses danger to his wellbeing. Whether Gargi could really work miracles assigned to her by K. is disputable but she certainly could hold a shattered Som together by her motherly affection. Like a mother sometimes withholding a precious gift from a wayward child to punish him, Gargi hands him over the trinket (i.e. the bundle containing shares) and withholds the prized treasure, Anuradha. It is a severe punishment she deals out to him.

Between these two benign figures—Gargi and mother—Som has come into contact with many women but the three around whom his life revolves are Leela, Anuradha and Geeta. Leela Sabnis, a Professor of Philosophy, is the new woman with ultra modern ideas about free sex, individuality and the like. Unconventional as she is, she has no qualms in having physical relations with Som just for the fun of it. Som is fond of her but he is impatient (with her) when she seeks explanations and gives philosophical analysis of his problems and steps into the intellectual field. He enjoys her company when she talks, behaves and submits like a woman, but the moment she becomes an overbearing intellectual, he loses interest in her 'muddled' talk. We meet Leela twice in the narrative but since Som remembers her often, we get sufficient clue to believe that though he does not love her, he seeks her company as 'a mechanic of the spirit' (p. 75). It is like turning to a male friend for solace.

Interestingly, Som describes her with a touch of humour, 'Dr. Leela Sabnis, a professor, descendant of a long line of professors, M.A. and Ph.D. from Michigan, something else from London, short, shapely small-breasted, skinny, trained in philosophy, emancipator of women, married and divorced, believer in free love, harbinger of a new order of things, reformer of the body and a mechanic of the spirit, a good lover' (p. 75). We can compare this with his description of Geeta and Anuradha to see the difference in his attitude. Geeta, he says, 'stood adjusting her sari, child of another world, traversing, like a plane at a higher altitude, a corridor separate from the dark vestibule that I had just crossed' (p. 69). About Anuradha he says,

> I noticed, then, the tracery of *mehndi* on her pink palms. A little hot wave, tinged with sorrow, travelled down my spine. The delicate curlicues, golden arabesques, roadsigns of fate, wound and unwound, turned upon themselves. I had seen that hand before: as a child, as a boy, in my fantasies of lust. I stared at her not quite understanding what was happening to me. (p. 14)

The tender touches and the fine nuances of feeling in the latter two are missing in the former. Leela has the 'peculiar neatness and straight carriage' of a working girl, she has 'intelligence in her face and conversation' (p. 111), but she is not 'extraordinary' like Geeta or 'different' like Anuradha. Som Bhaskar makes fun of her obsession with books and passion for analysis. Her flat is crammed with books, 'books on the floor, books against the walls, on the toilet, inside the laundry bag, on the bed' (p. 77), and Leela claims proudly that her husband 'divorced her for her reading too much' (p. 77). Som calls her a 'muddled creature' with a penchant for analysis. She becomes a 'pain in the neck' when she reels off 'diagnoses, half sense, half poppycock' (p. 78). Obviously, she cannot attract Som for long and the affair 'fizzled out' within six months, but neither he nor Leela is pained. Both accept the break as inevitable, and while Leela rationalises the parting, Som looks for 'something, somebody, somewhere' (p. 82), in which his two worlds—the material world and the world of spirit—would meet.

In Anuradha, Som sees his two worlds meeting. She fascinates him, becomes his *Shakti*, his 'dark terrible love' with something stronger and deeper than physical satisfaction. He turns to his 'pock-marked phantom' (p. 105) again and again in spite of Aftab's displeasure, Anuradha's occasional rebuffs, and his own better judgement. It is as though she is 'gifted with a vision, a vantage point high above the earth, from where she could see the melee below as ordinary men could not' (p. 58). Som is enchanted by Anuradha as Billy is by Bilasia in *The Strange Case of Billy Biswas*. Bilasia, the primal force is as difficult to explain and understand as the elements. Romi asks, 'What was Bilasia? What is the playful effervescence of a mountain stream? What is sunlight filtering through a glade? What is the thunder of a volcano or the hardness of granite? What is the vengeance of a cobra whose mate has been killed?' (p. 225). Som too cannot understand Anuradha. He uses a number of metaphors and similies to define her to himself and to the readers: She is an 'antique person' (p. 138), she is 'different' and the 'daughter of disturbance' (p. 106), she is unfathomable 'like the ocean' (p. 132), and above all she is 'a city of ruins' (p. 9). The nearer he goes, the more mystified he is.

Anuradha leaves a traumatic impact on Som whose crazed state of mind leads a reader to search for those esoteric qualities in her which the protagonist assures him she possesses. Critics and scholars, by and large, are unimpressed by Anuradha's supposed stature. Some refer to her in derogatory terms as Aftab's 'concubine' and Som's 'mistress' while others call her a 'strange' woman with spiritual powers, an enigma embodying 'the concept of sacrifice'.[10] A close study of the novel, however, reveals that Anuradha is neither a mystery not a spiritual shaman. She is an ordinary woman whose charm lies in her inaccessibility. Som who has experienced success with women and has never seen the pain of frustrated love is not ready to accept that she should be available to Aftab, an unsuccessful businessman and not to him, a brainy millionaire. To possess Anuradha and Aftab's shares becomes his obsession. That she is one of his 'obsessions' is clear from his words, 'I was . . . obsessed with her, just as I had been obsessed with all those other women. The one-shot obsession' (p. 59). Our difficulty in understanding her as a woman stems from the very nature of the first person point-of-view which does not afford us a sufficient clue to her psyche. Som Bhaskar, the narrator-protagonist, records his experiences with her without letting us know what she feels; though we have no reason to doubt his account, we cannot thrust his opinions on her and accept her on his terms. After all, Anuradha has a specific role to perform in Som's life.

To be fair to Anuradha, we must take into account her qualities as a woman. Anuradha is frank, sincere and naïve; she is gentle yet strong; and she has a balanced mixture of the mundane and the spiritual. She is candid enough to tell Som, '. . . you are not as clever as you think. You are wrong about many things. You are wrong about yourself. You think you know a lot, when, in fact, you don't' (p. 61). The egoistic millionaire is left spellbound by this revealing remark. Anuradha's attitude to marriage is bold and Som is amazed at it, 'You can't marry everyone you love. So, why marry anyone at all?' (p. 43). Once she tells him, 'I can imagine I am married to Aftab. I can imagine I am married to you. My mother used to imagine she was married to Krishna' (p. 123). She is naïve in her faith in Krishna, and sincere in her love for Som. Like a typical Indian woman, she sacrifices herself for his welfare. Thus, she remains a mystery for Som, with the mundane side of her life open like a book to be read freely, and the spiritual side closed firmly never to be understood. In a way, she is a combination of Leela and Geeta—unconventional like the former and traditional like the latter. She is probably the only person who can give Som Bhaskar the 'mystical identification' he wants. Arun Joshi substantiates this when he tells us, 'Anuradha's role in the novel is to lead Bhaskar through the unconscious.'[11] Even if we do not consider the spiritual aspect of her personality and think of the psychological impact upon Som, we find that she exercises tremendous influence on him by her uncanny power to understand him. Her remark, 'It is not me you want' (p. 58), has obvious psychological overtones suggesting that Som wants to possess her to derive the satisfaction of a vindictive triumph over Aftab. She does the work assigned to her by her creator, i.e. Arun Joshi, guides Som successfully through the labyrinth of the soul, awakens him and leaves him to Geeta.

Geeta is Joshi's ideal Indian woman—innocent, vulnerable, calm, tolerant and gentle. Som admires her 'cool strength' (p. 46) and her ability to trust 'like birds fly, like fish swim' (p. 63), which shows her spontaneity. Moreover, Geeta is 'a great, big giver. . . . If discontent is my trademark, trust is Geeta's' (p. 63). He admits that he cannot 'imagine life without her' (p. 73). According to a critic, Som is 'neutral to his wife',[12] but I believe, he (Som) gives her all credit for being a perfect wife, the 'same loving, marvellous, gentle person' even after ten years of marriage (p. 70). We, however, do not know what Geeta thinks of her husband's whims and fancies. But, though we are not told, we can construe, from occasional actions or remarks, that beneath her silent acceptance there is a woman deeply distressed. Her sudden interest in Sadhus and astrologers is an indirect indictment of Som's behaviour which leaves a void within her. With the children in the hostel and a husband on the run, where could she look to for an anchor? Her religious beliefs become a source of strength and sustenance for her. Som tells us:

> Of late, she had become a great enthusiast of temples, shrines, tombs of the godly. Ten years with me and she had developed her own guide-book of grief. Saints, sadhus, miracle-workers, astrologers, they drew her. Was it my rages that had driven her? My fornications? Her brother's death? Or some urges of her own? (pp. 62-3)

Geeta is educated and sophisticated; she is intelligent and is aware of her husband's various escapades, but instead of creating trouble for him and subsequently for herself, she maintains a quiet dignity which disarms Som. She impresses with her amazing capacity to compromise with the hard realities. She is serene and submissive but not passive, she takes decisions when required, and faces her husband's irate mood with heroic resistance. Som comes back after the debacle because she is there, and more importantly, 'she understands' (p. 224). Had she behaved like Meena, Billy's wife, could she have gained back Som? Geeta stands by him all through and we know she will be there to give him strength by her sympathetic understanding, patient nursing and self-sacrifice.

If we look back and consider Joshi's treatment of woman as wife, we find that he leads his readers step by step to the traditional Indian wife. Sheila's docility and gentleness attract Sindi Oberoi, Meena loses Billy because she refuses to suffer passively, and Geeta's patience draws Som back home after the traumatic experience. The image that emerges is of Sita, Sati and Savitri-stereotype. Clearly, in husband-wife relationship, the woman has to show intensity, depth and devotion, not the man. Gentle, patient, homely and affectionate women get the prize when their husbands choose to return to them. In one of his letters, Arun Joshi maintains that 'alienation in my novels which I have written so far ultimately leads them back to community. I realized that in my latest novel *The Last Labyrinth* for the first time it does not happen'.[13] The 'community' Joshi visualizes is the Indian society with its abiding values and old world charm, not the *modern* Indian society of which he is skeptical. It would be interesting to mention what one of his characters has to say about modern Indian society and modern Indian woman. Kewal Kapur, in the story 'The Survivor' declares:

> I am a survivor, gentlemen, of card parties, of wedding receptions, of five-year plans! Of nosy neighbours, of conjugal bliss, of well-meaning friends and of bloody-minded bosses. I am a survivor of life insurance schemes, of stock exchanges and family planning techniques. In brief, gentlemen, I am a survivor of that fantastic racket that passes for MODERN INDIAN SOCIETY. I am a survivor of mendacious mothers and of relentless fathers, of tuppenny politicians, of lawyers and of doctors. Above all I am the survivor of the greatest disaster of them all: THE MODERN INDIAN WOMAN.[14]

In *The Last Labyrinth*, Som does not go back to his community but to his wife, the epitome of all virtues.

Joshi's men have an ambivalent attitude toward themselves as well as toward their women. His cultured, well-travelled and wealthy men do not know what to do with themselves with all their knowledge and wealth. Similarly, they are not sure what to look for in their women. The new woman with ultramodern ideas about sex fascinates them, but she cannot hold them. Women with a combination of traditional values and modern spirit draw them irresistibly. But, somehow, they, the men, are destined to lose the battle to possess them. June dies leaving Sindi distracted. Billy has to pay with his life for possessing Bilasia. Anuradha's mysterious disappearance drags Som to a nervous breakdown and attempted suicide. According to Joshi, in snatching Anuradha away from Som he 'was hinting at the old classical dictum that you do not get anything without sacrificing something. So she is to be taken away from him.'[15] This reminds us of William Golding's *Free Fall* where Sammy Mountjoy's teacher exhorts him, 'If you want something enough, you can always get it provided you are willing to make the appropriate sacrifice. Something, anything. But what you get is never quite what you thought; and sooner or later the sacrifice is always regretted.'[16]

Sammy sacrifices Beatrice, his beloved, and suffers hell. Sammy's Beatrice and Som's Anuradha have an almost Dantesque touch. Like Dante's Beatrice, Anuradha has the potential to become an instrument of his spiritual salvation, but Joshi forces her to sacrifice her life for Som's sake thus reinforcing the traditional concept that self-realization and fulfilment for a woman lie in her sacrificing spirit. One cannot miss the distinctly Indian tone of Joshi's work when Geeta too mutely accepts her erring husband after he returns home, a defeated quester. For Joshi's men, the only stable prop is the wife—ever-suffering, ever-forgiving and never complaining. She remains the palpable reality of a man's life.

The archetypal images of woman as Mohini, Shakti and Sita make their appearance in Joshi's fiction. His heroes are lured by Mohini, and held spellbound by Shakti, but they invariably come back to Sita. Here, we do not have the strong emerging woman like Anand's Gauri, Narayan's Rosie or Markandaya's Rukmani or Mira or other heroines, nor do we meet the high-strung but individualistic women of Anita Desai. Unlike Nayantara Sahgal's women, Joshi's female characters are not 'strivers and aspirers'.[17] Geeta, Leela and Anuradha show some strength but in their strength lies their weakness. Leela submits to Som in the name of free love, modernity and self-fulfilment. She rejects the existing norms, traditions and social ethos, but her nonconformity remains at the superficial level as it does not achieve anything, nor does she herald the new order. Anuradha is so weakened by her love that instead of facing Aftab and Som, she disappears quietly. Geeta connives at Som's faults, compromises with life and achieves a make-believe peace. Geeta is modelled on the Sita, Sati, Savitri-image—symbols of sacrifice, true love and suffering. To be an ideal wife like Sita is a good enough precept for a woman, but then where is Ram, the ideal spouse?

NOTES

1. (London: Hogarth, 1929), p. 153.
2. Virginia Woolf, p. 152.
3. C.N. Srinath, 'The Fiction of Arun Joshi', *The Literary Criterion*, XII, 2-3 (1976), p. 127.
4. Arun Joshi's works referred to in this paper are: *The Foreigner* (New Delhi: Orient Paperbacks, 1968), *The Strange Case of Billy Biswas* (New Delhi: Orient Paperbacks, 1971), *The Apprentice* (New Delhi: Orient Paperbacks, 1976), *The Last Labyrinth* (New Delhi: Orient

Paperbacks, 1981), *The City and the River* (New Delhi: Vision Books, 1990); and a collection of short stories *The Survivor* (New Delhi: Sterling, 1975). All references incorporated in the text are to these editions.

5. See R.K. Dhawan (ed.), *The Fictional World of Arun Joshi* (New Delhi: Classical Publishing Co., 1986), and *The Novels of Arun Joshi* (New Delhi: Prestige, 1992). Both these anthologies contain papers dealing with different aspects of Joshi's novels and stories—the existential quest, alienation, art and vision, archetypal patterns, political overtones and technique. See also, A.N. Dwivedi's paper 'The Novels of Arun Joshi', in *Studies in Contemporary Indian Fiction in English*, ed. A.N. Dwivedi (Allahabad: Kitab Mahal, 1987). This is a general survey of the novels of Arun Joshi.
6. Quoted in Sujata Mathai's 'I'm a Stranger to My Books', *The Times of India*, 7 July 1983, p. 8.
7. Sujata Mathai, p. 8.
8. Usha Bande, 'Archetypal Patterns in the City and the River', R.K. Dhawan (ed.), *The Novels of Arun Joshi* (New Delhi: Prestige, 1992), p. 261.
9. Kamala Markandaya, *A Silence of Desire* (London: Putnam, 1960), p. 7.
10. R.K. Dhawan, 'The Fictional World of Arun Joshi', in *The Novel of Arun Joshi*, p. 33.
11. 'A Winner's Secret: An Interview with Purabi Bannerji', *The Sunday Statesman*, 27 Feb. 1983.
12. A.N. Dwivedi, p. 312.
13. Reply to V. Gopal Reddy, 8 Jan. 1981 in *The Novels of Arun Joshi*, ed. R.K. Dhawan, op. cit.
14. 'The Survivor', in *Modern Indian Short Stories*, ed. Suresh Kohli (New Delhi: Arnold-Heinemann, 1974), pp. 27-8.
15. 'A Winner's Secret'.
16. William Golding, *Free Fall* (London: Faber & Faber, 1959), p. 235.
17. Quoted by Jasbir Jain in *Nayantara Sahgal* (New Delhi: Arnold-Heinemann, 1978), p. 4.

Impressive Women but the Chains are no Fictions: Women in Rushdie's *Shame*

Uma Parameswaran

Salman Rushdie is an ardent crusader for women's rights and strengths. He delineates the freedoms and oppressions faced by women in their traditional roles, and portrays a diversity of strong women who make their own space, and reach out for controlling their own destinies sometimes despite and sometimes because of traditional codes of conduct. No sooner do I type these words onto the computer screen than other voices jam the system, clamouring to be heard:

> He is what's-its-name a doubledyed chauvinist, look how he uses women as sex objects and nothing but, look at Madame Jocasta, Pinkie Aurangzeb and Farah the Parsee.
>
> That's right, and a racist to boot, charging Parsees with unbridled sexuality, poor Shahbanou.
>
> Racist all right, denying his own race, country and religion, desecrating women right left and centre, stripping Bilquis nude to her dupatta and stretching his filthy hand even to the wives of the Prophet, upon whom be peace. Racist pig.
>
> Bloody brown sahib is what. So why doesn't he ever say anything against Christianity huh? or Judaism? Always coming down on eastern religions, giving goddess names to Padma and Parvati, illiterates and magicians.

If we were to tabulate a case history of Mr. Rushdie and take cognizance of the inter-relatedness of his fiction with his own life and training in the West since the age of fourteen, it would not be illogical to deduce that the dysfunctional-family syndrome that we see in his fiction is symptomatic of larger problems at the personal and ethnocultural levels.

As an avant-garde intellectual, it is not at all surprising that Rushdie should project the Lacanian paradigm of the conflict between the imaginary state of bonding with the mother and the symbolic state of developed consciousness. The situation becomes more complex when one sees that the process of individuation is hindered by cultural repressions.

Is there a single person in his novels who is plainandsimple faithful to the spouse?

Or any scene saying halleluiah to plainandsimple marital love? Always perverted, always and only brutish carnal cavorting, shame shame.

Who he thinks he is? How he can know anything about parents' love and Shakil Sisters' mourning for their son? Poking fun at old people, Reverend Mother and Bariamma and Dolores O'Toole, so what if god gives one a moustache, another baldness or a humpback?

Exactly, god makes some children empty in the breadbin as Bilquis says; so who is Salman to drag poor Sufiya and Toxy Catrack for all the world to see?

The voices go on, more insistent than the radio waves set up by Midnight's children.

One could retract the first line of the first paragraph and go on to substantiate all the rest and prove that what's-its-name is a double-dyed male chauvinist. Given the excesses of sexual acrobatics in *Grimus,* and Padma's preoccupation with Saleem's 'other pencil', and the much publicized polemics of the brothel in *The Satanic Verses,* it will not be too difficult to advance an argument that women are trivialized and exaggeratedly sexualized.

Or, one could erase all but the first line and bring forward Robert Graves and Leslie Fiedler, Edward Said and Jacques Lacan, Derrida and Kristeva, to show that Rushdie is indeed weaving patterns—mythic, historical, anticolonial, psychoanalytic, deconstructionist, semiotic—which delineate women with an authenticity of detail that characterizes Rani Humayun's eighteen shawls.

This route is tempting, for these are contemporary criticism's gods and one must pay due homage to these outer shrines before entering the inner shrine where cultural sensitivity and common sense are the perambulatory paths to a more down-to-earth form of apprecia-ting the sculpted beauty of the text against life as lived rather than as dissected by literary pundits. However, in the present context of tradition and modernity, it is practical to restrict oneself to one of the other shrines—The White Goddess.

Graves, in *The White Goddess*, divides women into three mythological representations: Diana, virgin goddess; Venus, goddess of love, sex and fertility; and Hecate, goddess of death and oracles. The White-Goddess is all three; she is the Moon in its three phases—New, Full and Waning. Graves traces how all ancient cultures had the same central concept of the triple female identity that represented the three phases of youth, maturity and decay in Nature's cycle. He quotes from Apuleius' vision of the Queen of Heaven who reveals herself to be Ceres, Diana, Minerva, Proserpine, Juno, Hecate and indeed mother of all creation.

The concept of the Triple Goddess, as feminist critics such as Mary Daly have discussed, was present in all ancient cultures, but was displaced in each by patriarchy. Daly summarizes the identity of the Triple Goddess in various ancient religions: Hera-Demeter-Kore of pre-Hellenic times, Thetis, Amphitrite, Nereis of Hellenic mythology, Neith Triple Goddess of Libya, Eire, Phodla, Banbha of Ireland, and Myrine who was mother of the gods in Phrygian lore. In Hinduism, Parvati, Lakshmi and Sarasvati could be the equivalent rather than the parallel of the White Goddess, in that they are the triple deity but do not correspond to virgin, lover and crone but to three traits fundamental to continuity of culture and civilization, namely, creativity, progress, and transmission of cumulative knowledge.

In Rushdie's fiction, we see the Triple Goddess vindicated both in individuals and as a principle. As individual, we see her in Naseem Ghani—Mrs. Aadam Aziz—Reverend Mother, changing from virginal goddess to be adored through a white perforated sheet in snow-covered Kashmir, to Venus and Ceres running a household of five children, husband and servants in Agra, to Hecate presiding over the Sinai household in Bombay. We see the Triple Goddess phases in Amina though she is never as dominant at any stage as Naseem. We see her in a perverted but identifiable form in Kamala Sutra-Media-Livia/Jocasta in *Grimus*.

As principle, Graves' White Goddess is present in *The Satanic Verses*. Lat, Uzza and Manat 'are the exalted birds, and their intercession is desired indeed' (p. 114). In *The Serpent and the Rope*, Raja Rao's Rama says that Catholicism became a universal religion once the Mother of God replaced the Son of Man. So it is with

Jahilia's new religion in *The Satanic Verses*. Rushdie recognizes this human need for the goddess; as soon as Mahound pays tribute to the patron deities of the town, Grandee Abu Simbel and Hind accept his new faith, and the populace follows their lead:

> both the crowd in the tent and the overflow of men and women outside it, begins to kneel, row by row, the movement rippling outwards from Hind and the Grandee as though they were pebbles thrown into a lake. (*SV*, 115)

The homage of Abu Simbel and Hind is motivated by politics but the crowd's homage is only partly dictated by the political powers of the day; they bow down because the new religion combined the best of the old tenets and infused new blood. Their goddesses were Allah's daughters. That history took a wrong turn in ousting the goddesses is another story.

The traditional *burqa*, that covers women from top to toe, is in a way symbolic of the banishment of the goddesses from human sight. In Rushdie, the *burqa* is a touchstone of the measure of one's negative traditionalism. One of the first rules that Aadam Aziz lays down to his wife is that she give up purdah. Culturally indoctrinated into certain ideas of what constitutes immodesty, Naseem reacts with dismay: 'You want me to walk naked in front of strange men'. When he argues that her dress covers everything but her face and feet, she cries, 'They will see more than that! They will see my deep-deep shame!' (*MNC*, 34). Aadam's mother had shed her *burqa* even earlier, rising to the exigencies of being a businesswoman. Both women quickly shed a tradition and enter modernity. For the women of *Shame*, it is not so easy to step out of figurative purdah whether or not they wear a *burqa*. However, despite their traditional handicap, they strike out for a certain measure of identity and independence.

Rushdie recognizes the strength there is in women and also the force of the chains that bind them. His women characters are strong and individualistic. They take over whatever space they are in; even if it is as narrow as the single bed on which Sufiya Zinobia sleeps, it is theirs and woe to the one who dares encroach on their personal space. Of this takeover, the author says in *Shame*:

> I had thought, before I began, that what I had on my hands was an almost excessively masculine tale, a saga of sexual rivalry, ambition, power, patronage, betrayal, death, revenge. But the women seem to have taken over; they marched in from the peripheries of the story to demand the inclusion of

their own tragedies, histories and comedies . . . It occurs to me that the women knew precisely what they were up to—that their stories explain, and even subsume, the men's. (*S*, 173)

He goes on to say:

it goes without saying that not all women are crushed by any system, no matter how oppressive. It is commonly, and I believe accurately, said of Pakistan that her women are much more impressive than her men . . . their chains, nevertheless, are no fictions. (*S*, 173)

These statements might well form the core of any study of Rushdie's delineation of women.

It is noteworthy that Rushdie uses the pronoun 'her' for Pakistan. This might be merely due to the translation involved from Urdu to English, assuming that the 'common' saying would be in the vernacular. However, since this is the only place where Pakistan is personified and given a gender, it should be taken as significant. Despite Rushdie's impatience at Indians' propensity to confer allegory on literary creations (interview in *Kunapipi*) Pakistan has to be seen as a woman ravaged by an all-male domination. Like Bilquis', Pakistan 'was unclothed by change, but . . . wrapped herself in certainties' (*S*, 67) and in an existential sense, certainties are deceptive. Arjumand Harappa, contemptuous of her sex as many abused women are, rejects it, trains herself to be masculine, and joins the patriarchal group to the further abuse of the country. But Rushdie is right in disapproving of allegorical readings in that allegories tend to universalize situations and to distance the reader from the personal experiences of the characters as individuals. As Margaret Atwood says in *Survival*, victimization can conveniently be adduced to a 'necessity decreed by History, or Economics, or the Unconscious, or any other large general powerful idea' (*Survival*, 37).

Atwood's four basic victim positions—denial, explaining away as defined above, a will to change the situation, and being a 'creative non-victim' might be an appropriate chart by which to categorize Rushdie's women characters. However, as with the White Goddess paradigm, this will be restrictive. Neither in real life, nor in Rushdie, are women to be compartmentalized into one or other pigeon-hole. A more aesthetically productive approach would be to see them as living breathing women moving against the backdrop of a traditional culture that itself is continually evolving.

'Tradition' is an elusive word that defies definition because it ignites instant value judgements; some think of it as sacrosanct, others as hollow idols that must be thrown out. Moreover, different cultures superimpose their own value systems on other cultures; this is particularly dangerous in the light of Western critical imperialism which might see the Indian, Pakistani and Arab cultures delineated in Rushdie's novels as totally benighted and steeped in outdated oppressive 'traditionalism'. To confuse matters still further, there is some relevance to one of the imaginary voices quoted above—that Rushdie's intellectual make-up has been shaped by the West. Armed with the caveats, it is time to meet the women in *Shame*, and consider how each reacts to tradition and modernity. Each one's attitude towards certain key facets of tradition and modernity might yield relevant patterns. One could list certain items on this hypothetical questionnaire: attitude to gender-role expectations in appearance, social behaviour, speech habits, marriage, faithfulness in marriage, parental obligations, personal fulfilment and ambitions.

There are two distinct classes of people in the vertical hierarchy of society that forms the setting of the novel. Most of the minor women characters belong to the working classes, and the major characters belong to an affluent aristocracy. Rushdie eschews the middle class. None of the women is ever seen working in the kitchen or worrying about ration lines or school admission for children, though we are told that Bilquis ran her father's house and was given 'slightly more than her fair share of household duties' in the Bariamma household (*S*, 75). Rushdie excuses himself by saying this is not a realistic novel (*S*, 69) but in many ways it is. It gives a very authentic picture of women caught between the freedoms and oppressions of both tradition and modernity.

Among the minor women characters are those of the town of Q—Zeenat Kabuli and Farida Balloch, and those of the city—Duniyazad Begum. These women are stereotypically traditional but we remember their brief appearance because of the exuberance of their hatred. Zeenat and Farida ensure that Maulana Dawood does not snatch always their hour with his colourful curses; Duniyazad, a cousin in the Bariamma household, flings the most hurtful of all traditional taunts at Bilquis, that of barrenness, and the public fistfight that follows leaves clumps of hair and broken tooth on the dormitory floor.

Among other minor characters are the ayahs, or caregivers in current terminology—Hashmat Bibi in Q—, Isky's nameless ayah in

Mohenjo, and Shahbanou in the city. All three can be seen as stereotypically traditional domestics, totally devoted to their employers. Hashmat Bibi serves the Shakil sisters and their father, ministering to their material needs; Isky's ayah adores him, 'fawning over Iskander as if her were three years old, or a deity, or both' (*S*, 108); Shahbanou is more enigmatic. Her dedication far surpasses the bounds of duty and she ministers to Shakil's physical needs as well as Sufiya's material needs. In this, is she being traditional or modernist? Traditional in that she sacrifices herself in lieu of her mistress whom she genuinely loves, or modernist in being pragmatic about keeping Shakil's health under control, knowing that 'it is only a matter of time before you lose control or burst' (*S*, 211). One would think that these are the two ways of reading her motivation; but a third view, that emerged from a discussion with a friend, is that Shahbanou might just be satisfying her own needs. I do not quite see where the text implies this but I insert this in passing as an example of cross-cultural dialogue. Paul de Man speaks of 'misreading'. A good misreading is 'a text that produces another text which can itself be shown to be an interesting misreading' (1974, p. 51). A misreading turns a work inside out, reverses the traditional reading to reveal layers that are hidden. Perhaps, my reading of Rushdie's women as strong, individualistic characters who make their own space despite great odds is such a creative misreading!

The major characters are Bilquis Hyder and Rani Harappa in the city and the Shakil sisters in Q—. Dichotomy and pairs abound in Rushdie. The Shakil household parallels and contrasts the Bariamma household. Both are patterned on a form of traditional autocracy but the contrasts are gendered and through this gendering, Rushdie shows his appreciation of women's strengths. The first is dominated by a patriarch and the second by a matriarch. Whereas the oppression of the first are unmitigated, the oppressions of the second are mixed with a variety of positive qualities. Despite fearing and hating their father, the Shakil sisters end up imitating his arrogance (which ignores and thus alienates the local elite) and his heretical fanaticism (Omar comes into the world 'without benefit of mutilation, barbery or divine approval') and his unrepentant egotism. Arjumand is another product of a father-dominated family.

Given the recurrence of unloving and unlovable, unforgiving and unforgivable fathers in Rushdie's fiction, one might be tempted to say it is an autobiographical component, but given his positive treatment of women, it might be pertinent to hold that Rushdie is distinguishing between male-dominated traditions and female-dominated traditions.

While father-dominated Shakil sisters replicate their father's evil in themselves, the women under Bariamma's rule, even while fearing and hating the domineering matriarch, end up being influenced only by her good qualities, of which she has several, unlike old Shakil who has none. Tradition has much to give to contemporary life, and the sense of family that Bariamma nurtures is one of its positive contributions.

While it is easy to argue that the Bariamma house is traditional and that Bilquis strikes out for modernity by insisting on leaving it, one must ensure that it is understood that the dormitory is Rushdie's exaggerated and extended satire on the joint family system. Rushdie himself is careful to point out one positive aspect of the system: it promotes a sense of family. A.K. Ramanujan has a poem where the speaker says to his wife, 'Really what keeps us apart/at the end of years is unshared/childhood' and thinks, even if facetiously, of the wisdom in the old custom of child marriages which would have 'wed us in the oral cradle'.

In Bariamma's realm, each newcomer was brought into the oral cradle. Family stories, Rushdie says, 'were the glue that held the clan together, binding the generations in webs of whispered secrets'. After several additions and deletions, when Bilquis' story of her rescue by Raza settled down into hallowed text, 'Bilquis knew that she had become a member of the family: in the sanctification of her text lay initiation, kinship, blood' (*S*, pp. 76-7).

The family as centre was integral to the traditional culture of the subcontinent. Rushdie has said that he sees the leadership of Pakistan, and other dictatorships, as revolving around family cliques, and therefore the analogy fits at the literal and figurative levels. It is significant at both levels that the extended family is quickly reduced to three nuclear families—those of Isky, Raza and Mir. Even as it has all but vanished from contemporary life, the Bariamma model of family vanished with time within the novel. Of the forty thieves and their partners, only two pairs continued their interaction—Bilquis-Raza and Rani-Isky. Bilquis, Raza and Rani are from mother-figure-dominated families. Though Bilquis is brought up by her father, he is called Mahmoud the Woman because of his lack of aggressiveness and therefore Bilquis can be said to have the same background as Rani who grows up under Bariamma's tutelage.

Bilquis and Rani have conventional dreams of getting out of a confined environment and becoming queens by virtue of marrying a prince. To invert the fairy tale archetype, they expect to be transformed from moth to butterfly, from frog to princess as soon as the designated prince kisses them. Bilquis is chosen by Raza whereas Rani's marriage is arranged in a conventional manner; but both have the same partly romanticized, partly passive attitude to marriage. Both enjoy love making and seem to be fully satisfied and fully to satisfy their husbands. But married life changes a woman's course even in the most harmonious of unions, and for these two it changes drastically because of their husband's political ambitions. Isky peremptorily silences Rani when she, lulled with her first love making, speaks of his companion, the doctor 'that everybody in town is calling such a bad influence on you' (*S*, 80). This is an omen of what is to come in their future together. Isky will go his way and Rani must draw from whatever inner strengths family and genes have given her. Similarly, Bilquis' future with Raza is foretold in her beginning. Rescued during pre-partition riots, wooed with gifts from plundered booty, she starts her wedded life as a nomadic soldier's wife and ends it that way, though Raza at some point became primarily a soldier of Islam.

Both Bilquis and Rani are left alone for long periods of time by their husbands. Their friendship realistically shows the bond that often develops between women. They candidly share secrets and hopes in the Diana phase; they brag about their spouse's sexual prowess and their pastimes in the Venus phase; they can be quite cattish as seen in Bilquis retailing tidbits of gossip over the phone about Isky's philandering; but there is a bond between them that withstands their husband's bitter rivalries. The bond is due to the traditions they share and not due to similarities in character because they are very different.

They react differently to similar situations. When Rani hears of Isky's affair with Mir's woman, she continues to embroider, keeping her anger under control with regality, and in time becomes as

* grass-widow = women whose husbands are away, as with soldiers-gone-to-war

formidable a figure as Dickens' Mme. Defarge; when on the other hand Bilquis is told of Raza's unsuccessful wooing of Pinkie, she takes the comment as an insult and forces Raza to consider it as a matter of besmirched honour. When forced into grass-widowhood' by their husbands' absence, Rani takes recourse to embroidering her anger into her shawls whereas Bilquis has an affair with Sindbad Mengal, who is, ironically, a cinema man like her father. When their world turns topsy turvy around them, Rani withdraws into herself, both at the time of Mir's raid on Mohenjo and when placed under house arrest; but Bilquis loses her mental balance. The loo wind symbolizes change for Bilquis and she is terrified of it. Rani holds her own to the very end. Both are almost vengefully faithful to their spouses towards the end. Rani skilfully manoeuvers to find out that Isky had been murdered before being hanged, and Bilquis engineers Raza's escape from his house before Armageddon.

Bilquis, who yearned for fixities, is driven from Delhi to Karachi to Quetta and finally dies a horrible death. Her wedded life ends as it began, in flight but also with commitment to each other. Rushdie has little sympathy for Raza and the man he represents in real life, but as a good writer he has inscribed patterns perhaps despite himself. Raza might be a stupid dictator advised by a vengeful fanatic (Dawood); he might have been blinded by his desire for a son to the point of being traumatizingly cruel to his newborn daughter; but there are moments of infinite tenderness in him. For example, when he carries Sufiya in his arms after she has decapitated Pinkie's turkeys; when at Naveed's funeral he looks at Bilquis and sees her 'history as a slow retreat from that early nudity into the secrecy of the veil' and murmurs, 'Ah Bilquis, what happened to our lives?' (*S*, 228); and most poignantly, when he finds Bilquis in the far room of the Shakil dungeons:

> 'Don't worry, Billoo', he whispered to her, 'Raza is here. I'll clean you up good and proper and then you'll see . . . What's the meaning of this, you're not supposed to die?' (*S*, 280)

Raza is to a great extent a scion of Bariamma's matriarchal mould, after all. Through the references to the *burqa* image and the decay of love between Raza and Bilquis, Rushdie communicates the failure of Pakistan as well as the sadness of women's plight as the country regressed into a religious dictatorship.

Both Bilquis and Rani are more sinned against than sinning. We empathize with their limited options and their essential humanity. We admire Rushdie for his sensitive portrayal of their aspirations and the unjust suffering forced on them by their husbands' ambitions and infidelities. Having Rani Harappa sign her shawls as Rani Humayun is a fine touch of inscribing identity on one who deserved it.

Rushdie makes ironical use of setting and of choice of names to trace the two courses. Rani's last name, Humayun, recalls the Moghul emperor who spent most of his reign in exile. Rani's name changes to Harappa and she is immured alive in a baroque mansion in Mohenjo's unending arid landscape that is 'afflicted by chronic water shortage, populated by scornful monsters' (*S*, 94). Mohenjo, Daro and Harappa combine to recall the ancient civilizations of the past. Instead of focusing on the advanced aspects of these cultures that flourished when most of the world was populated by primitive barbarians, Rushdie uses the setting as symbolic of stagnation and obsolescence. Negative traditionalism has Rani in throe here; she is surrounded by peasant girls who help themselves to her trousseau and ancient servants, 'in this house it's still what Isky's ayah says' (*S*, 93-4); her home is raided by barbarians who see women as possessions; occasionally, when Isky feels guilty about the isolation he has forced on her, he descends with an entourage of pimps and floozies, as Naveed would say, and upsets her further. Here everything is ruled by *takallouf*, 'a form of tongue-tying formality, a social restraint so extreme as to make it impossible for the victim to express what he or she really means, a species of compulsory irony that insists, for the sake of good form, on being taken literally' (*S*, 104), as Rushdie defines it in the context of Bilquis and Raza.

Both women are victimized by tradition. But it is paradoxical, perhaps more ironical than paradoxical, that both find a measure of freedom because of tradition. Tradition dictates that a man support his family no matter what; tradition dictates that a woman run her household no matter what. Despite the erosion of love and trust, the accretion of veneers in time gives a measure of solidity and stability. Money, the earning and saving of wealth, keeping accounts, and all the paraphernalia that goes with the amassing and spending of money, is never mentioned; that too is *takallouf*. Old Shakil would have died in debtor's prison in Dickens, and Bilquis and Rani spent years in law courts over maintenance and alimony in modern day Eurocentric soap operas and real life, but in the cultural setting of *Shame*, mentioning money or lack thereof is tabooed. Bilquis and

Rani can and do have a material sense of security that is part of the package of this cultural misogyny. A man's home is his castle, the saying goes in one part of the world; in another part, a woman's home is her castle, even if it turns out to be a living tomb. Because of this, women can build a strange and sad kind of autonomy for themselves as we see with Bilquis, and especially with Rani.

But one trait that is absent in Bilquis and Rani is maternal love. Indeed, positive parental emotions are conspicuously absent in Rushdie's fiction. Whereas fathers are usually unforgiving and unforgivable in their dealings with their offspring, mothers have a cavalier spirit of abandonment towards their children. The mothers in his novels are not particularly maternal; none of them seems to have the character traits usually associated with mothers—gentleness, self-sacrifice, nurturance—; all that can be said in their faviour is that they do not inspire or instigate violence and abuse in their offspring the way fathers do. The mothers are indifferent, callous, or selfish. It is implied that Bilquis might have smacked or thrown Sufiya and brought about her retardation; the chasm between Rani and her daughter is wide enough to hold the Grand Canyon; Naveed has twenty-seven children but she is not a mother. The only one who is deeply desirous of having babies and loves them is Sufiya Zinobia. She plays with Naveed's babies as often she can.

> She likes watching them crawl, fall over, make funny noises, likes knowing more than them. She skips for them: O the wonder in their eyes. (*S*, 214)

Rushdie's handling of retarded children is sensitive and immensely poignant, as I have argued in my 'Girl Children in Rushdie's Novels' (ed. by Viney Kirpal, 1991). It is significant that he makes them girls. Through his women, and girl children, Rushdie covers a wide range of injustices. He sums up his view of the effect of these injustices in two authorial appearances—the key passage about the three characters who inspired the character of Sufiya Zinobia (*S*, 115-17) and where he talks of women having taken over his narrative, which ends with:

> If you hold down one thing you hold down the adjoining. In the end, though, it all blows up in your face. (*S*, 173)

A family that ill treats its women will destroy itself, as happens at the end of the novel.

But what of the other women in *Shame*? Farah Zoroaster, Pinkie

Aurangzeb, Arjumand Harappa and Naveed Hyder, strong characters every one of them, who march out and grabs father time/opportunity by the beard and drags him to their lair.

These characters' lives show they are a new breed of women, intelligent, astute, ambitious. Common to all is a braggadocio way of talking, a supreme confidence in oneself, an all out thrust at ignoring tradition in their search for self-fulfilment. All of them start or end with an uninhibited scorn for the opposite sex and the state of marriage.

Of the four, Arjumand is the only one who is trained for a profession other than housekeeping. Like the other women, her ambition is to be linked to a great man, to be the force behind his greatness. The man is her father, rather than the suitor fantasized by virginal Rani or the flesh and blood husband loved by bridal Bilquis. In words that echo Bilquis', Arjumand tells Isky, 'What things won't you do? Just wait and see' (*S*, 126). And when she echoes her mother's long-ago words about Omar Shakil, her father smiles in agreement. And when he tells her, 'It's a man's world, Arjumand. Rise above your gender as you grow. This is no place to be a woman in' (*S*, 126), she takes him at his word and thenceforward rejects her gender.

As she grows into womanhood, she spurns her body and makes herself look and behave like a man, flatchested and stern; she spurns men and when the crowd of suitors at the gate creates a perpetual traffic jam, she goes off to a women's college; but women fall in love with her as passionately and hopelessly as the men had, and she returns to her father, eager to be by his side as he rose to power. Then, Oedipus more than biology takes over; she falls in love with Haroun Harappa who looks exactly like her father did in youth. But Haroun's marriage is arranged with Naveed, and she retreats in rage, to be Virgin Ironpants then on. She is devastating as a lawyer. As a modernist, she reprimands her father for comparing his job of making 'this country as a man would build a marriage. With strength as well as caring'. She retorts, 'Polygamist . . . what an old-fashioned backward type at heart! It's just marriages and concubines you want. Modern man, my foot' (*S*. 183). But her father can do no wrong, and her world-view is that of a man, anyway. Women have no place in her life, not even her mother, Rani, whom she rejects because Rani refuses to go along with the Alexandrine myth that she builds around Isky.

In conclusion, Arjumand is a modernist who prepares herself to lead the country into progressive changes but she offers no model for the modern woman who feels it is her right to have both marriage and career. Arjumand is a prototype of the phase in Western feminism where women professionals paid the price of spinsterhood and/or childlessness. Moreover, her philosophy is too deeply imbued with the abrogation of human feelings and failings to be considered admirable. Most important, strong and independent though she is, she is too much a worshipper of a male hero to be an ideal new woman.

Farah Zoroaster is kindred spirit to foul-mouthed, brash Evie Lilith Burns of *Midnight's Children* and Azra who scorns the love of the postman early in *Shame*. Farah rides roughshod over Omar's amorous advances; her vocabulary and actions show not only her independence from traditional constraints but a conscious will to shock: 'I shit on your words . . . you got the hots, no more to it than that' (p. 29). 'Drop this jungle-boy business, you're no fucking ape-man, sonny jim' (p. 31). Like Evie, she kindles a passion that turns destructive when frustrated. Saleem Sinai, the voyeur, gets into Evie's head; Omar Shakil, also a voyeur, takes the more common route of rape. Rushdie has Omar repeat his rationalization, 'She was willing . . . she must have been willing, and everybody knows the risk' (*S*, 52) but in the slight variation, Rushdie encapsulates what psychiatrists and social workers have established as a clear pattern of self-exoneration in rapists and wife beaters: an illogical assumption that 'she *must have been* willing'. Rushdie excels in building up the reader's awareness of injustices meted out to women even while dealing with a quite unlikeable person.

Naveed is another such example. She alienates the reader from the moment she appears on stage as a pre-teenager. But looking deeper, the influence of traditional role-expectations is clear. Even at age ten, she is obsessed with the idea of getting married and wants long hair because she has heard that 'men grow crazy for shiny hair that you can put under your bums' (*S*, 136). It should be noted that her obsession is for marriage and not directed towards promiscuity. When Bilquis brings forward the name of Haroun Harappa as a possible match, Naveed is brutally pragmatic:

'I don't need to look at any stupid photograph', she told Bilquis, 'he's famous, he's rich, he's a husband, let's catch him quick'. (*S*, 155)

In her supreme self-confidence, she says she'll 'fix him' when Bilquis points out that Haroun is 'bad to his daddy'. She flouts tradition and throws family honour to the winds when she backs out of the betrothal with a characteristic, 'I won't marry that stupid potato'. Love, as Rushdie says, 'was the last thing anyone had been expecting to foul up arrangements' (*S*, 165). In a traditional set-up one married for fame, riches, political advancement, not for love. Naveed struck out for love, for modernity in making matrimonial relationship. And what happened? Her husband

> came to her once a year and ordered her to get ready, because it was time to plant the seed, until she felt like a vegetable patch . . . and understood that there was no hope for women in the world, because whether you were respectable or not the men got you anyway, no matter how hard you tried to be the most proper of ladies the men would come and stuff you full of alien unwanted life. (*S*, 207)

Again, in a single sentence Rushdie summarizes the oppressive lot of women through a character who is quite unlikeable and yet who is so clearly a victim of a male-centred society that the reader is moved to sympathy. Naveed's fertility is symbolic of Pakistan's population explosion at the level of political allegory, but at the level of social satire, it only slightly exaggerates women's lack of autonomy in deciding when or when not to have children.

Pinkie Aurangzeb's position *vis-a-vis* tradition/modernity is more complex. She is yet another strong, self-confident woman. She has scant regard for the sanctity of marriage vows. She is Isky's twin soul in many ways. She flirts outrageously and picks up whomever she wants whenever she wants. But unlike Isky and Raza who have attractive helpmeets, Pinkie has a doddering old husband who knows how to hold his drink without spilling a drop even when asleep but is clearly good for little else. 'Trapped in a marriage with a dotard, Pinkie finds her pleasures wherever she can' (*S*, 104). There is a hint of justification for her promiscuity.

Pinkie's is a complex case. Liaisons such as hers dot the pages of history, sometimes glamourized, sometimes held up an example of what not to be. So, one cannot rush to a hasty conclusion that she was being modernist in her unfaithfulness that modernist Rushdie seems to excuse, or that Rushdie has transplanted the salons of Paris to this locale. The pertinent question is, how does it all end? Thrown out unceremoniously by Isky, she remained faithful to him until 'the day of his death, when after setting fire to an old embroidered shawl she hacked out her own heart with a nine-inch kitchen knife' (*S*, 106).

It is difficult to surmise why Rushdie gave her this ending. Was it dictated by some real life analogy to the figures represented by Isky and Pinkie? Rushdie has obviously taken liberties with historical analogs in numerous instances in order to remain true to his muse; so why not now? or is this what his muse would endorse? Was it to redeem Pinkie's promiscuous image in the minds of traditionalists? Unlikely, given Rushdie's irreverent swipes at traditionalism. Was it to raise these lovers to some sort of Antony and Cleopatra level? Not likely, given his open dislike of fictional Harappa and historical Bhutto. Why then does he pack Pinkie off to the hereafter in this extremely traditional manner?

Pinkie Aurangzeb is the only woman in the novel who claims equality in terms of sexual freedom, doing what men traditionally do, namely, use the opposite sex for sexual gratification without any qualms of conscience. Farah is raped; Bilquis is seduced by a lewd-mouthed playboy. But Pinkie is her own woman, she picks and chooses, who excels in the game that is traditionally a male prerogative. Granted that two wrongs do not make a right and that the way to combat men's promiscuity is not by admiring or condoning the same behaviour in women; still, Pinkie's independence and initiative in sexual indulgence does arouse a streak of appreciation, and one feels regret that she turns out after all like the hundreds of heroines on the traditional Indian movie screen. Especially when taken in the context of the parade of women just analyzed, one wonders why Rushdie did not hold at least one example of an independent, strong-minded woman who approached sexual freedom with the same irreverent vitality that so many of his male characters assume. It is not indoctrinated traditionalism that restrained them for they were rebels as we have seen. It is not any saccharine sweetness of innate womanhood for most of them lack stereotypical womanly virtues and are quite unlikeable. It is Rushdie, in short, and not the characters themselves who shape this aspect of their fate.

Yes, one wonders with deep dismay why all these women who deviate from the traditional role of faithful wife and devoted child-bearer come to grief. It is small comfort to be told, in the mode of Professor Higgins' rejoinder when Eliza contrasted his rudeness to Pickering's politeness, that even women who do not deviate from traditional role expectations come to grief in Rushdie. Rushdie, as one sensitive enough to know that the chains that bind women are no fictions, as one courageous, or imprudent, enough to challenge long-established beliefs, could have given us a truly modernist woman. Perhaps it could not be Arjumand because the political allegory did not quite permit it, but it could have been Farah who could have come back to Q— to be other than the old crone he makes her, or Rani who could have come into her own after Isky's death, or Pinkie Aurangzeb. Making Pinkie another of the thousand 'good bad-girl', to use Fiedler's classification for the Marilyn Monroe prototype, who have died tear-jerker deaths on the silver screen of India is a lapse that is regrettable indeed.

REFERENCES

Makarand Paranjpe, ed., *Indian Poetry in English* (Madras: Macmillan, 1993), pp. 152-4.

Margaret Atwood, *Survival: A Thematic Guide to Canadian Literature,* Toronto: Anansi, 1972.

Mary Daly, *Gyn/Ecology: The Meta Ethics of Radical Feminism* (Boston: Beacon, 1978).

Leslie Fiedler, *Love and Death in the American Novel* (New York: Criterion Books, 1960).

Robert Graves, *The White Goddess* (New York: American Book-Stratford, 1948).

Paul de Man, 'Nietzsche's Theory of Rhetoric', *Symposium* 28 (1974).

Raja Rao, *The Serpent and the Rope* (London: John Murray, 1960).

Salman Rushdie, *Grimus* (London: Victor Gollacz, 1975).

———, *Midnight's Children* (London: Jonathan Cape, 1981).

———, *The Satanic Verses* (London: Penguin, 1988) (identified as *SV*).

———, *Shame* (London: Jonathan Cape, 1983) (identified as *S*).

———, 'Interview with Rushdie', *Kunapipi* 4.2(1982): 17-26.

The Crisis of Contemporary India in Nayantara Sahgal's Fiction

Makarand Paranjape

INTRODUCTION

I have set myself the task of trying to understand Nayantara Sahgal's novels in terms of how her women characters respond to the phenomenon of change. How do they cope with the rival pulls of tradition and modernity in their search for identity, independence, fulfilment, and love—whether within marriage or outside it? How, in their journey to selfhood, do they negotiate with various personal, social, religious, and political issues? In brief, how they cope with their lives in contemporary India.

But such a task begs more questions: what do we mean by tradition? By modernity? Why does the issue have special relevance to India? How does it change when it confronts women? What knowledge can a novelist give us in her telling of a story? Surely, my assigned task forces me to contend with such questions. Consequently, my text will contain my responses to them—either tacit, as is usually the case, or overt as it is here.

The article is divided into three parts. Part I defines the problem as I see it. Part II is, more or less, a survey of the critical opinions available on the problem. Part III is the paper proper, offering my response to the task at hand. This part is, in turn, divided into three sections according to the three senses in which the tradition-modernity problem finds its definition in Sahgal's work. The first section discusses tradition in the sense of the general religious and ideological inheritance of a society and the effect it has on women. The second section examines tradition in the more specific sense of tradition in politics as seen in the subplots of the novels. Finally, in the third section, I attempt to offer Sahgal's particular synthesis

* First published in the special Indian number of *World Literature Today*, 68:2 (Spring 1994) pp. 291-8.

between tradition and modernity by examining the values of her protagonists.

I must clarify at the outset that my paper is confined to five novels: *This Time of Morning* (1966, rpt. New Delhi: Hind Pocket Books, n.d., henceforth abbreviated as *TTM*); *Storm in Chandigarh* (New Delhi: Orient Paperbacks, 1969, henceforth abbreviated as *SC*); *The Day in Shadow* (1971, rpt. New Delhi: Penguin, 1991, henceforth abbreviated as *DS*); *A Situation in New Delhi* (New Delhi: Vikas, 1977, henceforth abbreviated as *SND*); and *Rich Like Us* (London: Heinemann, 1985, henceforth abbreviated as *RLU*). All these novels have women protagonists at their centre; three of them have women walking out of bad marriages; and all of them are concerned with the problems of single women trying to survive in a male dominated society. The first novel, *A Time to be Happy* (1958, rpt. New Delhi: Sterling Paperback, 1975) does not fall into this category. It is the portrait of three, changing upper-middle class families, the Shivpals, the Sahais, and the Mathurs, and lacks a strong female protagonist. Nor do the later novels, *Plans for Departure* (London: Heinemann, 1986) or *Mistaken Identity* (London: Heinemann, 1988) focus directly on the problems of women in a changing society. *Plans for Departure* is essentially about memory, time, and cultural perception. Its protagonist, Anna, is a Danish woman who recalls the years she spent in India. *Mistaken Identity* is an allegory against the divisive effects of communalism. The protagonist, a minor princeling, suffers from a severe sense of alienation as India moves towards independence. He falls in love with a Muslim girl, which leads to a riot, and spends several months in a jail because he is mistaken for a revolutionary by the inept colonial police. Hence, only the above-named five novels directly address the question at hand.

THE TRADITION-MODERNITY PROBLEMATIC

To me, Nayantara Sahgal's novels are meaningful as chronicles of a larger narrative, indeed, as I might argue most of Indian English fiction is. The work of Mulk Raj Anand, R.K. Narayan, Raja Rao, and all the other novelists featured (or not) in this anthology is meaningful, to me, as part of this ongoing and evolving 'big' story. So is this anthology and this paper itself. We are all simply a part of one big story or proto-narrative, our own 'little' stories adding to its totality. We are not only a part of it, but also, in our own ways, making it happen, altering it in trying to understand and define it in relation to ourselves. This big story is the story of the growth and development of modern India, starting perhaps at the beginning of the nineteenth century and continuing into the present times.

Like all stories, the story of the development of modern India has some key themes. These themes recur in all narratives on modern India. They are ways of organizing the contents, of making sense of the multiplicity and diversity, of imposing some order on the chaotic plenitude that inheres in the story of modern India. Some of them are: colonialism, nationalism, partition, independence, regionalism, communalism, revivalism, Westernization, Sanskritization, science, religion, caste, urbanization, feminism, capitalism, socialism, and so on and so forth. These themes constitute the keynotes of this big story. We see them being played out again and again, not only in fiction but in our daily lives.

One such big theme is 'tradition and modernity'. This theme seems to hold a lot of explanatory power because of the peculiar social formation prevalent in India. When measured against Western standards, we are a 'traditional' society; measured against our own past, we are 'modern'. This tension, conflict, and struggle between what we have inherited and what we wish to become recurs in our lives from generation to generation. In fact, one way of characterising modern India would be by considering it a society in transition: a great tradition, as Robert Redfield put it, modernising itself. In other words, the story of modern India itself is a tradition-modernity story. Every novel, every poem, every work of art in modern India, then, either explicitly or implicitly, is one version and articulation of this big movement of our culture and nation. The tradition-modernity paradigm, therefore, defines our culture and our culture, in turn, determines the thematic parameters of the texts which it generates through various authors.

The question for me is—what is Nayantara Sahgal's formulation of this problem? How does she see tradition? Modernity? And the struggle between them? How do her characters respond to this issue? No doubt, to tease out such answers from fictional texts requires some yardsticks I must myself own and accept. Like Sahgal I must, willy-nilly, have my own answers to these questions without which I may not be able to make sense of her responses in the novels. That is, this paper itself must have implicit in it some version of the story of modern India. Let me, briefly, try to give voice to the paper's own formulation of the tradition-modernity story.

To begin with, I do not see tradition and modernity as automatically opposed to one another. There is a tradition of modernity itself as there is the potential for modernity and change in tradition. Likewise, I see tradition as not necessarily evil. If by tradition is meant all that is handed down to us, then certainly not all of it can be bad. Tradition, then, is the repository of both good and evil and its use and abuse must be separated from tradition itself. Similarly, modernity cannot be all good if it simply means what is the latest. Everything in the present or from recent times cannot be of positive value; much of it, in fact, is more horrible both qualitatively and quantitatively than anything humankind has witnessed in the past. Both tradition and modernity are mixed categories, descriptive rather than normative. Because they are value-loaded, we cannot see them in simple unitary terms. We must be alive to their inner contradictions, tensions, and oppositions and also be aware of their overlaps and interpenetrations.[1]

If tradition-modernity is an important theme in our big story, the East-West conflict, by this or any other name, is another. Often, the two are seen as closely related. But surely everything modern is not Western just as everything traditional is not Eastern. True, the Occident has defined itself by its break with the past, while we seem to define ourselves by our continuity with it. But *satyagraha* is as modern as the atom bomb and as much as part of world culture. We have contributed to the making of modernity just as the West has contributed to our invention of our tradition. Because, in the ultimate analysis, tradition must be constructed or even invented; it does not merely exist as the given. From a vast multiplicity of possible meanings, our choosing one interpretation underscores the dynamism of the process of tradition-making. No doubt, the powers that be influence this process, even control it; but this only serves to underline for the rest of us that their version of tradition is not immutable, incontrovertible, and immaculate.[2]

TRADITION-MODERNITY IN NAYANTARA SAHGAL'S FICTION: SOME CRITICAL OPINIONS

Coming to Sahgal's novels, it would be salutary to begin with the conventional wisdom on the subject, both the critics' and the author's, before offering my animadversions.

In the last chapter of what was the first book on Sahgal, A.V. Krishna Rao addresses himself to this question of tradition and modernity:

> unlike some other Indian novelists in English who indiscriminately affirm the Indian cultural milieu, she seeks to excoriate the diseased and the decadent part of the Indian tradition. She does not however go with Mulkraj [*sic*] Anand in making loud and strident protests against the concept of conformity to tradition in favour of some alien idea of social justice; on the contrary, she dives deep into the sustaining springs of the composite cultural tradition of India and comes up to affirm that aspect of Indian tradition which possesses and promises a survival value. She is thus neither an out-and-out conformist nor a thoroughbred non-conformist. She is neither too submissive to the dictates of an orthodox tradition nor too much in love with revolutionary romanticism. She accepts the ***composite*** character of the Indian tradition and affirms its catholicity which allows for the human being maximum freedom. (*Nayantara Sahgal* Madras: M. Seshachalam, 1976, 91-2)

The passage is remarkable for its clarity and insight, more so because it was written before the later works, *Rich Like Us* (1985), *Plans for Departure* (1986), and *Mistaken Identity* (1988). Rao assigns for Sahgal the middle path between tradition and modernity. Unlike Raja Rao, who emerges as a traditionalist or Anand who is mostly anti-tradition, Sahgal is somewhere in the middle. However, to define her position as exactly as possible by evaluating the content of her work is something that Rao does not do. He merely provides us with a framework for analysis, a framework which I accept because of its continued viability. In fact, I would go further to assert that every Indian writer can be located on this axis of tradition versus modernity; in every writer we shall find a mix of both. But the task, ultimately, is to identify which aspects of tradition a writer endorses and which she opposes. This is something that I shall attempt to do later.

Jasbir Jain, whose monograph *Nayantara Sahgal* (New Delhi: Arnold-Heinemann, 1978) appeared two years after Rao's book, more or less endorses the latter's view without adding significantly to it. 'There is much in tradition which she values and a great deal in modernity which she rejects' (p. 33) says Jain. But she fails to point out, like Rao, exactly what Sahgal values in tradition and what she rejects in modernity.

The link between the question of tradition modernity and the position of women in India is supplied by Sahgal herself. In several interviews, she has stated that one of her major themes is the definition of the virtuous woman:

> right from the beginning my women have been a sort of new definition of the virtuous woman. The virtuous woman, according to tradition, is ideally a kind of 'sati', i.e. one whose life ends in self-immolation. She is there to suffer, to stay put, and to endure all the problems that come her way. My women, right from the start of my novels, have walked out. . . . (Varalakshmi, p. 282)[3]

The same idea is repeated in Sahgal's 'Meet the Author' address organized by the Sahitya Akademi in 1988:

> in every novel the heroine has moved one step further away from the stereotype of the virtuous woman into a new definition of virtue. . . . What does these three women [Rashmi, Saroj, and Simrit] walking out have to do with their virtue? The meaning of *sati* is a virtuous woman. And this is synonymous with self-immolation—a tradition arising out of the concept that woman is her husband's property and has no other life. Traditional virtue lies in staying put, suffering. The new woman does the opposite. No more *sati*, she is determined to live, and to live in self-respect. Her virtue is courage, which is a willingness to risk the unknown and to face the consequences. (Printed as 'Passion for India' in *Indian Literature*, Vol. 32, Jan.-Feb. 1989, p. 84)

These words echo, almost exactly, what Saroj says to Vishal in *SC*. When Vishal asks her, 'And have you no ambition?' she replies, 'I want to be a virtuous woman' (p. 230).

All these quotations emphasize Sahgal's commitment to change. She places the woman at the heart of the tradition-modernity issue; the woman becomes the site where the battle between the two is fought. It is clear that as far as the status of women is concerned, Sahgal is completely against what she perceives to be tradition.

But none of Sahgal's critics, to my knowledge, explains what aspects of tradition she endorses. This is not clear in Sahgal's own statements, though she does provide some clues. In 'Passion for India' she points out that the background for the personal crisis in her novels is usually political: 'And alongside the personal story there is a picture of political erosion, degradation and decay' (p. 85). It seems fairly clear that in novel after novel, Sahgal expresses her dissatisfaction with the 'new' in politics. The new, the modern is often corrupt, ruthless, and fascistic. The old, the traditional, is the

Gandhian, the humanistic, and the compassionate, which the modern displaces.

To sum up, critics have recognized that Sahgal works out a kind of synthesis between tradition and modernity. She accepts some aspects of the former and rejects others; likewise, she accepts some aspects of the latter and rejects others. But what she rejects and accepts are not clearly indicated, either by the critics or by Sahgal. The author, however, does tell us quite emphatically that she sees tradition as being the main cause for the enslavement of women. Her women rebel against such traditions which would force them to suffer silently, without redress. Instead, her women walk out, substituting courage for self-sacrifice, thereby redefining the notion of the virtuous woman.

Women and Change in Nayantara Sahgal's Novels

I will now go on to describe what I see as Sahgal's larger project as a fiction writer, with special reference to the tradition-modernity question and the position of women in her novels. I shall try to develop and critique the secondary sources which I have cited above, adding to them my own understanding of her novels. I would like to make some global assessments first before focusing in detail on what I consider her most significant novel, *RLU*.

It seems to me that Sahgal sees tradition in two related ways. In its broader sense, tradition refers to Hinduism—that set of beliefs and practices which determine the mental make-up of most Indians. Tradition, in this sense, is responsible for social mores and thus, ultimately, for how individuals, particularly women, behave within the family and in a marriage. Indirectly, it is also responsible for political attitudes, for how a particular culture responds to corruption and the abuse of power. However, in Sahgal' world, politics is an area in which we Indians have our own positive tradition because of the national struggle for independence. This tradition, chiefly, is the combined legacy of Mahatma Gandhi and Jawaharlal Nehru. There is in it the Gandhian emphasis on truth, non-violence, *satyagraha*, social justice, prayer, poverty, simplicity, and so on, and the Nehruvian emphasis on socialism, democracy, and progress. In addition, there is a third realm on which the question of tradition and modernity has a bearing. This has to do with the values and life-choices of the main characters, especially as they are revealed in intimate relationships. It is necessary to examine how these three kinds of tradition are depicted in Sahgal's novels. Only then can we form some idea of her own brand of synthesis between tradition and modernity.

THE MAIN PLOT: THE IMPACT OF RELIGION ON THE INDIVIDUAL

To begin with, what is Sahgal's view of Hinduism? Why is it a pre-occupation in her works? In 'Passion for India' she admits that Hinduism is one of the three important themes in her novels:

> What does it [Hinduism] mean today? How does this culture affect our conduct, our decisions, that sort of thing? What kind of person is the inheritor of this inheritance? Hinduism is of interest to me because most of us are Hindus, but even those who aren't, live under the social and psychological overhang of Hinduism. It is not something we can ignore, if we want to understand ourselves. (p. 85)

Clearly, Sahgal believes that the way we behave or rather the choices that society gives us have to do with this system of beliefs and practices called Hinduism. This is obvious when we take a closer look at her characters, especially the women. When Rashmi's marriage begins to disintegrate, she is forced to ask herself what system it is which expects her to suffer and suffer silently without reacting or trying to change her life. Significantly, Hinduism becomes an issue only in *TTM* (1966); we may recollect that Sahgal's own marriage was disintegrating around this time. Her divorce came through in 1967. *TBH* (1958), her first novel, shows no concern or conflict with the prevailing ideology of Hinduism. The conflict arises only when Rashmi in the next novel contemplates separation from Dalip. Hinduism, it would seem, is all right as long as you don't break any of its implicit codes. When you do, then you are forced to confront its hypocrisies, double standards, and oppressions. Only those who are burned, so to speak, by the system are forced to question it. They can no longer accept all that is perpetrated in the name of tradition.

It is Kailas in *TTM* who first addresses this issue in Sahgal's fiction. And Kailas seems to function as the author's spokesman in this case because he is invested with enormous narrative approval and authority. Not only is he a positive character who enjoys much authorial power, but his view of Hinduism is repeated, with slight modifications, by other 'positive' characters like Vishal, Raj, and

Sonali's father, Keshav. Hinduism, for Rakesh, is a puzzle because it seems so chaotic; 'the creed that he was born into' was 'the only baffling uncertainty' (p. 40). To help him Kailas explains:

> Hinduism was boundless enough . . . to encompass the loftiest of metaphysics, rigid enough to despise the Untouchable. It was goodness and piety and the living light of faith. . . . Yet it was the sufferance of disease and clamour near the temple. It was torpor that accepted maimed limbs, blind eyes and abject poverty as destiny, letting generations live and die in hopelessness, and at the same time it was the majesty of the mind engaged in lifelong combat with the senses.

The picture of Hinduism painted by Kailas underscores Sahgal's ambivalence towards it. This ambivalence is summed up by the narrator:

> You could not accept Hinduism in its entirety without harbouring ignorance and superstition too. You could not wholly reject it without destroying part of yourself, for it was the story of India. (p. 40)

Essentially, this is Sahgal's view of tradition. Such a view persists through all her work.

Rashmi, Saroj, Simrit, Mona and Rose, Sahgal's heroines, all suffer the brunt of the negative aspects of Hinduism. The prototype of the woman oppressed by marriage begins with Rashmi. When she decides to walk out on her husband, her mother, Mira, is unhappy:

> Rashmi's announcement was worse than bad news. It was a mortal blow to all she held sacred. . . . What reason under heaven could sever the marriage bond? Women stayed married, had since time immemorial stayed married, under every conceivable circumstance, to brutal insensitive husbands, to lunatics and lepers. (p. 146)

The last words would seem to echo *Manusmriti* itself wherein a woman is enjoined to remain true and faithful to her husband regardless of the latter's character or treatment of her.[4] This is a classic example of how conventional Hinduism oppresses a woman. It must be admitted, though, that we don't get to know exactly what went wrong between Rashmi and Dalip. Also, Mira's views don't seem to be true to her character because her own marriage to Kailas was so unconventional. Here she comes across as a very conservative person, while the father, Kailas, is more understanding.

Saroj and Simrit are clearly victims of patriarchal oppression. In both their marriages, there is a clash of values leading to incompatibility. I shall focus on the values involved later, but it is sufficient to note how in both these marriages, the women are not only considered automatically subservient by their husbands, but the final break comes because of the violation of the unstated rule of obedience which the husbands think their wives must follow. In both marriages, the woman is little more than chattel or property. Inder's fixation on Saroj's one-time sexual experience during her student days becomes an unscalable barrier in their relationship. Inder's ideas about his wife's supposed violation of chastity *before* her marriage are not irrational so much as tribal; though educated, unconsciously, he thinks of her as a fallen woman, soiled or second-hand goods, so to say. His wife-battering too comes from the same possessive instinct. Lalli, Som's friend in *DS* had killed his wife for being unfaithful; Som 'kills' Simrit financially through a very unfair divorce settlement. Similarly, Ram, though already married to Mona, marries Rose, and goes on to have an affair with Marcella, all with a frightening nonchalance which would imply that he considers it his right to behave this way. Therefore, all these women, are oppressed by tradition. The patriarchal version of Hinduism tolerates the oppression of woman by men. This version of Hinduism reaches its height in *RLU* where we see an upper-class/caste woman of an educated, 'progressive' family being forced to commit *sati* in 1905. This is Sonali's great grandmother. No wonder, the strongest indictment of Hinduism is found in this novel. Outraged over his mother's murder/self-immolation, unable to find any way of explaining it to himself, Keshav's grandfather writes: 'So I cannot believe in Hinduism, whatever Hinduism might be. Not because of such evils as *sati*, but because evil is not explained' (p. 136).

In addition, we are told of the rape and killing of lower caste/class women. This happens routinely in Uttar Pradesh and Bihar. Sahgal mentions the names of several cities and towns where women are fed to brick kilns after they have been abused—'Muzaffarpur, Samastipur, Bhojpur, Beguserai, Monghyr, Purnea, Gaya, Patna, Chapra' (*RLU*, p. 68). Finally, Rose herself is murdered by her stepson, Dev. All these, then are instances of the oppression of women by tradition.

If women are treated badly by tradition, what about men? The answer will depend on what our own values are. From one standpoint, Dalip (of whom we know little), Inder, Som, and Ram are triumphant. They dominate their women and seem to win, at least materially. But surely, these men are very unhappy; in fact, they end up losers in the end. Their marriages break up. Worst of all, their lives are completely devoid of love. I would argue that such men are also victims of patriarchal Hinduism. They have internalized the violence of the patriarchy and in turn directed it outwards at their wives. They have been handed down expectations about 'husbandhood' and 'wifehood' which are incompatible with contemporary reality. In brief, tradition has turned them into oppressors. Their tragedy is that they are incapable of introspection or change and must be abandoned by their spouses in the end.

There is another type of man, though, in Sahagal's novels. Sanad, Rakesh, Vishal, Raj, Osman, and to some extent, Ravi Kachru, are representatives of this type. All these men are liberal, compassionate, and seek more or less equal relationships with women. What distinguishes them is the fact that they do not aspire to dominate over females. These men, however, are almost always critical of tradition. Or, rather, they embody another kind of tradition. They are usually what I would call outsiders, critics of the establishment. Usually, they are Gandhians. Often, they allow the beleaguered woman to escape the tyranny to which she has been subjected. One reason that *RLU* is so depressing is because such a man is absent; there is no way out for Rose.

Hence, we have seen that the effect of tradition on Sahgal's women is, by and large, inimical. Women who are quite placid, passive, and conformist are forced by circumstances to rebel. Their oppression is so great that they have no choice. In Sahgal's novels divorce becomes a powerful symbol of revolt against tradition. The assertion of freedom by the women indicates their refusal to accept patriarchal gender relations. This freedom—which critics have pointed to repeatedly as a prime value in her work—to act, create, and live the way a woman wants to, includes sexual freedom. From *TTM* onwards, the heroines decide whom to make love to without being afraid of social consequences. Rashmi sleeps with Neil, a pattern repeated in Devi's affair with Michael in *SND.* Saroj and Skinny have had sexual encounters with their peers while still at college. Sonali and Kachru have been lovers at Oxford. The Sahgal heroine's attitude to herself is not influenced by conventional notions of purity/contamination. This is best summed up in Saroj's comments about herself to Vishai: 'I've always loved myself. . . . I've been able to say I mattered, that I was whole and clean. But today, for the first time, someone else has said it. It's like seeing a rainbow' (p. 198). In this passage we see, once again, a redefinition of virtue. It lies not necessarily in sexual purity, but in the kind of values one has.

Rashmi, Saroj, and Simrit, in choosing personal happiness over suffering affirm certain modern, post-renaissance notions about self-fulfilment over social obligation. Moreover, their actions assume a certain idea of individuality which tradition would seem to deny them. They seek freedom to act, to change, to combine, and to create—options not available to them within a conventional marriage. Tradition would appear to force men and women to stick to their given roles, discharging well-defined duties. In opposing their assigned roles, the women are choosing modernity over tradition. As Vishal tells Saroj: 'It has taken a million years of evolution for a person and his cherished individuality to matter . . . and no terror must be allowed to destroy that' (*SC*, p. 231). Life with Inder would have amounted to accepting not just the loss of individuality, but by extension, a kind of living death.

The right to choose, once again, underscores the value of freedom in Sahgal's work. Krishna Rao was the first to recognize that freedom for Sahgal was a cardinal value, an assessment which the author agrees with. He defines freedom as 'a deliberate choice or communication with one another or self-identity or courage of conviction [,] the fearless expression of one's personality or simply 'being' itself' (p. 92).

The underlying idea is that 'the human being is the nucleus of social dynamics'. If so, then Sahgal's idea of freedom is close to Jurgen Habermas' theory of communicative action. Considering the importance of Habermas' work, this similarity, if demonstrated would be an important new direction for Sahgal criticism.[5] Here, I shall only suggest the germ of such a project. Something like the following causality is implicit in her work: freedom→communication→common action or commonweal→peaceful solution of problems→social upliftment and prosperity. Here Sahgal seems to imbibe the lessons of modern European thought and uses them to question the oppressiveness of Hindu tradition.

Let me sum up. If tradition implies accepting repeated abuse and injustice within marriage, then Sahgal's women reject it. If, contrarily, divorce, separation, seeking fulfilment outside marriage imply modernity, then Sahgal's women opt for it. These women, who walk out of their marriages, obviously need the support system which only a modern civil society can provide. They also have to attain financial independence. This means that they must not face unfair discrimination in the job market. A whole society's acceptance of constitutional safeguards is assumed in this act of divorce. However, the problems of a working woman in our society are not directly addressed in Sahgal's novels. Sonali, the lone exception, is an IAS officer of the post-independence generation, who takes constitutional safeguards for granted. When she is transferred, it is not because she is a woman but because she doesn't accept the new culture of the emergency. Overall, though, so far as the status of women is concerned, Sahgal comes across as against the tradition inherent in the default mode of Hinduism. She questions patriarchal norms, endorsing humanistic modernity in place of the oppression of tradition. She clearly sees virtue not in self-immolation, but in rebellion.

However, if the woman is a victim of tradition, from where does she get the courage to rebel? It seems to me that this is a crucial question which will force us to qualify the above formulation. Sahgal herself says of Simrit:

> [she] is a passive creature to whom things happen. . . . Simrit is not an individual—she is culture, tradition, a patient enduring passivity. (Usha John, 'Interview with Nayantara Sahgal', *Femina* quoted in Uma, p. 26, see note 6.)

If Rashmi, Saroj, and Simrit all represent the traditional Sita type, passive and long suffering, what does their rebellion signify? It signifies, surely, that even a Sita will not remain forever passive. Even she will rebel when oppression becomes unbearable. Moreover, if Simrit is tradition or culture, then her rebellion means that our tradition must change, must rebel against its evil 'Other'. In other words, tradition itself must provide the impetus for change by negating those of its aspects which are inimical to its survival.

Hence, though Saroj and Simrit are oppressed by tradition, it is tradition which gives them the strength to rebel. At any rate, it gives them the inner resources to survive, to reach out to modernity, to seek help from the other side as it were. In fact, the women in Sahgal are always emotionally and spiritually stronger than their husbands. Simrit, for instance, walks out in spite of having an unspecified number of children and being saddled with a crippling financial contract. It seems that this inner strength is very akin to the traditional notion of the woman as Shakti. What Sahgal wishes to say, however, is that Shakti must express herself not through self-immolation but through a demand for equality in the present times.

THE SUBPLOT: POLITICS AND THE QUESTION OF TRADITION

As I have suggested earlier, tradition takes on a different meaning in the subplots of the novels. These subplots have to do with politics, a recurring preoccupation with Sahgal. Here, tradition acquires positive connotations as opposed to the negative connotations associated with it in the main plot. Tradition in the subplots usually refers to the Gandhi-Nehru brand of political action, the legacy of the freedom movement.

A typical Sahgal novel usually begins at a point of transition. The old, that is the Gandhi-Nehru brand of politics, is about to be replaced by the new. In *SC* and *DS*, the old ministers are on the point of death, about to be replaced by a newer, more corrupt, amoral breed of racketeers represented by the likes of Sumer Singh. Even in *TTM*, there is a sustained ideological opposition between Kailas and Kalyan. In this novel, Kalyan himself is seen as divided and in the end, his better instincts triumph. In the later novels, though, the split is complete and unbridgeable. The climax of this indictment of the new is reached in *RLU*. Here Dev, obviously modelled on Sanjay Gandhi, represents the abuse of power and the lumpenization of Indian politics. The old order is represented in Jayaprakash Narayan himself (p. 46).

The opposition between the old and the new in the politicians is also echoed in the bureaucrats. Sahgal knows that India is governed by politicians and bureaucrats. These are the two tiers of our political and administrative ruling class. A degeneration of our polity would occur only when the rot sets in into both these tiers. Hence, the erosion of values of the politicians must be followed by an erosion of values of the bureaucrats. We have several images of the old-style ICS officer. He is usually portrayed as a plodder, an obeyer of rules and regulations. He is not imaginative, but he is solid, dependable, and upright. Indeed, his probity and honesty are his chief virtues. Sir Arjun (*TTM*), Trivedi (*SC*), and Keshav (*RLU*) are prime examples. As opposed to this the new type of bureaucrat, best exemplified by Ravi Kachru (*RLU*), is alternately ignorant, venial, and opportunistic. All is not lost though; the new generation of bureaucrats also contains Vishal (*SC*), Raj (*DS*), and Sonali (*RLU*). It is interesting how Sonali has to resign from the IAS. The implication is that there is no place for an honest and law-abiding officer in the new regime.

The conflict between tradition and modernity in the political subplots, thus, privileges tradition over modernity. Tradition represents the positive Gandhian and Nehruvian values of compassion, *satyagraha*, nonviolence, social justice, combined with the democratic values of socialism, civil liberties, rule of law, and so on. Modernity is associated with corruption, expedience, illegal activities, fascism, political violence, suppression of civil liberties, dictatorship, the politics of the personality cult, and so on. The deterioration in public life is best shown in *RLU*, set during the Emergency of 1975-7.

However, the tradition-modernity question in the subplot has little to do with the lives of the women characters. What is interesting, though, is that all of Sahgal's heroines are instinctively on the side of tradition and the old values in politics. Saroj, Simrit, Devi, Rose, and Sonali are examples.

The two senses of tradition do, however, combine at times. When looking for the causes of the political malaise in India, Sahgal often goes back to Hinduism. Again, she seeks in the prevailing ideology the reasons for our failures. However, her analysis is not facile or naïve. She is aware of the complexity of our tradition. As Vishal says in *SC*: 'We seem to be in the grip of impotence, stuck for answers, because the most effective part of our inheritance isn't brought into play . . .' (p. 17).

It is this part of our inheritance which Gandhi reactivated so effectively, Sahgal would imply. Vishal's discussions with Trivedi and his proposed paper on Brahminism are all a part of his ongoing quest for the answer to the riddle of the Indian character. Where have we gone wrong? Where has our leadership failed? Such questions haunt him. The failures of independent India exasperate him. The disintegration of civil life in Chandigarh is linked to 'the funeral march of Hinduism': 'History will say, these were a people who couldn't survive modern times. The modern world was too much for them. They never came to terms with it. They just went to pieces. They could have lived if they had the courage . . . to change' (p. 92).

This is an important passage which, once again, links our political failures with the inertia of tradition. India is seen as a traditional society resistant to change. But the failure for Sahgal is not the failure of tradition alone but the absence of courage. Courage, of course, belongs to neither tradition nor modernity exclusively. So, once more, the key lies outside the tradition-modernity question in an independent groundwork of values which to Sahgal, are necessary for our survival and success.

TRADITION-MODERNITY AND PERSONAL RELATIONSHIPS

A final area where the tradition-modernity question operates is that of personal relationships. This is where, I believe, Sahgal is the most suggestive and allegorical, where her own brand of synthesis is most discernible. By personal relationships I mean the values that characters represent and endorse when they are intimately involved with another person. Again, when we examine the heroines, Rashmi, Saroj, Simrit, Devi, Rose, and Sonali, we see a whole web of traditional values being affirmed. I call these values traditional because they are found in the religious traditions of most of the major religions of the world. Thus we see a range of related oppositions: altruism-selfishness, compassion-cruelty, nonviolence-violence, materialism-spirituality, and above all, love-lovelessness.

To begin with, we may observe that the men, Dalip, Inder, Som, and Ram are all selfish. They put themselves and their needs, physical, emotional, and material, above those of others. This selfishness reaches pathological proportions in Dev who is portrayed as a monster. Dev, we should remember, murders his own stepmother. The other men don't go so far. The women, both biologically and emotionally, are givers. They long to share themselves with others. They are not totally self-centred. Rather, they are more sensitive to other people's needs. As mothers and housewives, they are almost always attuned to the needs of their children and husbands. Saroj and Simrit, when pregnant, have an almost ecstatic fascination with the new life growing in them. They are life-affirming and loving. Remember Rose's ministrations of the disabled beggar. The husbands, on the other hand, seem to be incapable of love. They have a kink in their characters which substitutes domination for love. Likewise, the women aren't materialistic, basically. They value comfort and prosperity but not above emotional and spiritual fulfilment. What happens to Simrit is illustrative. As Som get richer and richer, he also becomes more beastly, corrupt, and uncaring. He is noticeably dehumanized. Som's wealth comes from making weapons of mass destruction; the violence which he seems to abet in the world outside also returns to destroy his own family life. Inder, too, beats Saroj in the earlier novel. Simrit nearly goes mad in such an atmosphere of material greed and inhumanity.

If one word or category were used to sum up the whole gamut of traditional values which the women endorse, it would be love. In 'Passion for India' Sahgal implies that the goal of human relationships is 'true everlasting love, . . . real give and take, a love that transcends misunderstanding' (p. 84). The last phrase is, actually, a play on the Biblical notion of peace that 'passeth understanding'. Of course, it could be argued that love is no more traditional than courage is modern. True, but the kind of love that Sahgal seems to describe is what the religious traditions of the world emphasize; it is a set of values which the machine age of modernity is wont to destroy or suppress.

In brief, the women represent love, charity, compassion, kindness, altruism, and a preference of the emotional over the material. The husbands are selfish, cruel, violent, possessive, and materialistic. The contrast is so old as to be seen in religious terms. The values that the women embody are essentially the core of the ethical and moral code of most religions. I would say that at heart Sahgal's women are religious and traditional. That is, they believe that nonviolence and compassion and sharing will solve the problems of the world. The men are greedy, materialistic, violent and therefore represent the unpalatable underbelly of capitalism and modernity. Their actions, multiplied a millionfold, by implication, result in wars and poverty.

The values of the heroines are thus, essentially, conservative. As Saroj says, they involve a courage which consists in 'Not throwing things away, but holding on . . . and never giving up' (*SC*, 92). This tradition of cultivating virtue is basically idealistic-humanistic in that it refuses to accord primacy to the material. Sonali's critique of Marxism arises from her refusal to submit to the domination of either a Eurocentric world-view or to a master discourse: 'I . . . had no intention of chaining myself to any doctrine when I had just lost some of my chains' (*RLU*, 101). Liberal, humanistic, Gandhian, social reform—call it a combination of all these, the prevailing ideology in Sahgal's works, thus, retains the core of religious values from Hinduism, Buddhism, and Christianity plus a selective acceptance of essentially bourgeois values from modernity.

It is when the characters recombine that we get the best idea of the kind of synthesis that Sahgal endorses. I can express it in the following equations:

Rashmi + Rakesh
Saroj + Vishal } = The formula for contemporary India
Simṛit + Raj

Essentially, this synthesis consists of the humanistic and spiritual heritage which comes from tradition combined with reformative or heterodox Hinduism and Western liberalism. From the latter, ideas and values like individuality, freedom, and the quest for happiness are accepted. Overall, the package may be called liberal Gandhism.

It was Jain who characterized Sahgal as a person with 'the conscience of a liberal and the spirit of a non-conformist' (p. 9). This is an apt definition. Sahgal in a letter to this writer says, 'I am a conservative (i.e. careful about stepping out into the new) who has been constantly driven to being a revolutionary by the force of circumstances and the nature of events around me'.[6] With her privileged family background, she could have attained any high office she might have desired; instead she has consistently tried to be a 'VUP'—a 'very unimportant person' ('Passion for India', p. 87). Ultimately, what is significant about Sahgal is not her ideological position, which is that of liberal bourgeois, but the hardships and trials through which she has sustained this position. That is what makes for its continuing viability and authenticity in our times.

Below, I attempt a schema of exactly how Sahgal's position gets to be defined *vis-a-vis* the tradition-modernity question:

Tradition

Rejects:

— the *sati* idea of virtue:
— Manu's idea of an ideal wife:
— patriarchal gender relations;
— oppression of women in the name of religion;
— the inertia, passivity, and hypocrisy of Hinduism;
— social injustice sanctioned by religion.

Modernity

Rejects:

— materialism, organized violence, capitalism and its dehumanising effects;
— Eurocentricism, belief in a master discourse like Marxism;
— the new politics of the Indira Gandhi era;
— expediency, opportunism, corruption, authoritarianism, violence, and Fascism in politics.

Accepts:

— values, orientations, and life-choices offered in various religious traditions;
— compassion, charity, altruism, love, and other non-material values;
— the Gandhian ideology with its stress on nonviolence, truth, simple living, *satyagraha*, removal of social injustice, and so on;
— Nehruvian values of democracy civil liberties, freedom, progress;
— nationalism, liberal humanism, idealism

Accepts:

— concept of the autonomous individual;
— freedom, including sexual freedom for women;
— equal rights for women
— social reform
— protection of civil liberties;
— communicative rationality as a means of solving problems;
— choice as opposed to fate.

Ultimately, it is a judicious mixture of tradition and modernity which constitutes the underlying value system of Sahgal's novels. And at the crux of such a synthesis is usually a female protagonist, the crisis in whose life reflects the crisis in contemporary India.

NOTES

1. Ashis Nandy's long engagement with this question has produced several invigorating and powerful insights. See *The Intimate Enemy* (Delhi: OUP, 1983), *Traditions, Tyrannies, and Utopias* (Delhi: OUP, 1985). Also see his essay, 'Cultural Frames for Social Intervention: A Personal Credo', *Indian Philosophical Quarterly* (October-December 1984).
2. My thinking on the Indo-Western encounter has been influenced by two seminal texts, Gandhi's *Hind Swaraj* (1908; rpt. Ahmedabad: Navjivan, 1957) and Sri Aurobindo's *The Foundations of Indian Culture* (1953, rpt. Pondicherry: Sri Aurobindo Ashram, 1985). See my book, *Hind Swaraj Revisioned: A Primer on Decolonization and Development in India* (forthcoming).
3. The interview is appended to S. Varalakshmi's Ph.D. dissertation, 'The Changing Face of Nayantara Sahgal's Women' (University of Bombay, 1990). Varalakshmi was not only kind enough to send me copies of some of her chapters, but also wrote encouraging letters. I gratefully acknowledge her help.
4. Actually, Manu does allow a woman to leave her husband if he is insane (IX. 79), but he enjoins fidelity upon a wife whose husband is unfaithful (V. 154 and IX. 80); the husband, of course, can leave an

unfaithful wife (IX. 80). See Alladi Uma's *Women and Her Family: Indian and Afro-American: A Literary Perspective* (New Delhi: Sterling, 1989), p. 2.

5. Jurgen Habermas, *The Theory of Communicative Action*, Vol. 1 (New York: Beacon Press, 1984); Vol. 2 (New York: Beacon Press, 1987).
6. Dated 8 May 1991. I would like to record my profound thanks to Sahgal for replying to my queries and for her continued interest in this paper.

Cultural and Political Allegory in *Rich Like Us*

Makarand Paranjape

Nayantara Sahgal's *Rich Like Us* (London: Heinemann, 1985; abbreviated as *RLU* henceforth) is her most ambitious and complex novel. Its importance, both artistic and political, was recognized in its being awarded the Sinclair Prize for fiction and the Indian Sahitya Akademi award for the best book in English for the year 1986. It is also the key novel to consider if we are examining how women characters respond to the tradition-modernity issue. In it we find Sahgal's most scathing attack on tradition; it is also the most radical of her novels politically. Finally, with *RLU* Sahgal properly enters the fictional domain of post-modernism. From the more or less straight narratives of the past in which the fictional mode might be termed mimetic, Sahgal uses symbolism and allegory extensively in *RLU*. The earlier novels are, formally, somewhat dull and stodgy; they are boring in an upper class, well-bred, genteel, 'club' manner. But *RLU* attempts at an adventurousness in form which is both challenging and refreshing.

So far as the narrative shift is concerned, *The Day in Shadow* (1971, rpt., New Delhi: Penguin, 1991) marks the end of one phase. *A Situation in New Delhi* (New Delhi: Vikas, 1977) is a transitional novel in which the narrative becomes clipped and elliptical, the closure uncertain and abrupt. Sahgal has moved into new pastures formally. But the real breakthrough occurs, as I shall show, in *RLU*.

Critics have pointed out how the concern with women's issues is naïve in the earlier novels, acquiring a complexity only in *RLU*. There have also been attempts to suggest a break between the earlier women and Sonali. It is argued the earlier women are essentially drifters, while the later ones are actors, taking the initiative to change

---

* First published in *Indian Writing Today*, ed. C.R. Visweswara Rao (New Delhi: Indian Association for English Studies, 1996), pp. 133-46.

their lives. Actually, I don't see such a break. There is, as Jasbir Jain says, a gradual evolution from the earlier to later ones (*Nayantara Sahgal*, New Delhi: Arnold-Heinemann, 1978, pp. 45-67). Sonali is a type of Rashmi, Saroj, or Simrit. Their values are similar. The only difference is that Sonali is more self-aware and self-assured.

Thematically, then, I don't see a break in Sahgal's work in the middle phase. There is a fullness of harmony and realization as early as *Storm in Chandigarh* (New Delhi: Orient Paperback, 1969). In this significant novel, I find a clear articulation of not only Sahgal's values, but also of her solutions to the problems raised in her novels. The political conflict between the two chief ministers is averted; Saroj finds Vishal; Jit and Mara get back together; finally, when everything seems to have broken down, Vishal's typist, Man Singh, does show up to type his memo to the Home Minister. The reconciliation and breakthrough evident in this work are not surpassed in the later fiction. Yes, the subject shifts and with it the quality of realization too, but its basic ingredients are already available in *Storm in Chandigarh*. This novel celebrates the triumph of Saroj's spirit under every kind of adversity, and thus the victory of good over evil, the human over the *asuric* and so on.

As to thematic shifts, I see them in two places in Sahgal's career. There is a shift after the first novel from the description of the social milieu in a small town to the problems of the beleaguered wife in *This Time of Morning*. The middle phase consists of five novels—*This Time of Morning, Storm in Chandigarh, The Day in Shadow, A Situation in New Delhi*, and *RLU*—all of which have the women's question at their centre. With *RLU*, this problem seems to have been fully worked out, after which there is again a shift in subject in *Plans for Departure* and *Mistaken Identity*. Though *Plans for Departure* has a woman protagonist, she is not fighting the system as in the earlier novels. *Mistaken Identity* is entirely centred on a male protagonist, reminding us of *This Time of Morning*, the first novel.

The reasons for considering *RLU* a more mature and politically radical book are discussed very persuasively in Pankaj K. Singh's essay, 'Feminism and Nayantara Sahgal's *The Day in Shadow* and *Rich like Us*: From the Particular to the Ideological' (in *Feminism and Recent Fiction in English*, ed. by Sushila Singh, New Delhi: Prestige, 1991, pp. 135-46). Singh argues that Sahgal has been moving to a recognizable feminist position, from the subjective point of view in

The Day in Shadow to the objective evaluation of social conditions in *RLU*:

> Unlike *The Day in Shadow* which almost naturalizes the arbitrary power dimension between the genders, *Rich Like Us* firmly rejects the arbitrary distribution of power, be it on the purely political level as it was during Emergency or on the interpersonal and familial level as in the gender roles in the society. (p. 145)

Singh substantiates her point by analysing *The Day in Shadow* in detail. She sees a 'central paradox' in 'Simrit's over-dependence on Raj': 'In a novel that seemed to begin with a woman's decision to seek freedom, ironically it is man [sic] who constantly provides the norm' (p. 140).

She rightly points out that Simrit 'passes on from one man's world into another man's' and that she 'fails to see Raj's prejudices, biases, superficialities' (pp. 139-40). The book, in fact, ends with Raj's one-sided announcement of marriage before Ram Krishen.

Though Singh's article is full of insight, she tries to fit Sahgal into a feminist straitjacket whereas the novelist would appear to reject the hegemony of any master discourse. Indeed, Simrit's and Sahgal's feminism is imperfect. But it isn't very certain that Simrit sets out to be a feminist in the first place. Her decision to leave Som is not so much the assertion of equality or her quest of freedom as an act of survival. She is not a rebel to begin with. Moreover, Simrit has no quarrel with men or even with the apparent domination of men; what she rejects is a certain kind of man who embodies certain kinds of values. Under the circumstances Raj comes across as a miraculous example of the male sex, so different from the other shallow and oppressive men in her life. Yes, Simrit is blind to Raj's own limitations as both a man and as a human being, but this if at all, is a drawback in her character, not in her ideological make-up as a feminist.

But the point that *RLU* is the more complex novel is well taken. Its narrative technique, for instance, is polyphonic. The book alternates between a limited third person narration and Sonali's first person narrative. The third person narrative is largely from the viewpoint of Rose, except for Chapters One, Six, Fifteen, Seventeen, and Twenty. The following summary may help to explain the structure of the novel:

Chapters	*Point of View*
One	Objective (moves from Neuman to Nishi, to Rose)
Two	Sonali
Three	Rose
Four	Sonali
Five	Rose
Six	Nishi
Seven	Sonali
Eight	Rose
Nine	Sonali
Ten	Rose
Eleven	Sonali
Twelve	Rose
Thirteen	Sonali
Fourteen	Rose
Fifteen	Kishori Lal
Sixteen	Rose
Seventeen	Kishori Lal
Eighteen	Rose
Nineteen	Sonali
Twenty	Nishi
Twenty-one	Sonali

Out of the twenty-one chapters, Rose and Sonali each have eight, Nishi and Kishori Lal two each; the opening chapter is from a broader, though not omniscient point of view.

The Rose chapters tell the story of the Indo-British encounter, the gradual degeneration of modern Indian culture, and of Rose's life with Ram. The Sonali chapters are used to comment on the Emergency, to tell Ravi and Sonali's story, and also to trace the history of four generations of the Indian elite starting with Keshav Ranade's grandfather and coming down to Sonali. The Nishi and Kishori Lal chapters deal with the compromise of the new generation and the regeneration of the old.

To use Sonali's words in the beginning of the book, any reader of *RLU* soon becomes 'obsessed with symbols' (p. 31). We can use Roman Jacobson's famous categories of the metonymic versus metaphoric narrative modes to express this point. The novel operates simultaneously on essentially two levels, the literal and the figurative, the syntagmatic and the paradigmatic, the metonymic and the metaphoric, the synchronic and the diachronic. The first set refers to the narrative on the literal level which works on the basis of contiguity and succession. The second set refers to the figurative implications of the narrative, to its allegorical and metaphoric meaning, which work through substitution.[1]

At the literal level, *RLU* is the story of the Emergency as seen from the viewpoint of two main characters, Rose and Sonali. It is a compelling story even as it is. But it is on the metaphoric level that it assumes a stunning complexity and multi-valency. Indeed, seen from this perspective, the novel is a sustained allegory of modern India, especially of its relationship with Britain. What I offer below is a preliminary interpretation of the symbolic meanings of the major characters.

Character	*Description*	*Interpretation*
1. Rose	British, working class; in love with Ram; frank, clear-headed, compassionate, attractive.	The 'good' West: liberal values, fair play, honesty; British empiricism, common sense; antiromantic, against superstition; the England that loved India, fought against Hitler, etc.

Rose is that part of Britain which crossed over to India and became a part of our past. True, her love for India and Ram may be a bit of a mystery; why she puts up with so much abuse from Ram is also not clear. But, Rose represents that aspect of Britain which loved India and was willing to suffer for it. Her working class origins distinguish her from her imperialistic brethren. The name 'Rose' itself suggests the mystic core of goodness within the West. Rose's candour, self-awareness, compassion, charity, empiricism, common sense, and sense of fairplay are what Indian culture might benefit from.

2. Marcella	Crafted in terms of the 'classic', upper class English beauty; sophisticated and ageless; also in love with India;	Represents the ruling classes and their ambivalent attitude to India; Ram's affair with her symbolises the selling

	marries into the British aristocracy.	out' of Indian interests by our elite.

Marcella begins by being clearly aligned with imperialism; her interest in things Indian is a sort of 'orientalism'. Her affair with Ram suggests that the Indian ruling classes will finally realign themselves with British ruling classes. Interestingly, she changes in the end by helping out Sonali. Almost like the British upper classes turning collaborators of India after independence and bailing out modern India (Sonali) from the clutches of fascism.

3. Ram	Indian, upper class; dapper; male chauvinist; bigamist; fascinated by British women; sensitive, intellectual, connoisseur of beauty; comatose at the beginning of the book.	The moribund aristocracy; morally corrupt; duplicitous, hypocritical, oppressors of women, yet charming, attractive; the 'bad' aspects of Indian tradition somehow alluring; but, finally, helpless, confused, dying.

Ram is Hinduism or India trapped between the past and the present, tradition and modernity, India and the West. He is aligned both to traditional India (Mona) and Western modernity (Rose). But he is devoid of life-sustaining values. Ram is perhaps Hinduism or Indian tradition at its worst. In a sense, he is the real villain of the novel, not Dev. It is he who gives birth to Dev and does nothing to check the latter's misdemeanours. Dev's forging cheques in Ram's name refers to the misuse of tradition by modern politicians. Ram also represents patriarchal values; he is selfish, two-timing, and naïve, but oppressive and insensitive none the less. Ram also shows the helplessness, the spineless confusion, and inertia of the Indian elite.

4. Ram's father	The old Lalaji; anti-British; shrewd businessman; accepts Rose; honest and upright; the 'real' entrepreneur.	Lalaji represents the 'good', uncompromising, older generation, the real Indian tradition in a sense; he accepts Rose, which means he is not totally inflexible.

Rose and Lalaji together build up the fortunes of the family after partition. This means that the new Indian state is built upon the foundations of the 'real' Indian tradition and modernity learned from the British.

5. Mona	Ram's first wife; traditional, pious, devoted; opposed to Rose at first, but makes up with her; spoils Dev.	Mona represents Indian womanhood; her devotion to Ram is monistic; she is the traditional woman, a loser and a sufferer; backward, but not 'bad', a victim; the doting mother who spoils Dev.

Mona is the traditional Indian woman—a giver, a loser, and a victim. She is never treated as an equal by Ram and scarcely as a human being, but she puts up with his abuse without a whimper. She is loyal, devoted, and stubborn. Religious, irrational, and superstitious, but not wicked or malicious. When Rose saves her life, she forgets the past and becomes her friend. Modernity, thus, must save tradition; when the victim is saved, she accepts modernity. The typical Indian mother, Mona spoils her male offspring by not deconditioning him of the evils of his inheritance.

6. Sonali	Upper middle class, civil service background; daughter of an honest ICS officer; inherits the Gandhian legacy from her father but also liberalism from the West at Oxford; upright, though marginalized; the real India and the heroine of the book; survives in the end.	The 'good' India; has got the best of both tradition and modernity; heterodox Hindu and Westernized liberal; critic of the emergency; independent working woman; strong, courageous; the culmination of the earlier Sahgal women; liberated but not necessarily feminist.

Sonali is the most important character in the novel. She represents the 'good' India and also modern Indian womanhood. She combines the best of Indian tradition and modernity. She is aware of the evil in traditional Hinduism because of the *sati* of her great-grandmother;

she is the new virtuous woman for whom virtue is courage, not self-sacrifice. She is aligned with Rose and with the anti-emergency forces. Her remaining single points to the deficiency in modern Indian manhood. Ravi's failure to measure up to her is the failure of Indian men in general. Therefore, she is forced to remain single. Yet, she is neither helpless nor unhappy. She is marginalized, treated unfairly by the system, but she does not lose heart. Her survival in the end is a sign of hope for modern India.

7. Keshav Ranade	ICS; bureaucrat; withers away after the Emergency is declared on 26 June 1975.	Bureaucrat of the old school; kind, upright, reformist Hindu; not a part of the Kashmiri 'Mafia'.

Ranade seems to be modelled on Sahgal's own father, Ranjit Pandit. He represents the old bureaucracy which was nourished by the freedom movement. He has also inherited from his father the legacy of his grandmother's *sati*. This makes him critical of tradition. Sonali is closely aligned to him, certainly his heir emotionally and spiritually.

8. Ravi Kachru	IAS; Oxford educated bureaucrat; supports the Emergency; replaces Sonali; changes in the end.	The 'new' bureaucrat; guided not by norms but by expediency; essentially spineless; prefers readymade and easy answers to hard facts and analysis; also a victim in the end.

Ravi has been Sonali's lover at Oxford, but has somehow turned back on his essence. He exemplifies compromise; the pliant bureaucrat, he actually plays a key role in the success of the Emergency. He lacks both courage and convictions. Allows himself to be used by the politicians. Thinks he is in control when he is actually a puppet. Shows a superficial assimilation of the West and an inadequate understanding of India. He belongs to a very old type in Indian politics, the courtier. Ultimately a case of self-delusion and self-betrayal. Meant to contrast the bureaucrat of the old school, Ranade. Dev is the child of the worst aspects of Indian tradition. He represents violence, greed, selfishness, cruelty—in a word, Indian politics gone bad. His stupidity and amnesia indicate that the new breed of

9. Dev	Rich, spoiled brat; stupid and selfish; cruel, materialistic, opportunistic; becomes a new entrepreneur and finally a minister; Rose's killer.	A Sanjay Gandhi like figure; a monster who represents Emergency; the worst of both tradition and modernity; the lumpen element in Indian politics.

politicians have no knowledge of their past. They have learned nothing from the Indian freedom movement. His means are fascistic and violent. His killing of Rose suggests not only that he is utterly immoral, but that he has no use for the lessons of liberalism, democracy or modernity.

10. Nishi	Lower middle-class girl who marries well; another victim who accepts the lies of the emergency for personal benefit, but is betrayed by it, in her father's arrest.	Represents the survival instinct without a corresponding value-system; shares the failure of Dev's generation in forgetting the past; ultimately, also a victim more than an oppressor.

Nishi is a child of the partition. Growing up in a lower middle class home, she first tries to secure her future. She refuses to see that in her quest for affluence she is violating most of the laws of the country. Similarly, she refuses to see the evil that is in Dev. She and her socialite friends represent the failure of the elite to safeguard the interests of the country. Their active collaboration with the Emergency is motivated by self-interest and greed; this shows not just the apathy of the ruling classes but their willingness to sell the country for their own gains.

11. Kishori Lal	Another old timer like Ram's father; failed academic; post-partition, small-time trader; but still retains ambitions of doing good; stubborn and head-strong; his character really blossoms in jail, when he's tortured.	Exemplifies the breakdown of civil rights during the Emergency; victim of police brutality and torture; uses techniques of *satyagraha* in jail; again, shows the hidden strengths of the middle class.

Kishori Lal is an ordinary middle class person, a petty trader. His life is already a failure; the partition has defeated him. His arbitrary arrest shows the complete breakdown of law and order during the Emergency. This event, however, actually brings out the best in him. He learns to resist injustice and tyranny like a *satyagrahi*. His befriending the tortured student is an instance of heroism lurking within the middle class.

12. The crippled beggar	Landlords have broken his hands and legs; he lies by the tomb, passive, but not unintelligent; knows who killed Rose; may get a pair of artificial limbs by the end of the book.	The beggar represents the Indian masses who have been battered and crippled by the ruling classes. They are silent and helpless, but not yet dead. They are victims of endless oppression and injustice.

The crippled beggar is perhaps the most important symbol in the book. His arms and legs have been broken by the landlord whom he was trying to oppose. This shows the suppression of the Indian masses by the brute force of the ruling classes. Rose is the only one who befriends him, who treats him like a human being. It is only a Western sense of the autonomy of the individual and the respect for the dignity of each human being which will enable us to see the downtrodden people of India as our equals. Everyone else only thinks of him as an eyesore, the typical attitude of the elite to the suffering masses. The elites have failed in their obligations to the underprivileged. Only Rose's attempts to give him a pair of artificial arms might help restore his dignity and usefulness as a human being. He sees Rose's murder but is helpless. The masses, likewise, witness the atrocities, oppressions, and injustices that surround them but are powerless to resist.

Putting all these interpretations together, we see that *RLU*, though a bleak book, does not despair totally. Sonali survives and there is a hint at the end that the Emergency will end after all. The crippled beggar, too, may get his hands back. Also, Kachru becomes Ravi again, disillusioned by the excesses of the Emergency. So there is hope for the bureaucracy too. Overall, in *RLU* it does appear that India will survive—but just about.

In spite of this guarded optimism, it is Sahgal's most gloomy book.

The murder of Rose is the nadir of Sahgal's pessimism. Never before or after has a main character been murdered so tragically and helplessly. There is also a real *sati* in this book, not just reports of rape, burning, and torture. We see the brutality of the police, the politicians, and the landlords. Peasant women are raped and fed into brick kilns; their husbands are beaten or maimed when they try to resist oppression. We see the lumpenization of Indian politics and the abuse of power on an unprecedented scale.

But while the book is very self-critical, it is soft on the West. Everything about the West is seen favourably. Even imperialism, so obviously the enemy during the freedom movement, doesn't have strong critics in the book. Ranade is merely an agonized and confused spectator of the last days of the Raj. The book, thus, lacks a strong anti-Western centre. While India is viewed critically throughout, the West is seen as if with tinted glasses.[2]

Rose, Marcella, and even Freddie or Minnie are positive characters. While blaming ourselves and our traditions, Sahgal would appear to condone the violence of colonialism and capitalism. She sees the West as the repository of not just liberal values, but of human rights, decency, democracy, and civil liberties. India, by contrast, becomes a dark continent, dominated by disease, poverty, injustice, oppression, religious superstition, communalism, casteism, bigamy, *sati*, rape, torture, violation of civil rights, corrupt politicians and bureaucrats, greedy and callous socialites, exploitative ruling classes, crushed and defeated masses, and so on.

This, to my mind, is a drawback. It also makes the motivation for Rose's character weak. What exactly is it that attracts her and makes her hold on to Ram? Why does she put up with so much rubbish from him? This isn't clear. It would seem that Rose is mesmerised by Ram and India, tied by mysterious threads of destiny to both. The narrator tells us that after meeting Ram, she had 'entered an emotional labyrinth and she was drawn magnetically on . . . a victim of casual unthinking sorcery' (p. 38). Many years later, she tells Freddie:

> You know how it was with me, Freddie, when I came out here. It wasn't me making up my mind. It was outside me, bigger. If I was a Hindu and believed in other lives, I'd say I must've been here before and wanted to come back. (p. 107)

Sahgal appears to be falling back on those old stereotypes of the labyrinthine, complex, and mysterious mind of the Hindu versus the simple, straightforward, commonsensical Westerner. Surely, this is a mystification. The English came to India for profit; later they colonized us for profit. Moreover, in the novel, Ram isn't even complex in any attractive or superior way. His polish is merely superficial, a gloss or veneer which peels off on closer observation. Rose's motivations, then, are too vague to be convincing.

The only way to solve the mystery that is Rose is to consider herself as someone who has learned from India, not one who comes to teach us. She belongs to the Mrs. Moore type of Englishwoman who has a mysterious love for India, a spiritual affinity with our culture. This semi-mystic type doesn't quite fit Rose, as we know. Likewise, it would be hard to make a case for Rose's representing the best of Indian traditions because she never quite loses her Englishness. She not only retains her Cockney accent till the end, but her room, a small English preserve in an otherwise Indian household, is a marker of her identity, her attempt to preserve a continuity with her English past. A more charitable way of regarding her would be to see her as an adventurer, someone who crosses boundaries, whose zest for life is her motivating force. But, again, why would an adventurer stay on through the kind of travail that Rose endures, only to be murdered in the end?

Rose is not the only problem with the book. The depiction of the entire Indo-British encounter is, ultimately, unsatisfactory. This is an important issue because the book itself is dedicated to 'The Indo-British Experience and what its sharers have learned from each other'. If this is indeed the key theme of the book, then it turns out that they have, indeed, very little to learn from us while we have a lot to learn from them. This inequality in Sahgal's portrayal of the encounter is disappointing. While it is true that Sahgal would have us accept all those who came to us from the West and gave us, so to speak, their lives without dividing them into the 'good' and the 'bad', while she would have us own up to the totality of our mixed inheritance, she still fails to offer any lessons to our 'Other', the West. What have they got from us? If we were to believe Sahgal's account in *RLU*, then it would be bigamy, hypocrisy, intolerance, and finally a cruel death.

No wonder, because Ram or Dev are the worst possible representatives of India that Sahgal could have thought of. Ram's charm is superficial; actually, he is a self-centred and willful liar. He lacks both integrity and character. He is a shallow person, with little knowledge of either India or Europe. Quite inferior to Vishal, Raj, or Shivraj, he is a poor representative of India. And Dev, his idiotic, frighteningly amoral, and murderous son, a pathological case of a diseased Indian mind, is an even worse example of an Indian.

On the other hand, British characters are, invariably, portrayed at their best. Even Marcella, superficial, upper class, predatory, redeems herself in the end by extending a helping hand to Sonali. Does this mean that the British aristocracy will always retain their values while the Indian elites betray them? And must Sonali, the modern Indian woman if not modern India herself, live on the handouts of the West when the novel ends? Even in Sonali's grandfather's manuscript, Mr. Timmons, the Collector, comes out a real hero, a liberal, paternalistic *sahib*. His friendship with Keshav's grandfather is unconvincing; the turn of the century was the period when the sense of empire was, perhaps, the strongest. The divide between the ruled and the ruler, black and white, Indian and English, was then at its height. How implausible to suggest that Keshav's father recuperated at the Timmons' as he recovered the shock of his mother's *sati*. If Mr. Timmons was all that great, why didn't his assistants prevent the illegal self-immolation? Not just Rose, Marcella, or Mr. Timmons emerge angelic in Sahgal's novel, the minor British characters are also real 'good guys'. Rose's parents, limited but brave, working class people, who in their own way stand up to Hitler, and die in the blitz. Freddie, good old Freddie: such a nice loser in love, the typical British sport; brave Freddie who fights for his country and the rest of the free world against Hitler's hellish hordes. Minnie, part of the lower order of the British in India, is so cultured and polite to Rose nonetheless. If the Indo-British encounter were to be judged from this book it would appear that the British are the ones who are civilized, while we are the barbarians. Isn't this the image which colonialism sought to propagate? Remember the white man's burden and the civilizing mission of Empire? Isn't Sahgal, in her moments of despair with the Indian scene, unwittingly reproducing such colonialist stereotypes?

There are other flaws in the novel, the chief of which is the *sati* incident. That a *sati* could happen in a family so progressive and advanced is perhaps Sahgal's deliberate note of warning, if not the representation of an actual event. But the manner of its portrayal is still unconvincing. Ranade's grandmother doesn't seem to be the sort to be pushed around easily, let alone murdered. The motivation for her consent isn't worked out sufficiently: it seems that she agreed to commit *sati* as a part of a deal with her brother-in-law about her son's inheritance (p. 135). But this aspect isn't brought out clearly or emphasized. The self-sacrifice or strength of character of Ranade's grandmother are, similarly, not demonstrated in her sudden self-immolation. The whole effect is painful and confused, almost as if the event were too horrible, too unbearable to even fictionalize. Also, a *sati* after the cremation of the husband is technically impossible unless the widow was not available during the cremation (not true in this case) or if she were menstruating (not indicated in this case). So the whole incident seems somewhat lurid and hazy, however powerful in symbolic import.[3]

The chronology of the novel has been meticulously planned from the time of Sonali's great-grandfather. Similarly, Rose's story too has an elaborate chronology, going back to her birth in 1912. But at least at one point the scheme seems to fail. We are told that in August 1969 Ranade is fifty-two (p. 150). This means that he was born in 1917. We know that Sonali was born in 1937 (she is thirty-eight in 1975). This means that Ranade was twenty when his daughter was born. We know that Sonali is the younger daughter (p. 160); so Kiran has to be born before 1937. Wouldn't that make Ranade an implausibly young father?[4]

In conclusion, it seems to me that *RLU* is an important, ambitious, but flawed book. While its depiction of the Indo-British encounter is unsatisfactory, its handling of the problem of women is both insightful and socially relevant. Rose and Sonali embody two different versions of the story of the oppression of contemporary women. Rose doesn't give up, but is killed; Sonali, who also fights back against the system, survives. Is Sahgal suggesting that only through inner strength, self-reliance, independence even into spinsterhood, can women live with dignity and self-respect in India?

NOTES

1. See Roman Jacobson on the metaphoric and metonymic poles in his essay, 'Two Aspects of Language and Two Types of Linguistic Disturbances', in R. Jacobson and M. Halle, *Fundamentals of Language* (The Hague: Mouton, 1956). Also see David Lodge's *The Modes of Writing* (London: Routledge, 1977).

Federic Jameson's argument that Third World texts are often political allegories (*Social Text* 15, Fall 1986) is particularly apt in this context. However, to the best of my knowledge, mine is the first essay that attempts such a reading of *RLU*. The commonplace view of the novel, on the other hand, comes from reading it literally only as a political novel that indicts the Emergency. See Jasbir Jain's 'The Emperor's New Clothes: The Emergency and Sahgal's *Rich Like Us* ', in *The New Indian Novel in English*, ed. Viney Kirpal (Delhi: Allied Publisher, 1990), pp. 27-35, and O.P. Mathur's 'The Nausea of Totalitarianism: A Note on Nayantara Sahgal's *Rich Like Us*, *World Literature Today* 65.1 (Winter 1991), pp. 68-71 as examples.

2. Uma Parameswaran makes the following observation in her critical review of *RLU* in *World Literature Today* 60.2 (Spring 1986): 'One would think that the misguided stereotyping of the English as the cream of human intelligence, the milk of human kindness, the backbone of human fortitudes, would have been buried with colonial imperialism' (pp. 361-2). Despite the clumsiness and the mixed metaphors, Parameswaran's comment seems justified.
3. In a letter to this writer dated 26 August 1991, Ms. Sahgal acknowledged the *sati* in the book was based on an incident in her own family. Her paternal great-grandmother (Ranjit Pandit's grandmother) committed *sati*. But I am concerned with the fictional representation of this event within *RLU* and its appropriateness to its immediate context.

   I would like to express my deepest gratitude to Ms. Sahgal for being so generous and kind as to read a draft of this paper and to offer numerous, valuable suggestions on how it might be improved
4. May I be permitted to a small aside on the name, 'Ranade'? Keshav Ranade is described as a Saraswat Brahmin in *RLU*, but Ranade is a surname which only Chitpavan (or *Konkanastha*) Brahmins have. Perhaps, Sahgal ought to have chosen a different name.

Anita Desai's *Baumgartner's Bombay*: The Feminization of a Hero

Malashri Lal

Anita Desai's most recent novel, *Baumgartner's Bombay* (1988) was written as an experiment in trilingual writing. During a lecture at Yale University in 1989 she said, 'I wrote the book with a general feeling of release, almost abandon, at last able to employ the language of my infancy and childhood.'[1] Desai was alluding to her German mother, her English-medium education and her Hindi-speaking playmates in Delhi. Though *Baumgartner's Bombay* was, in this sense, a confrontation with her multi-cultural self, it also marked a change from her earlier 'psychological novels' and 'the language of the interior.'[2] She wrote her new book in a determined mood, 'It was a book I had to write if I were to clear away a pile of debris, or unload a heavy piece of baggage from my back, so that I could continue on my way.'[3]

I

This essay attempts to see a comprehensive change in Desai's repudiation of her past literary practices. The debris she cast away was that of timid, traditional adherence to what was expected of women writers in India—scenes of women's oppression in society, their passive suffering, their repressed modes of protest often leading to madness. Desai broke away not only from the standard English of Indo-Anglian fiction, its pretty symbols from nature, and the descriptions of persons and places, she broke away from the implications of such traditional language structure. She now wrote a novel that positioned woman in an intriguing way at the periphery of a weak, male narrative centre. For the critic this raises questions about the author's intentionality. Consequently, *Baumgartner's Bombay* calls for a feminist-deconstructive reading. This may well lead to the conclusion that the new direction in Desai is not just in trilingualism or social explication but a kind of alignment with feminist strategies in writing which bypasses geo-political and cultural barriers. The critic notes that the book is enigmatically titled *Baumgartner's Bombay* but the man is not too much in Bombay nor is he Indian. Moreover, he is entirely unsure of his existence anywhere. He feels dissociated from his changing social contexts and is unable to establish any meaningful human relationships. Did the writer ever mean to locate the dense texture of a metropolitan city through such a spectral character?

The indeterminacies of unspecified boundary are manifold in *Baumgartner's Bombay* though mainly gender-based and linguistic. The female writer's entry into the male mind and the immediate subversion of the expected machismo in the character points to Desai's deliberate erasure of male/female dichotomies. Recalling the origin of Baumgartner as a fictional figure, Desai spoke of her own German lineage through her mother. During a walk in New Delhi's restful Lodhi Gardens, the hero and the novel's title suddenly synthesized a host of memories. Says Desai:

> This name struck me: *Baumgartner's Bombay*. Everything began to fall into place. . . . It was like a magic word; it brought everything to life again. And I began to see that at last I would be able to use my mother's experience of India from the late 1920s onwards, and her memories of pre-war Germany she [had] talked a lot about, and the memories of her German friends who [had] actually been in concentration camps during the war.[4]

Consequently there occurs the feminization of Desai's German Jew 'hero' in India. The position and experiences of Anita Desai's mother, Antionette (Toni) Nime married to a Bengali engineer, Dhiren Mazumdar, could be just partly analogous to Baumgartner's. The Mazumdars left Germany to settle in Delhi two decades before the Nazi persecutions of the Second World War. Hence Toni's accounts of Germany, as told to the young daughter, were direct narratives of her own girlhood conjoined with indirect narratives of German associates in India. By a process of filtration, such life-material is inevitably transmitted in concentrated form without needling, fastidious particulars. The literary equivalent that emerged in Desai's own writing turned some of Antionette Nime's recounting to Baumgartner's own, but in its turn made Baumgartner nostalgic for an absent mother. Desai's linkage with her mother's Germany, tenuous as it was, broke when Antionette Nime Mazumdar died in the mid-1970s. Personal loss, sharpened by evocations of the past, played upon Desai so strongly that she did not hesitate to make public statements:

> Because my mother was German, the lullabies and nursery rhymes I learnt were German ones. German was the language we spoke at home, within the family . . . a whole area of my mind, the earliest and deepest level of my consciousness, was occupied by the German language.[5]

The nurture and tenderness of the remembered mother is fictionally transferred to the gentle ministrations of old Baumgartner—ironically, to cats, to his woman friend, and his treacherous visitor.

Along with the crossing of the gender barrier by the device of a feminized hero, the novelist insists upon the overcoming of the language barrier of Indian-English. A German exile in India would keep his own language and also imbibe a version of the local tongue. Hence the 'trilingual experiment' of *Baumgartner's Bombay.* Again, Desai is quite precise in stating her innate compulsion to do so:

> For years, while I wrote away in English and talked away in Hindi, I was searching for a subject that would allow me to use that part of my tongue that I had to silence for all my writing years because I could not find the key to unlock it. I could have written a biography of my mother but I flinched from that.[6]

Although the novel is primarily in English, passages in German, numerous colloquial phrases, and some Hindi too, are woven in. The canvas is linguistically diverse and enriches the repertoire of Indian English fiction to the extent that Desai sets afloat a new subject and a new mode of telling an expatriate's tale.

Perhaps one should note here Desai's theoretical pronouncements on 'Indian Fiction Today' as published in *Daedalus.* To Ruth Jhabvala she gives the best credits for 'reproducing Indian speech rhythms in English', but it is Salman Rushdie who 'finally brought the spoken language off the streets onto the printed page'. In the 1980s says Desai,

> the tongues of Indian writers—so to speak—have been set free from inhibition and have found confidence. Suddenly it was made apparent that the Indian writer had as distinctive and authentic a voice as the American or the Caribbean.[7]

'Indian Fiction' has moved away from its old evocations of 'antiquity, traditions . . . magical idyll', according to Desai.[8] An Indian story can take authentic form in the experiences of a German Jew in Bombay. Here again Desai was confronted with a problem of personal choice. Though familiar with Calcutta and Delhi, Desai had less immediate contact with Bombay. The notations of change, social and political, so poignantly recorded in the cityscape of *Clear Light of Day*, could not be repeated for Bombay. In any case, Desai is too versatile a writer to attempt easy replications. The social base of the new novel evolved from a mere seed of information, a passing vignette. Desai remembered a decrepit, old Austrian Jew in Bombay:

> He used to walk around in the backstreets looking for scraps to feed his cats. I never got to know him but I knew someone who did. He told me that he wasn't nearly as poor as he looked, he was actually quite wealthy and even owned racehorses. He died a natural death, and my friend went to his flat to tidy it up and see to all his belongings, because he had no family. And he brought away a packet of letters in German and gave them to me. I read them and found they were not important. They were obviously from someone in his family but they said nothing at all. It was only later that I realized that the stamp number which I had seen on each of the letters had some significance, when I began to read about concentration camps. I found out that in the early years people were allowed to write letters. Then it began to mystify me why the letters said so little. I began to wonder if there had been some kind of code. Perhaps because they had been so empty, they teased my mind. All that lay at the back of my mind.[9]

The novel foregrounded the whimsical and vulnerable old Baumgartner, living in a nebulous Bombay, caught in vivid memories of a German mother and thoughts of pre-partition Calcutta. Desai had successfully accumulated material from her own life. Selected facets of this amorphous whole would be polished by the writer's skill.

II

The initial difficulties raised by the novel's trilingualism and gender displacement are further problematized in the novel's perspective. In its obvious form, *Baumgartner's Bombay* is a male-centered novel but by giving us a constantly retiring, retreating, almost vanishing hero, Desai dethrones the apparent male centre and turns the reader's attention elsewhere. Interestingly her social critique is channeled through the women placed at the periphery. We have the robust, earthy Lotte who asserts her presence everywhere she goes, Baumgartner's dead mother whose absence pervades the novel, and the versatile Gisella/Gissy/Lily of Shanghai/Baroness von Roth who assumes many names to seize every opportunity. The women, particularly the two expatriates in India, establish a relatedness to their dwelling place such that Baumgartner is incapable of. Therefore I would suggest that the novel subverts its own avowed intention. It is neither about Bombay, nor too much about Baumgartner as a person with an inner life. Baumgartner and Bombay exist separately though in congruence. Desai may well have placed a comma in the title instead of an apostrophe 's'.

However, this is no inadvertent faux pas in an author praised by her readers for her acute observations. 'Moving to and fro over the years Desai evokes an European sickness and an Indian sickness, until they combine like toxic chemicals', says one reviewer.[10] The displacements of Baumgartner are deliberate. The novel marks out a strategy by which Desai develops her social critique through the women, showing them to have a greater significance in human endeavours than the man. Her feminist position in the novel is therefore both radical and subtle—radical because of the obliteration of the male centre, and subtle because the void at the centre is almost replaced by the female experience of India but not quite. Through Baumgartner, Desai expresses doubts about the male viewpoint as a measure of reality. The male is self-centred but unperceiving of the inner life, diffident, vulnerable to external criticism, and consequently incapable of offering an intelligent understanding of society as a whole. Between the polarities of the individual psyche and the impersonal, multifarious city hinges Desai's argument against man as mediator. Instead she posits woman as the better link between personal action and social interaction. Women are not necessarily survivors but presumably more hospitable and responsive to city experiences.

Such a male-female dialectic seems to form the background for Desai's novels of the 1980s. The decade began with the 'city novel', *Clear Light of Day* recording the transitions in Delhi through the spinster Bim Das. In 1984 came *In Custody*. Desai made her first tentative attempt to explicate her theme of city changes through a male character, an unsuccessful college teacher. Then in 1988, Desai made a more determined bid to centre her novel in the male consciousness.[11] Of her many tales of city experiences, the last is the only one ostensibly naming in its title the hero and the place. But one notices the undercutting. Baumgartner suggests a garden or open spaces, hardly consonant with Bombay's hectic commerce and human crowding. By contrast Desai's novels of the 1970s are remembered for their portraitures of women caught in the layered trap of family, society, city. In the male-centering of the new novels, she has not changed her essential concern but has adopted a clever subterfuge that demolishes the male viewpoint within some common assumptions about maleness and femininity.

For a moment, let us turn from Desai's practice to her theory. At the same time that she changed from the female-centred novel to the male-centred ones (mid-1980s) she was working out theoretical statements about gender compulsions in men and women writers. In an essay published in 1983, initially presented at the Commonwealth Institute, London, Desai supports the views of Coleridge and Virginia Woolf that the great mind is 'androgynous.' However she splits her own arguments into two parts. First, she states that there is an essential difference in male and female assessments of human experience, 'Whereas a man is concerned with action, experience and achievement, a woman writer is more concerned with thought, emotion and sensation.'[12] Second, Desai modifies her statement to say that gender is not always the decisive factor—that in her 'literary ideal', the male and female attributes will be 'undivided', 'wholly creative and powerful'.[13] Seeing the theoretical formulations somewhat refracted through the 1980s novels gives us clues to Desai's feminist critique. The questions to be asked are whether her men and women emphasise different aspects of reality, and to what extent this affects self-knowledge and personal behaviour.

To *Baumgartner's Bombay* again for illustrative examples—actually to Baumgartner's world, since there is plenty about Berlin, Calcutta, Ahmednagar; and Bombay constitutes only a small part of the total experience. At an early encounter in Dhaka, Baumgartner had thought of himself as illusory. A few years later, at Ahmednagar, in a camp for alien residents, Baumgartner's tendency to hide from reality has not changed. We may recall passages like these: 'He was like a mournful turtle—he carried everything with him, perhaps it was the only way he knew to remain himself' (p. 109).[14] 'Silence was his natural condition' (p. 117). 'He was able to live ostrich like, under the sands of his illusion' (p. 118). Later again, in the miserable corners of a rooming house in Calcutta during communal riots, Baumgartner still strains to keep his anonymity by disregarding the current enthusiasm for Tagore's patriotic lyrics, Subhash Bose and

INA (p. 176). No doubt, when he finally arrives in post-partition Bombay, 'a man without a family or a country' (p. 133), he slips into another venue for his anonymity, his silence. The fact that he is befriended by Chimanlal, stumbles upon success at the race course, and keeps a household of demanding cats can hardly be said to be enrichments of human life.

Peering through the half lights at a shabby street in Bombay, he sees his own past, not the city before him:

> It was a scene that was linked for Baumgartner with the one he had observed through the barbed wire fencing of the camp—of women going to their cowpat heap to fetch dry pats for fuel, Annemarie hanging up the washing, and further back in time—his mother putting steaming dishes on the table, preparing him for bed. . . . (p. 213)

Consequently after fifty years in India, the passive 'hero' with whom the novel opens and closes, has fallen into a comfortable state of inaction, trivial routine, physical and mental lethargy (p. 204). We are a little surprised to discover from Baumgartner's own musings that thirty of those years had been spent in Bombay. There has not been much evidence of inner or outer life to match this length of calendar time. As Baumgartner himself says towards the end of the book, Bombay had been 'the setting for his life, he had never actually entered it, never quite captured it; damply, odorously, cacophonously palpable as it was, it had been elusive still' (p. 214). Circumstances left Baumgartner 'as a man without a family or country', but his own endeavours did nothing to overcome these handicaps.

Baumgartner establishes few emotional bonds in his fifty years of residency in India. With Lotte, a friendship began in pre-war Calcutta where Lotte (with the stage name Lulu) would dance enticingly at the Princes night club, passing from lap to lap, throwing back her red gold hair with abandon of body and spirit. This friendship from the jolly days is revived several years later in post-war Bombay—Lotte still a woman of high spirits but a little thickened by age and her fake marriage to a conveniently absent Indian husband. Baumgartner desires her company because she 'keeps him in touch with the German tongue' and 'because she belonged to the India of his own experience' (p. 150). In Calcutta, she had been quite a 'turnip'—'a Jiddischer turnip too'—remembers Baumgartner. Eyelids painted violet, her cheeks carmine and her lips purple, she had shared raucous laughter with her companion. Once, glancing at an immense Russian at the next table she made a remark 'straight off the Berlin streets'. ('*Wo kauft sie dann ihr Brot*—I wonder where she buys her bread' (p. 98). Baumgartner assumes, wrongly, that Lotte suffers from a sense of isolation.

His only other human contact is with a stranger, the aggressive German youth he befriends quite needlessly at a cafe. Though he notices the young man's Aryan features and recalls his own fugitive departure from Nazi Germany, Baumgartner's sense of a shared 'fatherland' overcomes all hesitations.

> Baumgartner found his concern aroused in spite of himself. The boy was no different from a sick cat, he told himself in order to overcome the revulsion he felt from contact with this fair-haired boy that was instinctive and uncontrollable. To think of Nazi Germany now, after all these years, in faraway Bombay, it was absurd after all. . . . 'Perhaps I better take you to my home,' he sighed sadly. (pp. 142-3)

The stranger is brusque, rude and a drug addict. Yet Baumgartner cajoles him in German, invites him home, 'mothers' him through domestic civilities such as cooking, feeding, bed-making, tidying his bag, and staying up at night. 'The boy needed sleep, a bath, and then perhaps he would eat' (p. 149). Why such solicitations to a stranger from an expatriate in India who has refused connections with his neighbours? A distasteful suggestion points towards Baumgartner's racist preferences. Indefinite German origins in Lotte and the drugged youth evoke empathy in a man who has spent years ignoring the poor Indians crowded in a rooming house, and the even poorer Indians outside his window.

Baumgartner's 'reality' is therefore a pathetically narrow one of Germany from which he drags mother fixated memories—the favourite endearment he remembers is *Miene Kliene mouse*, indeed appropriate to his condition. For fifty years he has lived, not in India in any meaningful way, but locked in a sort of time capsule where only the German language holds meaning and significance.

Consequently, the male perspective on India or Bombay in this novel amounts to nothing significant. Desai declares a focus and then deliberately obfuscates it. Furthermore, the theoretical premise that she laid at the Commonwealth conference that 'man is concerned with action, experience and achievement' is not applicable to Baumgartner. He is feminized by his silence, passivity and separation from the mainstream of life; he displays attitudes of dependence that patriarchy associates with women.

As an obverse to Baumgartner, Lotte and Gissy experience India more richly. A lively scene from a Calcutta night club is recounted:

The girls struck the floor with their heels, swung their hips and gestured with their hands, the one with yellow hair and the one with orange, singing together:

> Lola and Lily
> Are fifteen and free
> Lola and Lily
> 'O give them to me!' (p. 96)

Desai gives clever contrasts to the India of Lotte and Baumgartner. During the war years Baumgartner went to a detention camp, the resourceful Lotte struck a bargain marriage and changed her nationality. The doting 'husband' removed her from trouble-torn Calcutta to a comfortable apartment in Bombay. She was bored in the gaps between the 'husband's' visits, so he obligingly bought her a hat shop. At a parallel time Baumgartner languished in jail, making neither friend nor foe but dreaming of his mother. Peacetime. Baumgartner, released from detention, longed for the school-like regularity of the prison camp but was pushed into minor employment in Bombay's small trade. There Baumgartner met Lotte and clung immediately to the vestiges of a remembered Germany. Lotte, on the other hand, was energetically building her local connections. She was dressing up the house and her aging self, instructing the hat making women on the intricacies of netting and lace, and occasionally keeping herself limber with cabaret kicks. Practical to the core, she challenges Baumgartner's passive acceptances. She exploded, 'Without money, one can live?' She slammed down her glass and refilled it immediately. 'You can't be memsahib without money. I did try, Hugo, but no, without money, I was only poor old Lotte, not grand memsahib' (p. 71). Hence the 'jhoota' marriage to the seth, as the servants gossip.

Gissy, the other woman, has been resourceful in her own way. She had set up as an art collector and gained a haughty look to match her new aristocratic name—Gala von Roth, wife of Julius von Roth. Always an opportunist, she had shed her dancing past and had cashed in upon the post war demand for 'artistic' acquisitions. She is in Bombay too, but considerably elevated by wealth: 'the von Roths ran their business from their own flat that Gala kept barred to all acquaintances from the past' (p. 210).

The women, then, have shown the enterprise traditionally attributed to men. In them, Desai shows the 'action, achievement, and experience' she denied to the avowed hero of the novel. The women have the feminine characteristics too that Desai described as 'thought, emotion and sensation', as depicted occasionally in Lotte's tenderness towards Baumgartner.

Here too, the understanding of life's sad limitations is given to Lotte. Much as the old people dream of a return to Germany, perhaps a home in some corner of a becalmed nation, Lotte speaks wisely, 'Europe was gone, all of it. Let us face it, *Liebehen*, there is no home for us. So where shall we go? Hah? Tell me.' Fatigued by useless thoughts of retreat to a past, Baumgartner falls into troubled sleep. Lotte comforts his old body with the warmth and sensations of her own. The woman, once again, takes the initiative in offering the opiate of sexual oblivion:

> Eventually he felt something press against his back. He thought with sleepy affection that it was his cats who had come to lie on his chest or beside his pillow, and purr. He put out his arm to enfold Fritzi and Mimi, Miese and Lulu. Instead of their stifling, adhesive fur, he met only Lotte's hairless smoothness and bareness. The human, womanly quality of her slack old skin, soft as flour, drew a groan of pleasure out of his empty stomach—it was good, like bread. (p. 82)

As a novel which focuses on the exile's adjustments to India, the intimacies of personal expression take a second place. Nevertheless one may surmise that any vitality which may attempt to regain the lost promises of life is to be found in Lotte, not Baumgartner. For Desai, the two characters and their actions create the stage for her larger philosophical query about valid subjects of writing. She says in 'Indian Fiction Today' that 'the magical idyll' of moralistic works is 'surely torn to shreds by today's strife, riots, and commotion, and the tranquil scene overtaken by events of ferocious injustice and the obsessive struggle for survival'.[15] The German characters in her Indian novel have encountered major historical events in the countries mentioned. The Nazi regime and the Indian partition riots bring anguish and disruption to the small lives of the characters within the novel. Desai asks of fiction writers, 'Does today's literature reflect the violence, plurality, and volatility of the Indian scene? Or its comforts, solaces, and exuberances?'[16] *Baumgartner's Bombay* offers a kind of answer. Against a large historical canvas of violence two old people offer solace to each other.

III

The novel, *Baumgartner's Bombay*, has its links with Anita Desai's earlier novels of the 1980s. I will touch upon these briefly only to elaborate my interest in Desai's social critique from the periphery rather than the centre. One recalls that the story of *In Custody* places Deven at the centre. The small-town college teacher hopes to catch literary limelight by publishing an interview with a famous Delhi poet, Nur Shahjehanabadi. Deven's self esteem takes a leap as he begins to see himself rather pompously as 'the custodian of Nur's genius'. The poet suffers from delusions of his own kind. He has published nothing for fifteen years but Deven's adulation makes him believe, falsely, in his continued importance. Both men are looking for boosts to the faltering ego—and, in a way, prop each other up as the world of action and achievement passes them by. In their minds and in their conversations, Desai shows them locked in images of past glory—the Urdu poetry once memorized in Delhi's Jama Masjid area, the glamour of *mehfils*, the birthday celebrations and other opulent rituals. Both ignore the realities of the present, that the poet has lost his creative abilities and that Deven has undertaken the impossible task of writing coherently about a drink-sodden, incoherent man. Around there two deluded figures, Desai creates the ancillary figures of the poet's sycophants, all corrupt, all seeking some aggrandizement through Deven's foolish devotion to Nur. The end is predictable. Deven's ineptitude is such that he cannot handle a simple gadget like a tape-recorder, and the poet's speech is, in any case, disjointed. There is no 'interview' but a rambling, befuddled monologue about petty matters. No poetry, no song. The aspiring college teacher, now disillusioned and financially broke, returns home to his long suffering wife, Sarla.

Deven is another version of the fragile male introvert—the ostrich, the turtle, the mouse were Desai's metaphors for Baumgartner. Similarly, Deven's pursuit of the old poet is merely an escape from confronting hurtful reality—the students are a mocking lot (p. 105), colleagues sneer at him, the college Principal is contemptuous, even the peon insults him (p. 104).[17] So the hero fantasizes about a world in which a magic recreation would lead him 'to another land, another element . . . it caused cobwebs to disappear, visions to appear, bathed in radiance' (p. 105).

In *Custody*, like *Baumgartner's Bombay*, has the essential features of Desai's subversive male-centering strategy. The men are ineffectual, limited, self-deluded, unwilling to meet social reality for fear of rejection. Moreover, *In Custody* experiments with a sort of multilingualism although the novel is written entirely in English. Desai attempts to create the rarefied nuances of Urdu poetry and differentiates it from Deven's mundane world of Hindi teaching. Yet, the narrative mode of the two novels is somewhat different. In *Baumgartner's Bombay*, as I argued, the male centre is displaced in favour of a female perspective on society. The feminist critique, levied from the periphery, is that much more effective for being indirect and moving towards centrification. It seems to me that in *In Custody*, the process remains incomplete. The 'hero' is decentred because we constantly see through his pretensions but Desai does not develop a female alternate to the hero's limited viewpoint. She could have used Sarla, Deven's neglected wife, for this purpose. Sarla is angered by Deven's moonlighting but her barbed remarks are few, and her presence in the novel is negligible. She once taunts, 'So still spending all your time in Delhi?' Another time she remarks caustically that their son must depend on grand-parents for new clothes and shoes. Nevertheless, the obdurate male thinks of solving his debt problems by selling his wife's jewellery (p. 302); this being the traditional solution to male insurgencies. The male centre of the novel is ridiculed and displaced, but not substituted. For this and several other reasons *In Custody* seems a literary prelude to the feminist subtlety of *Baumgartner's Bombay*. *In Custody* illustrates the transition tactics from Desai's earlier mode of keeping psychologically intense women at the centre of her novels. The heroines of *Voices in the City, Fire on the Mountain* and *Where Shall We Go This Summer?* come easily to mind.

Desai's novel of 1980, *Clear Light of Day*, brings the obviously woman centred pattern to a closure. Its link with *Baumgartner's Bombay* is to be seen in how woman is the measure of all things, whether at the apparent centre or the apparent periphery. *Clear Light of Day* speaks of the decay of old Delhi paralleled by the decay of the Das home and family. Bim Das, a middle aged spinster, becomes responsible for the ancestral place. She is to manage the crumbling house, the overgrown garden, the insane aunt and the invalid brother, while the more adventurous in the family move away to gain opportunities of the 'modern' world. Desai makes a direct connection between the novel's title and Bim who 'could see . . . by the clear light of day that she felt only love and yearning for them all, and if there were hurts it was only because her love was imperfect and did not encompass them thoroughly enough' (p. 165).[18] There is no subversion of the title in this instance because the novel describes the poignancy of such female destiny in India. Bim's self-deprecating statement about her 'imperfect love' puts her in the context of her parasitical relatives. Desai draws attention to the defective social order. The woman who had sacrificed her ambitions and abilities to be 'dutiful' is a tragic figure—she does not comprehend her own wasted potential. Her choices are based upon fixed notions of family solidarity and yet the substance of the old order has changed. In the traditional order brothers would have assumed charge of the home and other responsibilities. Desai sketches a situation where one brother has gladly rejected the old and the other is an invalid. The married sister lives abroad. Bim chooses spinsterhood and loyalty to the ailing relatives, stretching her teacher's salary to meet household expenses. 'Noble choices' one may say, but Desai would rather point to the tragic deterioration of the self. Unable to cope with the financial and psychological burdens, Bim turns prematurely gray, shabby, irritable and petty minded. The young woman of promise becomes a disillusioned introvert, Delhi home—as both structure and family—crumbles into disintegration.

Reviewing Anita Desai's productions of the 1980s, one can arrive at a few conclusions. First that she is impelled to make a social critique which examines the changes from old ways to new. Next, that women are appropriate vehicles for her critique—not men. Further, she gives to her women attributes generally given to men—action, achievement, experience. She also keeps her women within the purview of traditional feminine expectations of 'thought, emotion and sensation'. This androgynous personality, though of female gender, becomes Desai's strategy for mounting an attack on patriarchal structures. Up to 1980 this attack came directly from the centre of her narratives where the woman was firmly placed as perceiver, interpreter and victim of social systems, yet with nowhere to flee. By mid-1980s, both in theory and practice, Desai made a categorical shift in strategy. While taking account of the binary oppositions of femaleness and maleness, she cleverly placed feminized males at the centre of two novels and put the women at the periphery. Nominally in *In Custody*, and more effectively in *Baumgartner's Bombay*, the attack from the periphery demolishes the male centre of the novels, and by implication, posits the feminist perspective as the only viable measure of the world around us.

However, Mrs. Desai's bodkin is so sharp and so cloaked that her critics and reviewers have preferred, so far, not to seek out her latent feminism, though several have pointed to Baumgartner's nebulous existence. Newspaper reviews often used epithets such as 'solitary', 'nowhere-man', 'a phirangi'.[19] Detailed analyses of the novel by literary critics are just getting to be published. In a useful essay by Kamal N. Awasthi, '*Baumgartner's Bombay*: The 'new' novel of Anita Desai', observations are made on the hero as a 'marginal man', as representative of 'the larger humanity which is marginal, unheroic'.[20] While these viewpoints are valid, I have tried to magnify the marginal world of *Baumgartner's Bombay* which has its own dynamics. It seems important to highlight Desai's deliberate obfuscation of gender and linguistic barriers, not only to reflect the pluralities in the external world but also to bring in view a major innovation to Indian-English woman's writing.

NOTES

1. Anita Desai, 'On the English Language in India', *The Commonwealth of Letters*, Vol. 2, No. 1 (June 1990), p. 9.
2. Ibid., pp. 4-5.
3. Ibid., p. 9.
4. Andrew Robinson, 'Interview [with Anita Desai]', *The Statesman*, 13 August 1988, p. 2.
5. Anita Desai, 'On the English Language', pp. 8-9.
6. Ibid., p. 9.
7. Anita Desai, 'Indian Fiction Today', *Daedalus* (Fall 1989), p. 212.
8. Ibid., p. 208.
9. Andrew Robinson, p. 2.
10. Rosemary Dinnage, 'Exiles', *The New York Review of Books*, 1 June 1989, p. 35.
11. Details in my article, 'The shift from female centered to male centered narrative in the novels of the 1980's: A study of Anita Desai and Nayantara Sahgal', in Viney Kirpal (ed.), *The New Indian Novel in English* (New Delhi: Allied Publishers, 1990), pp. 279-86.
12. Maggie Butcher (ed.), *The Eye of The Beholder* (London: Commonwealth Institute, 1983), p. 57.
13. Ibid., p. 58.
14. Textual citations in parentheses refer to *Baumgartner's Bombay* (London: Heinemann, 1988).

15. Anita Desai, 'Indian Fiction Today', p. 208.
16. Ibid.
17. Textual citations in parentheses refer to *In Custody* (London: Heinemann, 1984).
18. Textual citations in parentheses refer to *Clear Light of Day* (New Delhi: Allied Publishers, 1980).
19. Rosemary Dinnage, 'Exiles', *The New York Review of Books*, 1 June 1989; Ranjita Basu, 'Nowhere Man', *The Times of India*, 26 March 1989; Sushmita Ghosh, 'A phirangi's search for home', *The Hindustan Times*, 2 July 1989.
20. Kamal N. Awasthi, *Contemporary Indian English Fiction: An Anthology of Essays* (Jalandhar, 1993), pp. 47-54.
    See also Usha Bande, 'The Outsider Situation in *Baumgartner's Bombay*', in R.K. Dhawan (ed.), *Indian Women Novelists*, (New Delhi: Prestige, 1991).

From Purdah to Polo to Politics: A Study of Gita Mehta's *Raj*

Naresh K. Jain

Raj (1989) is a story of change set in princely India. The protagonist is a princess whose fortunes are intertwined with the fortunes of two princely states of Balmer and Sirpur and with those of the country at large. It is a success story that reads almost like failure. Change comes in the life of the princess in two principal ways: through a succession of deaths in the family (she loses her brother and father, and after marriage her brother-in-law, husband and even her son)—and the changing political reality in princely India and British India culminating in the freedom of the country in 1947. And she has little control over either. But though grounded in traditional values and pieties and partly because of it, Jaya responds to change in her personal and political life with surprising openness and resilience and manages to hold her own in the male-dominated world.

Her saga is all the more remarkable when we see it against the background of the lives led by the royal widows and the concubines in the harem. The only other woman, besides herself, who makes anything of her life is her mother. *Raj* is an ideal text for our purpose for perhaps nothing provides a better setting for the study of the working of tradition and the need for change than does princely India, particularly with regard to the status of women. This comes out with telling effect in the letter written by a Maharani to the Editor of *The Bombay Chronicle* quoted in the novel.[1] In the traditional set-up of a princely state a woman is more dependent on man and her marriage is even less a matter of personal choice, marriage being a political arrangement than it is elsewhere. There is much in this tradition as depicted in the novel that is decadent and obnoxious. And since it is a patriarchal system, women are the innocent victims of it. One example of this moribund tradition is the treatment meted out to a widow. She is ritually cursed by the old women assembled at her husband's funeral as unfortunate, unclean and unholy, fit only to be cast out and abandoned (p. 159). Jaya who in her revulsion at this humiliating practice on the occassion of her father's death hits out at the old women shouting a litany of abuse, herself suffers the same humiliation when she loses her husband (p. 355). Her own hair are shorn as the hair of her mother had been cut at her widowhood.

But if the novel dismisses the ill-treatment of widows, it also tries to rediscover or redefine tradition. The true *sati*, says the ascetic called Sati Mata, is not a woman who jumps into the funeral pyre of her husband but one who has 'the will to continue when the familiar world fragments around her' (p. 127). In this sense both Jaya and her mother are true *satis*. This true meaning of *sati* is expressed through the recital of the tale of Queen Pushpawati described here as the greatest queen of India who lost her father, brother and husband but who endured the taint of widowhood because of an unborn child in her womb. She finally delivered the child and then ascended the pyre (pp. 12-13). This tale which recurs in the novel like a refrain is recited near the end also but its final recital stops at the point of the widowhood of Queen Pushpawati (p. 455). The implication is that Jaya will continue the tradition of Pushpawati but will give it a new meaning. This redefinition of the meaning of true *sati* has other implications also which we shall discuss later.

Jaya's education which is comprehensive is at once traditional and modern. Her father who perhaps has a premonition of the future changes decides that she must be educated outside purdah. Accordingly, she learns riding, hunting and shooting and above all to confront her fears. This, according to her father, is essential for a ruler: 'Rulers are men and men are always frightened. A man cannot govern unless he confronts his own fear' (p. 5). Her teacher on the field is Major Vir Singh who is indifferent to the fact that she is a girl. Another tough teacher is the Raj Guru who gives her lessons in *rajniti* and to whom she turns for advice later on. Her mother, on the other hand, fears that her father is bringing her up as a son, and sees to it that she is taught the *sola shringar*, the traditional art of personal decoration in order to please a husband, music and also the aesthetics of colour and design. Another major influence on her is that of Miss Roy who teaches her English but who also passes on her nationalistic ideas to her. All these influences, sometimes contradictory, enter into her mental make-up and determine, among other things, her ambivalent response to monarchy *vis-a-vis* democracy. They also enable her to see things from a longer perspective.

Up to a point Jaya's story is essentially the story of an unwanted Indian wife who in spite of her humiliation at the hands of her husband proves to be his good angel. The catalogue of humiliations that she suffers begins even before her marriage and has a familiar ring. After her father's death she is considered a potential rival by her cousin, Raja Man Singh who usurps the throne and is married off in haste to Prince Pratap *in absentia.* It is almost two years before he returns from abroad and meets her and another five years before their marriage is consummated. And when she appears in her traditional bridal finery, he rejects her saying, 'I'm afraid you won't do, Princess. You really won't do at all.' And later: 'Wash all that nonsense off your hands and feet. And change out of these Christman decorations' (p. 189). In the second meeting he makes his motives clear. With chilling bluntness he tells her that theirs was a marriage of convenience and adds: 'Should the necessity for children ever arise, I am sure we can both rise to our duty, but until then . . .' (p. 190). The British consider him to be an 'irresponsible playboy' who would be permitted to travel abroad only when accompanied by a wife. 'That's why I agreed to our marriage. You cannot eat quail or wear a sari. You know no languages. Yet through you I must outmanoeuvre the Empire which forced me into this marriage' (p. 191).

When the marriage is consummated what should have been an act of tender love turns out to be a captor's assault. Jaya feels 'soiled' and 'violated' and screams silently in protest. 'The urgency with which he fulfilled his need left Jaya bitterly regretting an intimacy which soiled her as his remoteness had never done' (p. 287). When she becomes a mother she is forbidden to breastfeed her child, thus depriving her of the 'rights of maternity' just as he had robbed her of the dignity of being a wife. The moment of greatest shame comes when she discovers that on a visit to a Calcutta brothel he had worn the Sirpur crest not on his turban but on his feet.

So far Jaya has suffered and protested silently but this last example of his ignominy proves too much for her and she bursts out to Lady Modi, questioning the tradition that 'demanded only obedience from a wife' (p. 328):

He can't touch his own wife until she is turned into a toy who no longer represents a woman. Or until he himself is so drunk he can no longer pass for a man. He shrinks from the sight of his wife giving breast to his son, but not from wearing his ancient crest on his feet to visit a brothel. Is this the conduct of a husband? Of a king?' (p. 329)

But, though she endures a good deal, Jaya never gives up; she fights for her rights and proves to be a hard bargainer. However, Jaya is no iconoclast. She works within the given tradition, makes a place for herself *within* it and then empowers herself.

Jaya is a strong woman and though she goes to great lengths to win over her husband she has a mind of her own. For instance, she summarily rejects the advice of Lady Modi who has been employed to teach her the intricacies of polite society, to have her hair cut, saying: 'Long hair is one of the emblems of a married woman. I will not cut it off. It would be inauspicious for my husband' (p. 195). Notice that her reason is still traditional. Later she refuses to wear a glove and greets the Prince of Wales with folded hands. In an atmosphere where everyone is mindlessly fashionable and trendy, there is a positive merit in being traditional.

On two occasions she actually strikes a hard bargain with her husband who wants to create the right impression on his imperial masters. First, she agrees to play polo with the visiting Prince of Wales but will 'never allow a strange man, not even the King Emperor himself, to put his arm around her body' (p. 202). The following exchange between them is quite revealing:

'My grandfather had to impress the Prince's grandfather by swearing my grandmother would not commit sati. But if you were to play polo with us, could the Empire doubt Sirpur's commitment to progress?'

Jaya freed her arm. 'In exchange, Hukum, you will excuse me from the ball'.

Prince Pratap slammed the car door. 'Out of the question. You are Victor's hostess'.

'Then let me say I do not dance'.

Jaya saw the combative glance in his eyes, as if her exhibition of courage were eroding the barrier between them. 'It's a bargain, Princess. Play polo and you don't have to dance'. (pp. 221-2)

Her 'goal', as the Prince of Wales said later, 'was the best goal in the game' (p. 225). The polo marks a great accession to her strength.

The other occasion is more serious—her husband's infatuation for Esme Moore and the possibility of her blackmailing him. She tries to save him but once again she drives a hard bargain, harder than the earlier bargain. This time the price she exacts is *power.*

'So what is the price of your husband's honour, my dear?'

'I wish to be named Regent Maharani of Sirpur, in the event of anything happening to you, until Arjun is of an age to take the throne.'

Gita Mehta adds: 'Clearly, after a lifetime as power's victim she wanted to be its executor . . .' (p. 333). The role reversal is complete.

As a Regent Jaya is left alone but she conducts herself with dignity and restraint and gives a good account of herself as a ruler. As the nationalist movement gathers force in British India, she naturally feels anxious about saving the kingdom for her son. She is in a dilemma and she leans upon her childhood friend James Osborne who is now Political Officer to Sirpur for advice but at the same time she tries to cultivate the nationalist leader Arun Roy. Since she is clear-sighted and her democratic instincts are sound, she takes the right decision at the right time.

If, as suggested earlier, the novelist presents Jaya as a true *sati*, she does not consider her seeking sexual fulfilment in the arms of Arun Roy inconsistent with being virtuous. If she sleeps with him she does so with dignity and does not abase herself. The event is significant because it shows that Jaya is no ascetic and because it brings her the long denied sexual fulfilment and also because it wipes away the humiliation she had suffered at the hands of her husband. It is also an earnest of her expanding consciousness because she defies conventional morality and notions of purity.

Jaya stared at the night sky, so low the stars seemed caught on the branches of the tree. Arun Roy's lips brushed her neck, and his fingers stroked her hair. Jaya was afraid to breathe, but on the platform high above the night animals, enclosed by leaves like black stains against the thick branches of the tree, she felt the lawyer's tenderness burning away the violent humiliations of her past, allowing her to repossess her soul each time her name was whispered into the darkness.

. . . She felt herself expanding to contain not just Arun Roy's desire, but the jungle itself, seething with its predators and prey. (p. 416)

Earlier at the house of Mrs. Roy in Calcutta she had felt herself to be adulterous at the mere touch of Arun Roy's lips on her own

(p. 243). Obviously there has been a sea-change since. In this attempt to redefine virtue Gita Mehta is with Nayantara Sahgal.

In Jaya Gita Mehta is attempting to present her ideal of an androgynous woman combining devotion, affection, care and endurance with fearlessness, courage and ambition.

Jaya is truly Janus-faced looking back to the past and looking forward to the future. She is a battle-scarred woman who does not remain locked in the memories of past glory but is ready to seek new pastures in the fiercely competitive world of national politics. When we meet her last, she is filing her nomination papers as a candidate for election in free India. Her laughter as she does so is the laughter of a triumphant woman who is sure of her own destiny.

NOTE

1. (Bombay: India Book Distributors, 1989), pp. 237-8. All subsequent references to the book will be indicated by page numbers within parantheses in the text.

Jasmine: A Study

Usha Anand

Bharati Mukherjee's *Jasmine* (1990) is primarily a novel of cultural transplantation. It deals with a young Indian widow's successful attempt to reshape her destiny and achieve happiness. At seven, Jyoti is doomed to 'widowhood and exile',[1] but though the prophecy turns out to be literally true, she cancels out her fate and 'repositions' the stars as she had said[2] she would, achieving happiness with a man of her choice in her chosen land of adoption. The Jyoti born into a poor, backward Punjab village is, in the course of the novel, transformed into the Jase of the closing chapter, speeding with Taylor to California 'greedy with wants and reckless from hope'. The transformation is complete. Inevitably, the tradition—modernity issue becomes central to the concerns of the novel.

Bharati Mukherjee has presented tradition and modernity more or less as polar opposites in the novel. India or the India that Jyoti is familiar with is conservative and tradition-bound, indeed feudal in its attitudes to women and is particularly cruel to them. Linked with this are the opposition between old and new, death and life.

> . . . daughters were curses (p. 39).

> All over our district, bad luck dogged dowryless wives, rebellious wives, barren wives. They fell into wells, they got run over by trains, they burnt to death heating milk on kerosene stoves (p. 41).

America on the other hand comes across as the land of freedom and promise and self-fulfilment where there is a premium on individual effort and where man-woman relationships are based on mutual and equal partnership.

America, in the novel, is also synonymous with a liberated sexual morality where sex outside marriage is not sinful and is unburdened with guilt. The new woman in the novel Jasmine rejects the moribund Indian values and avidly accepts America and American values. The scales are heavily loaded in favour of new, Western values.

The impermanence of things and the suddenness of change in America does not escape her for long come to her during her first job with Taylor and Wylie as a 'care giver' for their little girl Duff: 'In the early summer of my second year, Wylie fell out of love with Taylor and into love with an economist named Stuart Eschelman . . . . She told me her problem before she told Taylor. 'It's all so messy. Taylor's such a sweetheart, and there's Duff and Stuart's three kids, but this is my chance at real happiness. What can I do? I've got to go for it, right?' Later on she says: 'I realized for the first time in at least a year that America had thrown me again. There was no word I could learn, no one I could consult, to understand what Wylie was saying or why she had done it. She wasn't happy? She looked happy, sounded happy, acted happy. Then what did happy mean? Her only chance?' (pp. 181-2). Eventually the lesson goes home: "In America, nothing lasts. I can say that now and see it doesn't shock me, but I think it was the hardest lesson of all for me to learn. We arrive so eager to learn, to adjust, to participate, only to find the monuments are plastic. . . . Nothing is forever . . . (p. 181).

What surprises her about Wylie at this stage will soon be incorporated in her behaviour later in the ease with which she becomes friends with Taylor, then moves to Iowa and starts living with Bud, and then at the end, abandons Bud to accompany Taylor to California. In the process, she even forgets Prakash, her first husband who had first aroused in her an awareness of America and the freedom it stood for.

Jasmine's rejection of India is complete, irrevocable. Though only seven years separate her from her life in India, she refers to it in the first sentence of the book as 'Lifetimes ago' (p. 3). The image of *rebirth* implicit in this reference, is made explicit at several points in the story. Later she uses the motif of rebirth hinted at here, explicitly. This she does while referring to the efforts of 14-year-old Vietnamese orphan, Du, adopted by Bud to forget his past and transform himself into an all American youngman: 'We *murder* who we were so we can *rebirth* ourselves into the images of dreams' (emphasis added) (p. 29).

But for the protagonist rebirth is not enough. In the process of her discovery of her true identity Jyoti of Hasnapur becomes Jasmine, Jassy, Jase and Jane before finally settling for Jase. The ruthlessness suggested by the word *murder* is part of her evolving consciousness as she comes to terms with America *vis-a-vis* her past.

Jasmine sees this past as an encumbrance that she gets rid of. Her first break with the past comes when her husband Prakash ('a modern man') changes her name from Jyoti to Jasmine ('He wanted to break down the Jyoti. I'd been in Hasnapur and make me a new kind of city woman. To break off the past, he gave me a new name, Jasmine') (p. 77). Jasmine takes a giant stride towards modernity when she gives up the idea of *sati* but the mention of it in the novel seems forced and historically inaccurate. The reference to the practice is not accidental but rather central to the meaning of *Jasmine. Sati* is mentioned as a highly desirable behaviour on the part of widows. Jasmine's friend Vimla tried to burn herself on a stove after the death of her husband at 22. Jasmine's own mother was prevented from committing *sati.* Most of all, Jasmine plans to burn her husband's suit and herself along with it in front of the institute in America where he had sought admission. But her Kali-like encounter with Half Face forces her to change her mind and instead of dying she kills him and decides to live and complete Prakash's mission of making good in America.

Now the practice of *sati* is a cruel part of Indian tradition and Bharati Mukherjee is right in making her heroine Jasmine reject it in favour of life. But the mention of *sati* in the context of Punjab involves her in historical inaccuracy. No one expected a widow in Punjab in the seventies/eighties to commit *sati* or immolate herself. It seems Mukherjee brought in the idea of *sati* in order for Jasmine to reject it and strengthen the impression of her modernity. She apparently had a Western audience in mind. Eventually Jasmine does burn her husband's suit and her widow's white *sari* and also the clothes in which Half Face had defiled her outside the motel but this burning symbolizes her throwing away the burden of death-dealing Indian tradition like *sati.* With the weight of the dead and deadening past discarded, she begins her journey to life and adventure and happiness in America, 'travelling light' (p. 121).

In the rapid Americanization of her consciousness Jasmine has little space not only for bitter memories but even for happy memories connected with Prakash. This is surprising because Prakash it was who gave her her first taste of freedom and equality. For instance he had insisted that she call him by his first name (p. 77). In fact Prakash suffers in comparison with Taylor who she falls 'head over heels in love with' (p. 186). Taylor's wife Wylie leaves her husband for her lover Stuart. Taylor reacts differently from how, she believes,

Prakash would have behaved. 'He [Taylor] acted forbearing even when aggrieved. Prakash would have slugged and raved. Prakash would have been impossibly possessive. He would have put in new locks and bars on the *outside* of the front door to the apartment' (pp. 182-3). But not Taylor. Obviously he had replaced Prakash as her hero.

There is another bit of the old world that she discards: that is her dutifulness. Among her several identities is her identity as a care-giver to Bud, who is a cripple: 'I am Jane with my very own Mr. Rochester . . .' (p. 236). And she is bearing his child. But when Taylor comes for her with Duff whose day-mammy she was in her earlier incarnation as Jase, there is no conflict or not much conflict in her mind about who or what to choose. Her first reaction is—'I can't leave. How can I?' and her unspoken words are: 'I want to do the right thing. I don't mean to be a terrible person' (p. 239). That means, that she considers leaving and going away with Taylor as morally wrong, as *not the right thing*. But Taylor's advice to her to just say no—'It's a free country'—is like saying no to an unwanted object that you had ordered through post but later changed your mind—clinches the issue for her.

'I am not choosing between men. I am caught between the promise of America and old-world dutifulness. A care-giver's life is a good life, a worthy life. What am I to do?' she asks herself.

This old world dutifulness is traditionally Indian and is rejected in favour of a life of adventure and happiness promised by America. Clearly people do not matter for Jasmine; what they promise to Jasmine does. The net result is that she cuts her cables with Bud whose child she is carrying without any feeling of guilt and switches her loyalty to Taylor easily. The case is of a piece with her earlier discarding of Prakash's memories. The past recedes more and more into the remote unusable past and what matters are the present moment and the promise it holds for the future.

The absence of any feeling of guilt over leaving Bud on Jasmine's part is significant in another way. It goes well with her permissive sexual morality. Bud wants to marry her but though she is carrying his baby she will not tie the knot because she has only affection for him, not love. In fact, the question of sexual morality is not raised in the novel in any important way, suggesting thereby that Bharati Mukherjee does not consider it important for Jasmine.

Besides there is a serious inconsistency in the character of the protagonist. Jasmine, we are told, had earlier wanted to be a doctor. 'Like the mustached doctor in the bazaar clinic, I wanted to scrape off cataracts, fit plastic legs on stumps, work miracles' (p. 51). This also means she wanted to be economically independent and also wanted a profession for herself. But apart from acting as day-mammy for Duff and some casual work she does at the University, she is not shown as engaged in any other kind of employment. All along she is shown as dependent on the people whom she is living with. Even in the final scene as she prepares to accompany Taylor to California, she is still neither economically independent nor trained for a vocation. This is an inconsistency which Bharati Mukherjee seems to have overlooked.

The novel reads almost like a fairy tale more in the nature of a wish-fulfilment than grounded in the harsh realities of life.

NOTES

1. (New Delhi: Penguin Books, 1990), p. 3. All further references to the text are to this edition.
2. If we [She and Prakash] could just get away from India, then all fates would be cancelled. We'd start with new fates, new stars. We could say or be anything we wanted (p. 85).

Voicing Women's Experiences in *Tara Lane*

Jaiwanti Dimri

In recent years, the marginalised groups, communities and races all over the world have shifted from the margin to the centre. This globalisation of ethnicity, in some ways, can be interconnected with the current feminist and post-modernist theories. Post-modernist writers such as Foucault, Derrida, Rorty and Lyotard have rejected stories that claim to encompass all of human history and have waged war on totality thereby rejecting the 'grand narrative of legitimation' and proposing a social criticism that is *ad hoc*, contextual, plural and limited. The emphasis on smallish, localized narrative and the belief that social identities are complex and heterogeneous has invariably provided an impetus for literature of small or minor communities and groups. One may agree or disagree with these feminist and post-modernist theories, but there is no denying the fact that these theories have largely been responsible for the global upsurge in ethnic minority writing. When Nancy Hartsock problematizes a fundamental feminist issue, whatever the context may be, her arguments authenticate the position of a marginalized/minority writer: 'Why are we—in all our variousness—systematically excluded and marginalised?'[1]

Among women writers, Bapsy Sidhwa and Dina Mehta (Parsee) and Farhana Sheikh and Shama Futehally (Muslim) are a few such noteworthy voices that have emerged in the Indian subcontinent over the years. In India, following the footsteps of Attia Hosain, the author of *Phoenix Fled* and *Sunlight on a Broken Column*, Shama Futehally, a young Muslim writer from Bombay has beautifully and picturesquely delineated the world of her narrator/protagonist, Tahira or Tara, in her maiden novel *Tara Lane* (1993). She has published two anthologies of short stories, *The Inner Courtyard* (1990) and *In Other Words* (1992) and her articles and reviews have appeared in various journals. With the advantage of education abroad in the University of Leeds and experience of teaching English for eight years in Bombay and Allahabad, her mastery of English language is well understood.

Tara Lane,[2] a small novella running into 174 pages, centres round the Mushtaqs, a cultured, upright business family of Bombay confronted with a crisis which is partly economic and partly ideological. But as the novel proceeds through the memory lane of the female narrator/commentator, it turns more and more into a monologue thereby unfolding the whole picture of the protagonist's life, first as the eldest child in the parental joint family set-up, and later on in the nuclear family as a young woman with her husband, Rizwan. The novel can be read primarily as a feminist text for it provides an implicit feminist discourse on the patriarchal set-up and the subservient position of a Muslim woman in the patriarchal social structure. The three major women characters, namely, Tara, her mother, and her grandmother, present three role-models for women in the Muslim patriarchal hierarchy. These role-models in their relationships with their spouses offer a critique of gender relations where the stereotyped pattern of male domination and subordination of women persists with degrees of variation. At a deeper level, the novel reinforces the conflict, the legendary battle between tradition and modernity. Thus, while on the one hand, the female protagonist's filial and wifely loyalties criss-cross and clash, on the other she encounters a hostile husband, the eternal male chauvinist, as an impediment in her quest for identity and self-assertion.

Tara's grandmother, a widow, fully conforms to the traditional model of Indian womanhood, where women willingly submerge their identity and accept a subservient position in the patriarchal set-up. She prefers to reside in her past, with the fond memories of her deceased husband, the founder of the factory. His ancient rosewood desk has a place of honour in her room and the ritual of hanging a fresh garland of marigolds around his portrait every morning is performed without fail. That Tara's grandmother intends to bequeath to her granddaughter the age-old legacy of traditions and conventions is evident on many occasions, especially when she admonishes Tara for dilly-dallying in the acceptance of the proposal for marriage. 'Why, when I got engaged the proposal came in the morning and by four o'clock the families were sitting down to sherbet' (p. 67). Later, when the betrothed couple steps into the grandmother's room for her blessings, she proudly introduces her grandson-in-law to her late husband's photograph. 'This was my husband. He was the founder of the business. At one time, it was the most famous business in Bombay' (p. 70). For her, the yardstick for measuring people's achievements or failures is her late husband: '. . . when my husband was alive, his people stuck to him through thick and thin . . .' (p. 154).

Tara's mother, with minor variations in her situation, initially submits to the traditional mode. Like her mother-in-law she too can be seen blithely basking in the glory of her husband's achievements, but quite characteristically, the wisdom that she shares with her marriageable daughter is imbibed with a kind of feminine anguish. 'My dear', she had said with a kind of bitter tenderness, 'make no mistake. You will have to give in, and give in, and give in' (p. 86). The repetitive verbal phrase 'give in' attains a kind of religious and mythical undertone combining in a way the destiny of three generations of women. Tara's grandmother, the strongest upholder of tradition, stands as firmly as a rock on all crucial, critical moments in her life. Tara's mother, on the contrary, falters in the face of a crisis. Her response or reaction to the enormous crisis in the factory is initially comic but finally tragic. When Tara's father and brother are sitting tense at the dining table in the aftermath of the strike in the factory, Tara's mother is stupidly fussing over the lack of decorum and dining table accessories caused by the absence of Simon, the servant, who has been employed by the men on a far more serious assignment than the laying of the dining table. Her comical antipathy to a crisis of great magnitude, as a matter of fact, critiques the patriarchal set-up where the womenfolk are assiduously confined to the domestic sphere for the 'perpetuation of housewifery' as Betty Friedan (*The Feminine Mystique*, 1963) would call it and this distancing of the womenfolk from the public sphere consequently renders them antipathetic or inimical to the public sphere,—the men's domain. Gradually when she realises the enormity of the crisis, she indignantly retorts with the perennial woman's question—'Why can't you include us more?' (p. 97). Dissatisfied with her husband's vague flattering explanation, she retreats to her room upstairs, quite like Savitri in R.K. Narayan's *The Dark Room*. As the narrator/commentator explicates, in her parents' conjugal relationship harsh words or insults were tacitly avoided, '. . . when the edge of decorum was reached my mother simply went upstairs' (p. 97).

That Tara's mother is greatly troubled with the 'woman's question' is evident from her mental sickness bordering on insanity. All her built-in pressures, her pent-up emotions and feelings subsequently give way to her mental sickness, a symptom of her psychic disturbance. Her mental disorder can be treated as a sign of her passive protest. No doubt her health ultimately becomes the prime responsibility and supermost concern of her husband, but Tara's mother has reached a nihilistic state of mind where all this facade is nothing but a 'tamasha' to her. Her passivity is in a way, the best form of protest, for her indispensability within the domestic sphere is unchallengeable. The novel ends with an outward show of solidarity and unity on the point of 'Amma's health' but the object of concern has by then acquired a nihilistic pose.

Tara's grandmother and mother are referred to in the novel by their familial denominators, i.e. as Dadi and Amma. Thus they have virtually conceded their identities as individuals. Both of them can be classified as 'women as victim' while Tara, the third and the most vital role-model falls into the category of 'women as truth-teller'—to use the classified categories of women in Robin Morgan's *Planetary Feminism*.[3] Robin Morgan has constructed women's experience within two categories—women as victim and women as truth-teller. Here a comparison of *Tara Lane* with Farhana Sheikh's *The Red Box*[4] will not be out of context. In Muslim communities of the Indian subcontinent, the hold of tradition is comparatively far more binding on the older generation of women than on the younger ones. The female protagonist Raisa in *The Red Box* is a liberated researcher, researching problems of identity for Asian girls and women in Britain. It is only after her mother's death that she realizes from her mother's hidden diary that her mother too was a victim of double identity. The daughter of a noted industrialist in Pakistan and the wife of an affluent barrister in England, Raisa's mother hid the true nature of her job as a daily-paid worker in a factory for the sake of men's family honour and social status. Raisa's father, though educated and rich, had allowed his ailing wife to suffer the strain and humiliation of working in anonymity. 'How had he let her suffer that strain and humiliation? He was a barrister; he was educated: he should have been earning enough. And how could her brothers have been so greedy? They were also to blame.'[5]

Tara is a highly sensitive, introspective and dutiful child with a restless self-consciousness. 'You see, I am very scared of my dutiful daughter' (p. 35), says her father jokingly when Tara is insistent on personally visiting the houses of Tara Lane vicinity for collecting donations for drought relief. She is by temperament mutinous but knows simultaneously that mutiny never succeeded. Therefore when she accepts the proposal of marriage from Rizwan, her cousin, conceding to the wishes of the family elders, the readers can very well anticipate a replication of the traditional behaviourial pattern. But in the portrayal of Tara, especially in her role of a wife, the author subverts the traditional model. Tara, a bildungsroman character, grows more and more assertive and persistent in her search for identity and in her insistence to be included in the public sphere. As an educated, emancipated and conscientious person she is restless over the socially assigned and family-approved role-model of a subservient wife. There is a consistent reference in the novel to a little worm: 'whatever you did it was there—crawling or turning or still but it was there' (p. 29). As a child, life had seemed to her like a piece of cloth which was stretched too thin, so that at any moment one could discover a large hole underneath. Later in college she had experienced a kind of alienation when she felt miserably isolated from her friends and environment. There had always been a gap, a space which had remained unfulfilled. At the initial stage of marriage Tara is elated, jubilant and confident that her husband 'has filled in the space effortlessly' (p. 79). She too, like her female predecessors in the novel is eagerly endeavouring to please her husband and appears to have accepted the 'perpetual housewifery' without the least hesitation, doubt or resistance.

Rizwan, Tara's husband is now the centre of authority in the nuclear family. He too, like his counterpart in Tara's parental family does not brook any kind of interference in his public sphere and resents being discussed with servants. 'So you gossip about me when I'm not here?' (p. 85). Tara is soon initiated into the knowledge that marriage was like a warm bath where '. . . you were either inside it or freezing outside' (p. 86). Literally after three days of her marriage she is disillusioned with marriage. The first quarrel of the newly-wed couple is patched up with the acceptance of defeat by Tara. Tara at this stage can be seen entering into a bond of sisterhood with Katreen, her young maid-servant. 'They will do that, bibi' (p. 87).

The theme of sisterhood is an integral part of feminism. Oppressed by men, women tend to unite in a sisterhood. The best example of this sisterhood occurs in the writings of Afro-American women writers. Glocia Naylor's *The Women of Brewster Place* as the title suggests, abounds with such women who find solace in the company of women. Alice Walker's *The Color Purple*, Toni Morrison's *Sula, The Bluest Eye* and *Beloved* also deal with such women who counter the male oppression with the help of sympathetic women. The reference to men as 'they' by Katreen therefore is very significant. This linguistic denominator 'they' connotes the polarization of gender. The novel critiques gender relations in patriarchy with the help of the above mentioned role-models for women. The prospect of motherhood momentarily plasters Tara's emotional hurt, but she is now quite often craving for a 'room of her own': 'Above all, there was a desire to be left alone, to stop having things flung at me, what had I done that I couldn't look out of my garden in peace?' (p. 91). Unlike her mother, Tara's involvement in the public sphere, i.e. in the factory is far more intense, but Rizwan attempts to thwart her involvement with his cryptic, monosyllabic replies: 'Talk was over for the day. And I was no longer the sort of wife who would ask questions which were not wanted' (p. 92). Rizwan, the eternal male, zealously safeguards his positioned superiority, Tara is therefore alienated in her marriage.

The nature of Tara's crisis so far is purely emotional but the crisis attains an altogether new dimension when Rizwan's involvement in an underhand deal of bribery is foiled. The battle for Tara is now one of conflicting loyalties on the one hand and a matter of principles on the other. Tara, nurtured in an idealist, uprighteous family, is hurt beyond measures by Rizwan's failure to live up to the standards of honesty and righteousness and her life is filled with a dreadful chasm. In desperation she turns towards the baby in her womb, ' . . . the baby would arrive into this chasm' (p. 127). Again, a comparison with African and Afro-American women would reveal that a marginalised, disillusioned woman has the tendency to turn towards motherhood. The African women writers, Flora Nwapa's *Efuru* and *Idu*, Buchi Emecheta's *The Joys of Motherhood* are a few such examples where the lives of female protagonists centre around motherhood. Similarly, in the writings of Afro-American women too, the harassed, disillusioned wives turn towards their children as Alladi Uma[6] too posits in her book.

In Indian fiction, says Shanta Krishnaswamy,[7] intense introspection on the part of the women is followed by a paralysis of will and cessation of all action. This period of inactivity, though brief but chaotic in Tara's life, roughly corresponds to an existential poise. 'I was imprisoned in a spacc the size of the rug, and when I walked up and down the room I carried my rug-sized prison with me' (p. 129). The birth of her son averts a prolongation of her dilemma and Rizwan too is willing to cooperate and compromise in the altered circumstances, 'Just relax now', he said. 'I'll settle that business, okay? I'll manage it. I'll settle things . . . with your father', says he to his wife in labour. Tara's world is whole again. 'Trust my husband. Trust them all' (p. 130). Tara is safe again within the folds of patriarchy.

Tara, the new, emerging woman, is capable of voicing her views and opinion as an individual—this can be inferred from her conversation with her mother-in-law. Keeping her voice within the limits of what was allowed to a daughter-in-law, Tara undauntingly expresses her difference of opinion. 'Thank you for your concern, Khalajan. But I think my father would prefer to suffer rather than to be practical, which only means dishonest' (p. 137). But still the best illustration of Tara's positivism towards life is the way she responds to the news of the closure of the factory. Her grandmother who had all along stood as firmly as a rock is in tears, while her mother escapes into her semi-insanity. It is Tara, the sole female in the novel, who takes a positive step to cope with the tragedy with her job-hunting effort. Tara is not a 'career woman' but with her newly acquired poise of responsibility, the novel entails the possibility of her transformation into a 'would-be-career woman'. That she has acquired an increasing adaptation to reality and a sense of social responsibility is indicated by her response to the news of the death of Katreen's son. She casts off her own tragedy in the face of Katreen's bereavement and is prepared to minimise Katreen's economic disaster. She is no longer an alienated being, her own suffering has bound her with Katreen, with a renewed bond of sisterhood.

NOTES

1. Nancy Hartsock, 'Foucault on Power: A theory for Women' in *Feminism/post-modernism*, ed. by Linda J. Nicholson (New York: Routlege, 1990).
2. Shama Futehally, *Tara Lane* (Delhi: Ravi Dayal Publisher, 1993). All the textual references are taken from this edition.
3. Robin Morgan, 'Planetary Feminism, The Politics of the 21st Century', in her *Sisterhood is Global: The International Women's Movement Anthology* (New York: Anchor Press, Doubleday, 1984, pp. XIII-XXIII).

4. Farhana Sheikh, *The Red Box* (London: Women's Press, 1991). First Published in Rupa Paperback, 1991.
5. Ibid., p. 5.
6. Alladi Uma, *Woman and Her Family: Indian and Afro-American—A Literary Perspective* (New Delhi: Sterling, 1989).
7. Shanta Krishnaswamy, *The Woman in Indian Fiction in English (1950-1980)* (New Delhi: Ashish Publishing House, 1984).

Contributors

USHA ANAND is Reader in the Department of English, School of Correspondence Courses, University of Delhi, Delhi.

USHA BANDE teaches English at the Govt. Post Graduate College for Women, Shimla.

KAMAL BHASIN is Reader in English at ARSD College (University of Delhi), New Delhi.

SHASHI DESHPANDE is a novelist and short story writer.

T.N. DHAR is Professor in the Department of English, Himachal Pradesh University, Shimla.

JAIWANTI DIMRI is Reader in the Department of English, Himachal Pradesh University, Shimla.

NEETA GUPTA teaches English at the School of Correspondence Courses, University of Delhi, Delhi.

NARESH K. JAIN teaches English at the School of Correspondence Courses, University of Delhi, Delhi.

MALASHRI LAL is Professor in the Department of English, University of Delhi, Delhi.

SARLA PALKAR is Reader in the Department of English, M.S. University of Baroda, Baroda.

UMA PARAMESWARAN is Professor in the Department of English, Winnipeg University, Winnipeg, Canada.

MAKARAND PARANJPE is Associate Professor of English at the Indian Institute of Technology, New Delhi.

G.R. TANEJA is Reader in the Department of English, R.L.A. College (University of Delhi), New Delhi.